"Placing psychoanalysis and the discourse of intersectionality in direct dialogue, this collection consolidates new and refreshing clinical approaches to the ways in which modern subjects construct their identities, consciously and unconsciously. Thinking race, gender, and sexual orientation together, the contributors update and expand the theoretical insights of an older discourse of 'identity politics,' situating processes of self-formation and interaction with difference firmly in the space of relational rather than individual dynamics."

—**Michelle Stephens, Ph.D.**, practicing psychoanalyst and author of *Skin Acts: Race, Psychoanalysis and the Black Male Performer* (Duke UP, 2014)

"*Intersectionality and Relational Psychoanalysis* is an essential and invaluable contribution to our field at a moment when psychoanalysis has finally begun to embrace the challenge of analyzing the social and historical contexts that organize our psychic experience—particularly the effects of collective trauma and intergenerational transmission. Each of these illuminating essays provides a uniquely thoughtful and complex answer to the question of how we integrate a perspective that recognizes the interpenetrating effects on psychic life of the relationships between race, sexual orientation, gender, class, and ethnicity. This volume represents an impressive work of vision, originality and depth that invites us, the readers, to immerse ourselves in the vital reflection on how we are formed by and express the social in our psychic lives and our clinical work."

—**Jessica Benjamin, Ph.D.**, author, *Beyond Doer and Done To: Recognition Theory, Intersubjectivity and the Third* (2017)

"Through a series of powerful essays, White and Belkin bring a collective voice to the marginalization of 'the other' and locate the challenges and opportunities that are available within the therapeutic situation. These papers, through rich clinical material, compel us to step into the intersection of race, gender and sexuality with our patients, moving away from being a 'perpetrating bystander' (Leavitt and Harris) in our clinical function. Regardless of one's theoretical approach, these are valuable insights that promote seeing ourselves and our patients more complexly, mitigating the tribalism that is ascendant in modern society and impacts our therapeutic capacities. Many of the chapters are written in the current relational idiom involving a degree of self-disclosure and a flexibility of psychoanalytic framework that may be regarded with varying degrees of acceptance by schools of psychoanalytic thought and readership. This book offers fertile ground for consideration of issues of otherness in psychoanalysis, thus serving a valuable contribution to breaking our silence to the monolithic conclusions that regard the other and impact our relevance in modern society that yearns for this form of inquiry."

—**Dionne R. Powell, M.D.**, author of *Race, African Americans, and Psychoanalysis: Collective Silence in the Therapeutic Situation* (2012)

Intersectionality and Relational Psychoanalysis

Intersectionality and Relational Psychoanalysis: New Perspectives on Race, Gender, and Sexuality examines the links among race, gender, and sexuality through the dual perspectives of relational psychoanalysis and the theory of intersectionality. This anthology discusses the ways in which clinicians and patients inadvertently reproduce experiences of privilege and marginalization in the consulting room. Focusing particularly on the experiences of immigrants, women of color, sex workers, and LGBTQ individuals, the contributing authors explore how similarities and differences among the patient's and analyst's gender, race, and sexual orientation can be acknowledged, challenged, and negotiated.

Combining intersectional theory with relational psychoanalytic thought, the authors introduce a number of thought-provoking clinical vignettes to suggest how adopting an intersectional approach can help us navigate the space between pathology and difference in psychotherapy. By bringing together these new psychoanalytically informed perspectives on clinical work with minority and marginalized individuals, *Intersectionality and Relational Psychoanalysis* makes an important contribution to psychoanalysis, psychology, and social work.

Max Belkin, Ph.D., is fellow, supervisor of psychotherapy, and faculty at the William Alanson White Institute, associate editor of *Contemporary Psychoanalysis*, and adjunct faculty at the Department of Applied Psychology at New York University. He is a licensed clinical psychologist in private practice in New York City, specializing in treating individuals and couples.

Cleonie White, Ph.D., is fellow, faculty, and supervisor of psychotherapy at the William Alanson White Institute, adjunct clinical assistant professor at New York University's Postdoctoral Program in Psychotherapy and Psychoanalysis, and faculty and supervisor at the Stephen Mitchell Center for Relational Studies. Dr. White maintains a private practice in New York City.

Psychoanalysis in a New Key Book Series
Donnel Stern
Series Editor

When music is played in a new key, the melody does not change, but the notes that make up the composition do: change in the context of continuity, continuity that perseveres through change. Psychoanalysis in a New Key publishes books that share the aims psychoanalysts have always had, but that approach them differently. The books in the series are not expected to advance any particular theoretical agenda, although to this date most have been written by analysts from the Interpersonal and Relational orientations.

The most important contribution of a psychoanalytic book is the communication of something that nudges the reader's grasp of clinical theory and practice in an unexpected direction. Psychoanalysis in a New Key creates a deliberate focus on innovative and unsettling clinical thinking. Because that kind of thinking is encouraged by exploration of the sometimes surprising contributions to psychoanalysis of ideas and findings from other fields, Psychoanalysis in a New Key particularly encourages interdisciplinary studies. Books in the series have married psychoanalysis with dissociation, trauma theory, sociology, and criminology. The series is open to the consideration of studies examining the relationship between psychoanalysis and any other field—for instance, biology, literary and art criticism, philosophy, systems theory, anthropology, and political theory.

But innovation also takes place within the boundaries of psychoanalysis, and Psychoanalysis in a New Key therefore also presents work that reformulates thought and practice without leaving the precincts of the field. Books in the series focus, for example, on the significance of personal values in psychoanalytic practice, on the complex interrelationship between the analyst's clinical work and personal life, on the consequences for the clinical situation when patient and analyst are from different cultures, and on the need for psychoanalysts to accept the degree to which they knowingly satisfy their own wishes during treatment hours, often to the patient's detriment. A full list of all titles in this series is available at: https://www.routledge.com/series/LEAPNKBS

Intersectionality and Relational Psychoanalysis

New Perspectives on Race, Gender, and Sexuality

Edited by Max Belkin and Cleonie White

Routledge
Taylor & Francis Group
LONDON AND NEW YORK

First published 2020
by Routledge
2 Park Square, Milton Park, Abingdon, Oxon OX14 4RN

and by Routledge
52 Vanderbilt Avenue, New York, NY 10017

Routledge is an imprint of the Taylor & Francis Group, an informa business

British Library Cataloguing-in-Publication Data
A catalogue record for this book is available from the British Library

Library of Congress Cataloging-in-Publication Data
A catalog record for this book has been requested

ISBN: 978-0-367-36174-7 (hbk)
ISBN: 978-0-367-36171-6 (pbk)
ISBN: 978-0-429-34431-2 (ebk)

Typeset in Times
by Apex CoVantage, LLC

Contents

About the contributors

Neil Altman, Ph.D., is faculty, William Alanson White Institute; editor emeritus, *Psychoanalytic Dialogues: The International Journal of Relational Perspectives*; and author, *The Analyst in the Inner City: Race, Class, and Culture through a Psychoanalytic Lens* and *Psychoanalysis in Times of Accelerating Cultural Change: Spiritual Globalization.*

Max Belkin, Ph.D., is fellow, supervisor of psychotherapy, and faculty at the William Alanson White Institute, associate editor of *Contemporary Psychoanalysis*, and adjunct faculty at the Department of Applied Psychology at New York University. He is a licensed clinical psychologist in private practice in New York City, specializing in treating individuals and couples.

Sue Grand, Ph.D., is faculty and supervisor at the New York University Postdoctoral Program in Psychoanalysis and Psychotherapy; faculty, Trauma Program at the National Institute for the Psychotherapies; and faculty, the Mitchell Center for Relational Psychoanalysis. She is associate editor of *Psychoanalytic Dialogues* and *Psychoanalysis Culture and Society*. She is the author of *The Reproduction of Evil: A Clinical and Cultural Perspective* and *The Hero in the Mirror: From Fear to Fortitude.*

Adrienne Harris, Ph.D., is Faculty and Supervisor at the New York University Postdoctoral Program in Psychotherapy and Psychoanalysis. She is on the faculty and is a supervisor at the Psychoanalytic Institute of Northern California. She is an editor at *Psychoanalytic Dialogues*, and *Studies in Gender and Sexuality*. In 2012, she, Lewis Aron, and Jeremy Safran established the Sandor Ferenczi Center at New School University. She, Lew Aron, Eyal Rozmaren, and Steven Kuchuck co-edit the book series Relational Perspectives in Psychoanalysis, a series now with more than 100 published volumes. She is an editor of the IPA ejournal Psychoanalysistoday.com, which is developing cross-cultural communications among the five language groups in the IPA.

Lynne Layton, Ph.D., is Assistant Professor of psychology, Department of Psychiatry, part-time, Harvard Medical School; supervisor at Massachusetts Institute for Psychoanalysis; and adjunct faculty at Pacifica Graduate Institute. She is the author of numerous book chapters and articles on race, class, gender, and sexuality in clinical work.

Julie Leavitt, M.D., graduated from the Psychoanalytic Institute of Northern California in San Francisco, where she is currently president. Her career interests are anchored in ethically bridging classic institutional psychoanalysis with surrounding social psychoanalysis, including pedagogy, praxis, and politics.

Hannah Pocock, LCSW is a psychotherapist in private practice in Charlottesville, Virginia, specializing in the treatment of trauma. She is a candidate for certification in Sensorimotor Psychotherapy.

Avgi Saketopoulou, Ph.D., is on the faculty at the New York University Postdoctoral Program, the William Alanson White Institute, the New York Psychoanalytic Institute, the Stephen Mitchell Relational Center, and the National Institute for the Psychotherapies in New York City, where she teaches courses on gender and sexuality. She serves on the editorial boards of *Psychoanalytic Dialogues*, *Journal of the American Psychoanalytic Association (JAPA), The Psychoanalytic Quarterly*, and *Studies in Gender and Sexuality (SGS).*

Pratyusha Tummala-Narra, Ph.D., is Associate Professor in counseling, developmental and educational psychology at Boston College, and in independent practice in Cambridge, Massachusetts. She has served on the American Psychological Association's (APA) Task Force on Immigration, APA Task Force on Re-envisioning the Multicultural Guidelines, and the APA Division 39 Board of Directors.

Cleonie White, Ph.D., is fellow, faculty, and supervisor of psychotherapy at the William Alanson White Institute, adjunct clinical assistant professor at New York University's Postdoctoral Program in Psychotherapy and Psychoanalysis, and faculty and supervisor at the Stephen Mitchell Center for Relational Studies. Dr. White maintains a private practice in New York City.

Acknowledgments

MB and CW

This anthology owes its existence to the moving and thought-provoking contributions of Neil Altman, Sue Grand, Adrienne Harris, Lynne Layton, Julie Leavitt, Hannah Pocock, Pratyusha Tummala-Narra, and Avgi Saketopoulou. It was an honor to collaborate with such wonderful clinicians and writers. Thank you.

MB

Don Stern's guidance as a mentor, supervisor, and editor of *Psychoanalysis in a New Key* has been invaluable not only in the development of this project, but also in my becoming a psychoanalyst.

Deep thanks are due to Cleonie White, whose wisdom, sense of humor, and patience made this project possible. I thank Toni Helllmann for introducing me to the work of Kimberlé Crenshaw and for encouraging me to think intersectionally about psychoanalysis. I am also grateful to Sue Kolod and Melissa Ritter for helping me find my writing voice and for generously sharing their expertise and enthusiasm. The following supervisors and analysts have been my role models and patient teachers: Mary Commerford, Sandra Buechler, Richard Gartner, Robert Langan, Richard Loewus, and Warren Wilner. I am especially grateful to Philip Bromberg for inspiring me to be a better analyst, writer, and human being. And to my friend, Helen Fronshtein, for always making time for me and for having my back.

Thank you, Mila Belkina and Patrick Haffner for supporting me in everything that I do! I am very fortunate to have such a loyal, fun, and loving family. Finally, I thank my patients for entrusting me with their sorrows and triumphs and my students at NYU for exploring with me the perils and joys of the human condition.

CW

For Max Belkin, the time is now to make public the voices of psychoanalytic practice and theorizing at their intersecting best with the cultural, and socio-political, realities of our time. Thank you, Max, for inviting me to join you as co-editor on this critical journey. Your brilliant mind, your thoughtfulness, and your keen attention to detail shepherded this work to its readiness for publication.

It takes a village: Thank you, Don Stern, for our long-standing friendship, and for your unwavering encouragement and support of me as a psychoanalyst and as a writer. I am also deeply indebted to Lew Aron who, having heard my voice, literally, and figuratively, invited me to write a paper, on – broadly – "reggae music and psychoanalysis." You saw, and fully understood, the shaping power of my Jamaican heritage. Thank you, Lew.

So many colleagues and friends at the William Alanson White Psychoanalytic Institute have played pivotal roles in my thinking about race, class, and Otherness. I am especially thankful to Lori Bohm, Tomás Casado-Frankel, Cynthia Field, Anton Hart, Toni Hellman, Jenny Kaufmann, David Koch, Sharon Kofman, Sue Kolod, Kimberlyn Leary, Maria Nardone, Jean Petrucelli, Michelle Stephens, Carol Valentin, and Kathleen White for our wonderful exchanges of ideas in our Study Group on Race and Psychoanalysis, in the Center for Public Mental Health, and at the Conference Advisory Board. My colleagues at Black Psychoanalysts Speak deserve my gratitude as well. What we do together in the name of those less well served within, and outside, our profession is invaluable. I am enlightened by your minds and your determination to challenge established norms, and to transgress.

Thank you, Janine dePeyer. With humor and a critical ear, you have been a dear, and very supportive, friend. Melanie Suchet: Thank you for your wisdom, your energy, and your unfailing love and support. You do keep me on my toes! I express my thanks and gratitude to my friend, Carolyn Clement, who, for so many years, has generously read, and edited, my work. Thank you, too, for the music – for Nina Simone.

Dear Philip Bromberg: I have traveled. . . . Your stubborn, unfailing, support has been my sure and steadying force during the waxing and waning of my many moons. For that I am forever thankful. Kathe Hift is a rare, one-of-a-kind friend. You have been my constant support when I am strongest. And you are always at my side during my most difficult times.

To my dear mother, Mrs. L. Victoria Hines White: How you have managed to maintain a positive outlook on this world after nearly one hundred years of living, and seeing, of learning, and knowing; of profound loving, and unspeakable losing, remains your mystery. Thank you for believing in me and for always pushing me forward. Thank you for being. You are our rock! To the Giniger Clan: Sy, Evan, Cheryl, Melissa, and Alexandra. I simply cannot imagine what my life would have been without you in it. Thanks for your persons, your smarts, your thoughtfulness, and your love. Love you back. You have given me stories to write.

Finally, my patients are the shine in my psychoanalytic diamonds. I love my journeys with you into places we did not think it possible to risk going until we got there. Thank you all for helping me into constant states of growing. And, dear Trevor: Thank you for traveling Uptown where you could see me, and for taking me Downtown to show me who you truly are. You changed my life.

Introduction

Max Belkin and Cleonie White

The papers presented in this volume examine the interplay among patients' race, gender, and sexual orientation in psychotherapy through the lens of relational psychoanalysis and the theory of intersectionality.

Part I: Queer identities

Chapters 1 and 2

In Chapter 1, "Who Is Queer Around Here? Overcoming Rigid Thinking and Relating in Patient and Analyst," Max Belkin explores the exchanges between a white gay male analyst and his straight female patient of color using the notion of intersectionality and relational psychoanalysis. The chapter describes the psychoanalytic process of moving beyond dissociated, binary modes of perceiving one's self and the other. This interpersonal process involves acknowledging the shame- and guilt-riddled aspects of patient's and analyst's experiences of privilege and marginalization. The author maintains that a playful, curious, and soul-searching engagement in enactments can lead to the emergence of a transitional space in which the similarities and differences between the patient's and analyst's gender, race, and sexual orientation can be acknowledged, challenged, and negotiated.

Chapter 2, "Minding the Gap: Intersections Among Gender, Race and Class in Work with Psychotic Gender-Variant Children," by Avgi Saketopoulou, discusses in depth the author's analytic work with a queer child. Her clinical material illustrates the centrality of thinking intersectionally and argues for the importance of considering the interdigitations among class, race, and gender in inpatient settings. Theorizing gender as a category of experience that can be appropriated towards multiple psychic ends, the author focuses on how race and class were interimplicated with gender. She proposes that adopting an intersectional approach to think about how one identity category can inflate others can help us navigate the space between pathology and difference.

Part II: Sexual exploitation of women

Chapters 3 and 4

Hannah Pocock, in Chapter 3, "Subordinated Selves: Integrating Intersectional Oppression and the Unconscious Mind in Prostitution Discourse," brings intersectional theory into conversation with relational psychoanalytic thought to examine how the interlocking oppressions of race, class, and gender shape and sustain the commercial sexual exploitation of women. The author bridges the gap between structural and intrapsychic analyses of prostitution, examining the interaction between structural oppression and intrapsychic processes that script marginalized women for prostitution. In particular, she challenges the notion of the universal "sex worker" subject, examining how the perpetuation of this narrative obscures the profoundly raced and classed aspects of commercial sexual exploitation. Furthermore, Pocock illuminates the ways in which contemporary relational thought, in conjunction with intersectional analysis, inform nuanced theoretical conceptualizations of prostituted women seeking treatment, and psychotherapeutic approaches that honor women's experiences of oppression, internalized subordination, and complex trauma.

Chapter 4, "Skin Memories: On Race, Love, and Loss," by Sue Grand, argues that the ubiquitous rape of African-American slave women by their masters was intersectional at its core: greed, racism, and sexism shaped the very origins of the U.S. economy, constructing a class system that continues to be marked by both racism and sexism. According to Grand, while this history is written into the skin of U.S. analysts, it has not penetrated psychoanalytic theory, practice, or consciousness. The chapter traces the trans-generational effects of this exploitation through an intimate and intersectional analysis in which the author, a Russian-Jewish patient, is treated by a light-skinned African-American analyst. In the transference, the history of slavery emerges: the analyst's apparent whiteness echoes with rape on the plantation. Racial guilt and conflict are threaded through issues of gender and class. These threads are worked through motifs of loss, forced separation, and internalized racism.

Part III: Immigrant experiences

Chapters 5 and 6

In Chapter 5, "Intersectionality in the Immigrant Context," Pratyusha Tummala-Narra describes the intersections between the intrapsychic and interpersonal experiences of immigrants and the children of immigrants. The author maintains that mourning of loss associated with immigration is closely connected with the intersections of multiple social locations and identities, privilege and marginalization, in pre-migration and post-migration contexts. This chapter underscores the importance of recognizing both sociopolitical and unconscious processes that underlie complex identifications concerning gender, race, and sexuality.

In Chapter 6, "Strangers in Paradise: Trevor, Marley, and Me: Reggae Music and the Foreigner Other," Cleonie White examines the ways in which the analyst and patient negotiate mutual experiences of alienation in a shared culture of origin as they encounter experiences of foreignness in a foreign land. As with relational spaces, the construct, "immigrant" is positioned as a thing in itself – a transitional space – in which Otherness might be interrogated. The work of crossing boundaries at the intersections of race and class is discussed, as two Jamaicans, embedded in the power of reggae music, engage in psychoanalytic and socio-political "talk."

Part IV: Clinical theory

Chapters 7, 8, and 9

Chapter 7, by Lynne Layton, "Intersectionality, Normative Unconscious Processes, and Racialized Enactments of Distinction," outlines the ways in which simultaneously interlocking local and global oppressions are subjectively and relationally lived in the clinic. The author articulates an intersectional analysis with her concept of normative unconscious process, which focuses on the ways that clinicians and patients unconsciously reproduce simultaneously interlocking oppressions in their work.

In Chapter 8, "Intersectionality Encountering Laplanche: Models of Otherness and the Incomprehensibility of Perpetration," Julie Leavitt and Adrienne Harris examine how the concept of intersectionality brings forward a consciousness of perpetration and difference. Furthermore, this chapter interweaves Crenshaw's ideas of intersectionality with the model of Laplanche, in which interpersonal relationships give rise to different aspects of subjectivity: gender, sexual desire, racial identity, class and cultural formation, and historical markers of trauma. To illustrate these ideas, the authors analyze clinical examples involving white female patients, whose whiteness intersects with their gender and sexuality while at the same time obscuring the effects of their white privilege.

Finally, Chapter 9, "Intersectionality: From Politics to Identity," by Neil Altman, draws a distinction between the way racial, gender, and sexual orientation are structured in language and the way they are lived. In particular, Altman posits that whenever race, gender, and sexual orientation are viewed as isolated and polarized categories of identity, they turn into stereotypes and fail to do justice to the complexity of lived experience. In fact, he argues, a person's location on the racial, gender, and sexual orientation continuum changes over time along with shifts in the interpersonal context. When race, gender, and sexual orientation intersect, as they always do, the complexity of lived experience increases geometrically as each dimension interacts with the others.

Part I

Queer identities

Chapter 1

Who is queer around here?

Overcoming rigid thinking and relating in patient and analyst

Max Belkin

"Who Are You?"

One day, a couple of months into my work with a Mexican-American graduate student named Ana, I casually inquired about her reactions to me. First, she offered her usual "I am glad that you share my background in philosophy and can understand me." But then I heard something new and baffling: "I had to stop watching *House of Cards* recently," added Ana with an anxious laugh. "Kevin Spacey looks too much like you. I mean, like you, he acts straight, even though he is totally gay." Taken aback, I asked Ana, "Are you wondering whether I am gay or straight?" To my surprise, instead of saying something reassuring and deferential, which used to be her habit, Ana continued: "When I googled you before our first session, I found out that you are from Russia, that you are Jewish and gay. But now I read you as a white, privileged straight man. I don't hear your accent. When I tried telling you about my campy side, like *RuPaul's Drag Race* being my favorite show, you were dismissive and condescending. I don't know what to make of you anymore."

Now it was my turn to feel confused and frustrated. Suddenly I heard my own indignant internal voice: "How dare this straight woman pontificate whether or not I am gay enough! This is preposterous." I took another incredulous look at Ana and thought to myself: "Do I know you? I don't believe that I have met *this* woman before. Has she been here all along?"

Queer theory

A few weeks following this exchange, upon entering the waiting room to greet Ana, I found her immersed in reading *White Girls* (2013) by

Hilton Als. Ana inquired whether I had already read it, and after learning that I had not, told me to check it out. While embracing his own black queerness, Als at the same time challenges the binary, essentialist categorization of people as black or white, gay or straight, male or female. For example, the author refers to his bi-gendered best friend as "SL" (Sir or Lady). "Since America is nothing if not about categories" (p. 12), Als and his friends struggle to subvert and transcend the narratives and stereotypes that justify and maintain their marginalization.

As I was reading Als's thoughtful analysis of the ubiquitous oppression of women, gays, and people of color, I was wondering about the impact of racial, gender, and sexual orientation differences between me and Ana on our ability to understand and empathize with each other. What does being homosexual, gay, or queer mean to her and to me? In what ways am I not "gay enough" for her?

At first, I became defensive. I get uncomfortable whenever a straight person raises questions about my sexual orientation. It makes me feel objectified, vulnerable, judged. According to Michel Foucault (1990), since the end of the nineteenth century there has been a marked proliferation of medical, legal, and religious discourses about homosexuality as an immutable and dangerous pathology that allegedly invades every corner of the homosexual's personality. Furthermore, viewing homosexuals as a separate group has been a powerful weapon of discrimination and persecution. Unfortunately, more than one hundred years later, in the words of Jack Drescher (2007), "homosexual" still remains "a medical term – usually with pejorative connotations – that takes one aspect of a person's identity, his or her sexual attractions, and treats it as if it were the sum of the person's entire identity" (p. 207).

Inspired by feminism and the gay liberation movement, several philosophers and literary scholars (Butler, 1990; Foucault, 1990; Sedgwick, 1993) have challenged the discourses and practices that pathologize sexual minorities. As a result, a new academic discipline, queer theory, was born. The word "queer" means *across* as in "across genders, across sexualities" (Sedgwick, 1993). By exploring people's sexual identifications in historical and cultural contexts, queer theory treats all sexual identities as socially constructed and contingent, rather than immutable. In fact, according to Siobhan Sommerville (2000), " 'queer' may be understood as pointedly critiquing notions of stable lesbian and gay (or 'straight') identification" (p. 6).

In addition to describing one's sexual identity, queer can also be a playful, subversive performance of difference, at once personal and political. The popular Pride Parade slogan: "We're Here, We're Queer, Get Used to It!" demands respect and equal rights for all. As Mark Blechner (2009) points out, "queerness is not about a particular form of sexuality; it is about an attitude – an attitude of acceptance" (p. 159). Thus, the word that used to serve the oppression of sexual minorities has been rehabilitated to affirm and celebrate them.

The meaning of queer depends on the interpersonal context in which it is being used. Whenever LGBTQ people call themselves queer (whether tongue-in-cheek or as a matter of fact), the implied connotation is usually one of pride and respect. And this kind of affirmation tends to employ the first person: "I am queer," "I am coming out," or "I will survive!" (Sedgwick, 1993, 2003). However, when straight people describe an LGBTQ individual as queer, the intention is not always clear or benign. It is similar to the difference between stating "I am a Jew" and the experience of being called a Jew by somebody else. For instance, had Ana wondered out loud whether I am "Jewish enough," that would have also made me uncomfortable.

Ana and I explored what queer meant to each of us, the parallels and tensions between her sexual identity and mine. Although same-sex eroticism initially formed the core of the term "queer," it has since transcended the limits of any given sexual orientation or sexual identity. According to Sedgwick (1993), "many people of varying sexual practices, too, enjoy incorrigibly absorbing imaginative, artistic, intellectual, and affective lives that have been richly nourished by queer energies – and that are savagely diminished when the queerness of those energies is trashed or disavowed" (p. 20).

Although the meaning of queer keeps shifting and remains elusive, its epistemologic and political agenda is clear: to deconstruct and debunk any one-sided, monolithic definitions of who we are as subjects and objects of erotic desire. While heterosexual and homosexual, gay and straight are binary categories, queerness occupies the transitional, metaphorical space between them. Refusing to be pigeon-holed or typecast, Hilton Als (2013) repeatedly insists throughout his book that "metaphors sustain us."

In retrospect, I view Ana's question about my gayness as an invitation to be queer together: to transcend the rigid binary categories of homosexual and heterosexual, white versus person of color, male or female, to create new meanings and possibilities for each other. In fact, this question seemed important not only to our work together, but also to my own personal and professional growth. One of the benefits of being a therapist is that our work forces us to confront our limitations and blind spots. Both patient and analyst can only access their dissociated parts via participating in jointly created enactments and by examining their personal contributions to them (Stern, 2010).

Articulating and exploring the differences and similarities between me and Ana seemed not only important, but also fraught. According to Russell Meares (1993), "the therapist's state of mind should resemble that to which the patient's should be moving" (p. 184). Unfortunately, that is easier said than done. Acknowledging and accepting the vulnerable, shame-laced aspects of one's self is not for the faint of heart; we keep them outside of our conscious awareness for a reason (Bromberg, 1998; Stern, 2003). In particular, a psychoanalytic inquiry into Ana's and my own experience of privilege and marginalization required a nuanced examination of the interplay among gender, sexual orientation, and race.

Intersections among sexual orientation, gender, and race

Sumi Cho, Kimberlé Williams Crenshaw, and Leslie McCall (2013) describe intersectional studies as context-specific inquiries into legal, economic, and other kinds of discrimination facing women of color and sexual minorities. These authors view intersectionality as an analytic approach to social issues. For them:

> What makes an analysis intersectional – whatever its field or discipline – is its adoption of an intersectional way of thinking about the problem of sameness and difference and its relation to power. This framing – conceiving of categories not as distinct but as always permeated by other categories, fluid and changing, always in the process of creating and being created by dynamics of power – emphasizes what intersectionality does rather than what intersectionality is.
>
> (p. 795)

Since the 1980s, Crenshaw (1989, 1991), a prominent legal scholar and activist, has made important contributions to both feminism and critical race theory by focusing on the intersection of sexism and racism in the professional and personal lives of women of color in the United States. For example, in 1989, Crenshaw critiqued the existing antidiscrimination law for its failure to recognize the cumulative effects of gender- and race-based oppression on working African-American women. In particular, the law viewed black claimants as similar either to black men or to white women, thus overlooking black women's particular experience of marginalization. In contrast, Crenshaw's intersectional analysis of legal cases of work discrimination revealed that many black women had been excluded from the workforce "both as women who are Black and as Blacks who are women (Cho, Crenshaw, & McCall, 2013, p. 790)." Over the past thirty years, Crenshaw's concept of intersectionality inspired a broad movement against gender, racial, and sexual discrimination in the workplace, housing, and the legal system (Verloo, 2013; Spade, 2013).

Building on the critical psychoanalytic inquiry into gender and sexual orientation, Adrienne Harris (Corbett, Dimen, Goldner, & Harris, 2014) suggests that we expand the "queering of psychoanalysis" by examining the intersections of race, gender, and culture in the consulting room. Many gay and lesbian studies focus on gender and sexuality while at the same time downplaying the role of race (Collins, 2005). Although queer communities value inclusiveness, just like society at large, they also struggle with racial divisions and stereotypes. For example, Hilton Als (2013) reports that for many black gays and lesbians, queerness itself reads like a form of whiteness. In addition to homophobia, black gays and lesbians also face racial oppression and prejudice (and sometimes at the hands of white gays and lesbians).

At the same time, research on race and ethnicity often overlooks issues around sexuality, and especially homosexuality (Sommerville, 2000). By contrast, contemporary intersectional scholarship examines how race, gender, and sexuality might mutually construct one another in historically situated social practices (Collins, 2008). The intersectional approach to gender, race, and sexuality as historically and culturally contingent markers of identity has opened the door to exploring how our notions of heterosexuality and homosexuality, masculinity and femininity might inform and be shaped by our shifting representations of race.

In the nineteenth century, prominent American and European sexologists, such as Havelock Ellis and Edward Carpenter, viewed homosexuals as sexual "inverts" who reversed traditional sexual roles (Sommerville, 2000). To describe "inverts" as a discrete sexual group, nineteenth-century sexologists employed the methods of scientific racism, the so-called American School of Anthropology, that maintained the myth of white superiority over other races. Guided by the erroneous belief that anatomy can predict intelligence and behavior, American sexologists and anthropologists developed a hierarchy of human beings that relegated African-Americans, all women, and homosexuals to inferior positions.

In Somerville's account (2000), the bodies of black women and lesbians became the primary sites of medical inquiry into racial and sexual differences. According to the prevailing anthropologic and sexologic views of that time, women's genitalia and reproductive anatomy reflected the "natural" racial and sexual hierarchies. Therefore, many case studies published in nineteenth-century medical journals included physical examinations conducted by comparative anatomists who claimed that both African-American women and white lesbians were endowed with unusually large clitorises. This "genital excess" supposedly invoked male anatomy, thus indicating that both lesbians and African-American women were allegedly less sexually differentiated than their white heterosexual counterparts. At the same time, few case studies focused on the genitals of heterosexual African-American men or white homosexuals.

According to Sommerville (2000), the first quarter of the twentieth century saw a gradual decline in the popularity of both the biologic model of racial difference as well as the notion of homosexuality as a sexual inversion. However, they were replaced by the infamous cultural myth about black rapists who desire white women and the concept of homosexuality based on the "abnormal" sexual object choice. In Somerville's reading, "racial and sexual discourses converged in psychological models that understood 'unnatural' desire as perversion: in these cases, interracial and same-sex sexuality became analogous within later conceptions of sexual object choice" (p. 37).

The invitation to view race, gender, and sexuality as fluid and intersecting markers of difference *simultaneously* poses serious challenges to scholars and psychoanalysts alike. In the words of Muriel Dimen (2011), "in the clinic, all these map onto each other, winding under and over and through each other like superhighways in a vertiginous sequence of cloverleaves" (p. 536). There is also a risk of spreading one's analysis too thin and saying very little while trying to account for everything.

To avoid these pitfalls, Patricia Hill Collins (2008) advocates focusing on the relationship between any two or three markers of difference at a particular time and in a specific space. For example, in *Black Sexual Politics* (2005), Collins examines the intersections of race and sexuality in the post-civil rights era of color-blind racism. In particular, she explores the mutual construction of racism and heterosexism. That means centering her analysis on the relationship between race and sexuality, while locating social class and ability in the background. Thus, Collins regards race and sexuality as the most salient markers of difference for *this particular study*, without reifying or privileging them. In fact, they are viewed simply as time- and space-specific points of entry. For instance, in my heated exchanges with Ana described previously, sexual orientation emerged as salient and emotionally charged, while our racial and social class differences remained in the background.

Building on the work by Foucault (1990), Collins (2008) emphasizes that while different systems of power (economic, educational, medical) operate in very different ways, their effects often intersect.

> Gender and sexuality operate as proximate systems of power, annexing the power of the erotic and the everyday, whereas race, class, and ethnicity tend to be organized in more macro-structural ways, through practices such as segregating social groups and the unequal treatment that can ensue.
>
> (p. 72)

At the same time, Collins continues, "clearly gender and sexuality have social policy implications and race and class shape individual lives" (p. 72).

The notion of intersectionality carries important implications for our ability to empathize with one another's experience of oppression or marginalization. Collins (2008) rightly cautions against viewing racial, gender, and sexual discrimination as the same or interchangeable. For instance, Ana's experience of prejudice as a Mexican-American woman is different from my own encounters with homophobia and heterosexism. However, in my work with Ana, exploring our racial and sexual differences gradually taught us a great deal about each other.

While Collins regards race, gender, and sexuality as systems of power, in my view, they also function as currency of social privilege, authority, and self-esteem. For example, every time I come out to a straight person, I fear that I will be perceived and treated as less competent or as less worthy. At the same time, being a white, educated, upper-middle-class man endows me with authority and privileges that many other people in this country do not enjoy. In addition, my race and social class affect the way other people perceive my sexual identity: I often pass as a straight man. Thus, it is no coincidence that Ana pondered my sexual orientation in the context of her experience of me as a privileged white man.

Our experiences of privilege or marginalization unfold in specific social-historical contexts. In the face of the government-sponsored backlash against the rights of women, people of color, and the LGBTQ community in the United States, psychotherapists face the growing need to assist our patients in examining and confronting their encounters with microagressions, microinsults, and microinvalidations both inside and outside of the consulting room (Sue, 2010). In particular, Sue cautions against imposing on patients the therapist's own subjective perceptions of what is happening in the therapeutic relationship because that implies that our patients are somehow less rational or less emotionally mature than we are. As therapists we need to acknowledge the power differential in the consulting room and treat our patients' reality with respect. However, we cannot entirely avoid the tensions and clashes between patient's and analyst's experiences of gender, sexuality, and race (Dimen, 2002). In fact, it is the very working through of these tensions that can lead to the emergence of a healing therapeutic relationship (Levenson, 1983, 2017, 2018).

To go beyond paying lip service to the individual differences between therapist and patient, we need to examine the shameful, guilt-inducing parts of both individuals that get dissociated and enacted in the therapeutic relationship. That includes examining the therapist's own unearned advantages and conferred dominance based on his or her race, gender, and sexual orientation (Campbell, 2011). In my own clinical work, relational psychoanalysis (Stern, 2015, 2017) provides me with a conceptual tool kit for addressing both differences and sameness between me and my patients.

Relational paradigm

Relational psychoanalysis is an open-ended search for understanding each participant's experience of difference that eschews certainty, embraces ambiguity, and opens the door to new ways of being together.

It acknowledges that one's understanding of one's self and the other are always ongoing and elusive, enriching and transformative. Guided by curiosity, psychoanalytic inquiry reveals the hubris of self-knowledge, clashes with our familiar representations of other people, and makes us reflect on our habitual ways of ignoring what we do know. Along the way, inquisitiveness often serves as a buffer against the anxiety generated by uncertainty and ambiguity.

Our experience of difference emerges and evolves in the context of our emotional attachments to important people in our lives. For instance, those of us who experienced relational trauma in childhood or adolescence, such as empathic misattunement or skewed mentalization (Fonagy, Gergely, Jurist, & Target, 2002), often rely on dissociation to sidestep the internal conflicts between the parts of ourselves that we cherish (the "good me") and those that we are ashamed of (the "bad me"). According to D. B. Stern (2003), dissociation is a stifling of imagination ushered in by the concrete (rather than metaphoric) use of language. Unfortunately, shame figures prominently in the public and private lives of many LGBTQ children, adolescents, and adults (Sedgwick, 2003). In the face of emotional rejection and physical violence, many of us grow up dissociating parts of our sexuality. This kind of dissociation often leads to myopic, rigid perceptions of others and to one-sided, emotionally stunted relationships.

Dissociation and curiosity are inexorably linked: whenever one of them moves to the foreground, the other one recedes to the background. While curious uncertainty never completely supplants defensive not knowing, the goal of psychotherapy is to foster curiosity and expand our relational freedom at the expense of narrative and interpersonal rigidity (Stern, 2015). Thus, psychoanalytic inquiry is akin to driving a car: one is always wondering where one is headed, while at the same time remembering that one always has blind spots.

From the one-person perspective, the patient is in the driving seat, while the analyst is a passenger-observer (Wachtel, 2008). However, in the two-person psychology that informs my thinking about the intersections among ethnicity, gender, and sexual identity, the "analysis-mobile" comes with two brake pedals and two steering wheels; both individuals are simultaneously a passenger and a driver; each of them is an observing participant (Fiscalini, 2004). Along the way, we can learn about not only who we already are, but also who we can become (Hoffman, 1998).

According to Goldberg (2002), a common problem of people in psychotherapy – regardless of their presenting concerns – is a lack of curiosity about themselves and other people. Thus, promoting patients' self-reflection is a central objective of psychotherapy. However, psychoanalytic curiosity goes beyond inquisitiveness. It invites both participants to examine their assumptions about themselves, as well as their expectations for each other (Stern, 2003). In particular, it is important to acknowledge and explore both participants' racial, gender, and sexual embeddedness. After all, our everyday experiences and internal representations of gender, sexual orientation, and race structure our very understanding of ourselves and others. Reflecting on the similarities and differences between the patient's and analyst's systems of reference and experience of difference can create interpersonal spaces for new meanings and new ways of relating to emerge (Stern, 2015).

Psychoanalytic examination of racial, gender, and sexual differences unfolds within the interpersonal field co-created by patient and analyst. The relational version of field theory (Stern, 2015) emphasizes the pivotal role of social interactions in shaping human identities. Through a joint exploration of their emotional exchanges in the "here and now," patient and analyst can describe both the privileged and marginalized aspects of their identities. For patients and analysts alike, each bridge across these different parts of the self is another step towards the expansion of self-awareness (Meares, 1993).

At the core of this restorative relational process lies witnessing (Stern, 2015): our attempts to recognize the privileged, marginalized, and dissociated emotional experiences both in the other and in ourselves. In psychotherapy, witnessing allows dyads to link the gendered, sexual, and racial aspects of their identities through metaphor. Given that the English word "metaphor" stems from the Greek "transference," it is not surprising that any analysis of transference is first and foremost an exercise in metaphoric thinking. In the grip of transference, a patient might experience her analyst to be just like her parent, while knowing the whole time that the two people are also different (Stern, 2010). In other words, analysis of transference is made possible by our capacity to juggle fantasy and reality simultaneously. Similarly, metaphors can capture the intersections among gender, sexual orientation, and race by making one category temporarily stand in for another. For example, when Ana says to herself "my therapist looks like Kevin Spacey, a privileged, straight-acting white man," she implicitly links white privilege to heterosexual privilege.

What makes metaphors different from stereotyped, binary forms of thinking is the "as if" transitory relationship between symbols and what they represent. For instance, Ana is fully aware that her gay therapist only looks and carries himself like a straight man. Like race, gender and sexual orientation inhabit transitional spaces between social reality and personal meaning (Leary, 2002). That means that they function simultaneously as facts of our social lives and as narratives that are open to interpersonal negotiation. Therefore, metaphoric thinking about our racial and sexual identities takes into account not only our everyday social experiences, but also the idiosyncratic meanings that we assign to them in various interpersonal contexts (Layton, 2002). For example, while Ana identifies as straight and I identify as gay, she and I might or might not be queer. It is by playing together with these metaphors that Ana and I eventually stumbled upon some new and interesting questions about the parallels and tensions between her and my experience of privilege and marginalization.

Beginning phase

Initially, Ana sought psychotherapy to help her manage the severe anxiety that was interfering with her ability to work on her doctoral dissertation in philosophy. She was feeling burned out and guilty about her lack of progress. In addition, she was suffering from low self-esteem, the fear of falling behind her peers, and guilt about not speaking to her troubled, estranged father.

Both narrative rigidity and curious uncertainty were woven into our interactions from the very beginning. To paraphrase Stephen Mitchell (1993), while both Ana and I were, on paper, committed to change, in our heart of hearts, both she and I also wanted to remain the same. Clouded in apprehension about uncertainty and ambiguity, our one-dimensional, rigid representations of ourselves and of the other remained under our conscious radar until they began to bump against her and my curiosity. From the onset of treatment, as we now suspect, the two of us had been ensconced in a comfortable illusion that we understood both ourselves and the other person.

Like many other therapeutic couples, Ana and I began to learn about each other even before our first meeting. After getting my name and contact information from her university's counseling center, Ana checked out my web site and googled me. She was pleased to find out that, similar to some of her closest friends, I was gay and Jewish, and had studied philosophy. She assumed that she and I would have much in common, that I would be able to understand and appreciate her intellectual side. At the same time, she also conceived of our relationship as professional and emotionless, so she would not have to share her vulnerabilities or take care of me. In that respect, she did not want me to be like her gay Jewish friends who frequently relied on Ana for emotional support. While one side of Ana enjoyed helping her friends, another side of her experienced their emotional dependence on her as burdensome.

Upon arriving to our first meeting, Ana glanced at the office décor and my clothes and remarked that aesthetics mean a lot to both of us. I was flattered that this attractive, sophisticated young woman chose me as her therapist. I had encountered many children of immigrants before and found it easy to relate to them. Furthermore, I have always felt a special bond with other students of philosophy, both because of our common interests and because of our shared penchant for intellectualization. Thus, I expected that Ana and I would hit it off.

During the first phase of treatment, Ana was open to my questions and frequently responded to my observations and interpretations with a reassuring "Yeah, it's definitely true." Although my narcissistic side was basking in what felt like Ana's approval, something felt a bit off. The very easiness of our interactions seemed too good to be true. More specifically, my skeptical mind began to wonder whether Ana was agreeing with everything I said in order to stroke my male ego.

"Ana," I offered, trying to sound casual, "I am a bit surprised that you seem always in agreement with everything that I say. I can't always be right." Ana smiled and admitted that she wanted to please me. Moreover, just as she does in other social settings, she had compiled a mental list of what makes me tick, and strategically complimented my plants and my outfits. And then Ana secretly disdained me (just like she despised others) for being so vain and gullible. "Why do I need to destroy people?" she later asked both of us. "I feel bad about being manipulative."

Over time, our curiosity-led inquiry into our perceptions of each other made holes in our co-created dissociative cocoon (Bromberg, 2006), and uncomfortable, rich, only partially formulated emotional exchanges like the one that opened this essay began to leak out. Our conversations became so emotionally charged for both of us that our ability to reflect on them would usually kick in only in between sessions. After yet another uncomfortable session, Ana would replay our conversation in her head and say to herself, "That was fucked up!" Likewise, our encounters often challenged my ability to maintain composure without getting defensive. Fortunately, we also felt curious about what was unfolding between us and eventually found a way of sharing those reactions with each other.

These exchanges made me wonder about the subsymbolic communication between us of the dissociated ("bad me") parts. Once the proverbial cat was out of the bag and we began to pay attention to the back and forth passing of uncomfortable truths about ourselves, we simply could not take our eyes off this fascinating and disturbing hall of mirrors. "*I* am a marginalized Latina, an underdog with a queer sensibility; *you* are a privileged, straight-acting white man," thought Ana. "No. *I* am the underdog here. After all, *I* am a gay Jewish immigrant, while *you* are a straight American woman from a rich family," protested my inner voice.

As D. B. Stern (2010) points out, "dissociation can only be enacted if the roles that constitute it are relevant in the psychic lives of *both* participants" (p. 151). In retrospect, it seems that both Ana and I were secretly jostling for some sort of moral superiority. While Ana was focusing on what she perceived as my "straight acting," she loathed acknowledging her grandparents' considerable wealth and social connections. Similarly, I perceived her as coming from a much more privileged family background than my own and underplayed the significance of my race and gender. Both Ana and I seemed married to our narrow and rigid perceptions of our own selves and of each other. Neither of us wanted to concede that we might be in any way the more privileged person. Moreover, focusing on the presumed privileged parts of the other allowed each of us to feel self-righteous (Davies, 2004). Until she and I became curious collaborators united by a common project, we kept swapping the roles of the domineering and the subjugated (Benjamin, 2004).

Patient's experience of difference

Whenever Ana attends philosophy conferences in the United States or Europe, she is reminded of her status as an ethnic minority: there are very few Hispanics in her field. However, whenever she visits her extended family and friends in Mexico, she is perceived and treated as an American. Furthermore, although her gay friends regard her as a straight woman, her politically conservative Mexican uncles look down on her as queer for having close gay friends. Although Ana comes from a wealthy family, she refuses to ask them for money and lives on a graduate student's budget.

Our discussions of Ana's attitudes towards me and other people gradually revealed that behind her pleasing, ingratiating demeanor often lay insecurities, resentment, and competition. Growing up as the only child of highly educated Mexican-American parents who valued professional success and good looks, Ana equated her self-worth with her academic accomplishments and her appearance. As a chubby teenager, Ana was very self-conscious and insecure about her body and her looks. These days, she puts a lot of thought and effort into putting together her sophisticated, slightly vintage outfits, closely watches her weight and diet, and gets her hair cut and highlighted only in cool hair salons. "I am not sure how to relate to my body," she once confided in me, "but I want to exude an urban, fashionable look."

Since our very first meeting, I was always impressed by Ana's remarkable facility with words and ideas. Yet, in her conversations with me and others, she worried a lot about coming across as unintelligent or inarticulate. So whenever she spoke or emailed someone, she carefully crafted her sentences and her emails. When she was working on her dissertation, she spent a lot of time editing and perfecting each and every sentence.

Ana divided people into two categories: the very few who seemed intellectually superior to her and the inferior majority. And she had trouble deciding where to place me. "I don't feel like you're equal. Are you superior or inferior to me?" Ana pondered out loud. Afraid of coming across as inarticulate or unsophisticated, Ana anxiously monitored and dissected both my verbal and nonverbal reactions. At times she felt so self-conscious that she requested to lie down on the couch.

Ana had difficulty bouncing ideas off her peers in her doctoral program out of fear that they might either ridicule her or steal her original ideas and get ahead of her in the competition for fellowships and jobs. As she put it, "I either dig them or hate them." In particular, Ana was envious of her more privileged peers who had grown up in more intellectual families, spoke more foreign languages, played musical instruments, and wrote more beautifully than she.

She also struggled to figure out how to get her advisor's attention and support without appearing pushy. Similar to wanting to be her advisor's favorite graduate student, Ana desired to be my most interesting patient. At the same time, she was reluctant to acknowledge that working with me was helpful to her. "Telling you about my sadness feels like giving into your expectations. You'll have a one up on me," she mused.

The only person whom Ana experienced as her equal, neither inferior nor superior, was her boyfriend, Matt. Upon meeting him through a mutual friend, Ana was instantly attracted to Matt's artistic talents, sweet personality, and somewhat childish sense of humor. She also appreciated his deeply felt compassion for marginalized people and his awareness of his white male privilege. After moving in together, Ana and Matt built a cozy home. In the evening, they enjoyed telling each other about the people they encountered during the day or watching *RuPaul's Drag Race* while cuddling on the couch.

However, after a couple of years of living together, Ana and Matt noticed that their erotic desire began to wane; their sexual encounters became less frequent and less passionate. The same qualities that Ana used to find so endearing in Matt – his sensitive, gentle, selfless nature – began to annoy her. "When it comes to sex, I want a man who knows what he wants, not some indecisive boy," Ana shared with me. To make things worse, Ana interpreted Matt's lack of sexual assertiveness as a reflection on her physical desirability. "I used to be a fat child, so sometimes I have a hard time believing that I turn him on."

Drawing on Mitchell's (2002) insights into the anxiety inherent in romance, I suggested to Ana that perhaps as their emotional connection deepened, they stopped taking emotional risks in and out of the bedroom. I also introduced Ana to Esther Perel's (2007) musings on the degradation of erotic passion in long-term relationships. To my surprise, Ana was turned off by what she perceived as Perel's condescending attitude toward an American insistence on honesty and transparency. It also made me wonder whether Ana sometimes experienced me as a patronizing European. And yet, the thought that she and Matt might be keeping their erotic life boring in order to make their love feel safe and secure seemed to resonate with her. In particular, she started to ask herself whether her perception of

Matt as sexually timid could also be linked to her experience of growing up with parents whose marriage was destroyed by sexual betrayal.

Ana's family history

I believe that Ana's insecurities and competitiveness originated in her relationships with her parents. Ana's mother insisted on waiting on her daughter hand and foot, which made Ana doubt her ability to take good care of herself. By contrast, being proud of his intellectually precocious daughter, Ana's father treated her like a trophy child, parading her around his intellectual friends. Having always identified with her highly educated father, Ana also internalized his insecurities about his social standing and his need to appear special in other people's eyes as central parts of her own self-concept.

Growing up, Ana was vaguely aware of her father's frequent disappearances and her mother's marital unhappiness. Yet, for several years, Ana was able to push these observations out of her mind by focusing on school, books, and friends. On the one hand, Ana protected her parents' secrets by colluding with their mystification of their shared family life; she disowned her own perceptions and intuitive understanding of how her family members were relating to one another. On the other hand, from watching and interacting with her parents, Ana learned that her own negative affect was potentially dangerous to others and had to be disowned and discarded.

Ana began to map out other people's minds, while at the same time masking the contents of her own (Schnarch, 2009). Furthermore, Ana's reliance on dissociation of her emotional and intellectual sides, as well as her ambition and insecurities, eventually led to a decline in emotional richness and diminished her capacity to modulate her affect states. For many years, Ana's 'work' self seemed walled off from the relational, emotional, and somatic aspects of her self. She could either work around the clock in isolation or stay at home with her family and friends and do nothing.

Soon after she turned 15, Ana's family and her sense of self imploded. It turned out that the father had run up a significant credit card debt, secretly remortgaged their house and spent the money on his mistress. A foreclosure and a bankruptcy followed, leaving in their wake public humiliation and identity crisis. Ana went from seeing herself as a beloved heiress of a very special father, to being an ashamed daughter of a con man and a pariah, from feeling superior to being inferior. It is during that challenging time that Ana experienced her first bout of depression and anxiety.

During her adolescence, Ana was so eager to become different from her parents that she had difficulty owning and processing the similarities between them and her. Ana initially sided with her father and secretly blamed her mother for the divorce. She had apparently bought into the narrative of her father's intellectual superiority over her anxious, ingratiating mother. Moreover, Ana learned to value her own ability to manipulate people and situations to her advantage, while concealing her insecurities from herself and others.

To preserve the illusion of a coherent self-concept, Ana had to cut the links between her confused, suffering emotional self and her thriving intellectual side. In Ana's own words, she began to view herself as "a brain in a jar," as opposed to a flesh and blood person with thoughts and emotions. As Philip Bromberg (2011) describes this experience:

> The effect of traumatic experience is that the person surrenders self-state coherence to protect self-continuity. When the illusion of unity is so dangerous to self-continuity that coherence cannot be maintained, experience that is disjunctive with the ongoing self-state that organizes core identity is denied simultaneous access to consciousness.
> (p. 68)

Similarly, Ana relied on externalization to manage her conflicting internal representations of her parents, what Fonagy et al. (2002) call the "alien parts of her self" (the "superior me" and the "inferior me"). For instance, Ana often projected her unintegrated desire to feel superior on the men who surrounded her: her father, her academic advisor, some of her male friends, and her therapist. And then she resented them. At the same time, she often disdained the women in her life whom she saw as inferior.

During graduate school, after many years of being her father's sole source of emotional support, Ana finally asked him to stop burdening her with his problems. Several months later, the father made an unsuccessful suicide attempt, which filled Ana with fear and guilt. It was at that time that Ana, stricken with anxiety and unable to work, decided to seek psychotherapy.

Analyst's experience of difference

The exchange that opens this essay also reveals the intersections of my own gender, sexual orientation, country of origin, Jewish ethnicity, social privilege, and white race. Overtly or covertly, sexual, gender, or racial similarities and differences permeate my therapeutic relationships with all my patients. Our internal representations and performance of our gender, sexual orientation, race, and social status are highly susceptible to interpersonal influence and cultural context. For example, when I was growing up in the Soviet Union, my most salient characteristics were my male gender and my Jewish ethnicity. After I moved to the United States at the age of 21, to my surprise, I discovered that I was attracted to men, that I was white and Russian. While in the old country I was perceived and treated as a member of a persecuted ethnic minority, in the United States, I carry many of the privileges of white men.

Although some of my patients, like Ana, do not view me as "gay enough," for others I might be "too gay." And sometimes their attitudes towards my sexual orientation evolve over time. For example, another straight Mexican-American patient of mine, Juan, fired me after learning on the Internet that I was gay. The only reason I know this is because about a year later he came back and told me so. After discovering that his trusted dentist of many years was also gay, Juan decided that working with a gay therapist was not that uncomfortable after all.

Throughout my work with Ana, I tried to keep an eye on the splits in my own sense of self. Ana's questions about my straight demeanor put me in touch with my own dissociated parts. In the former Soviet Union of my childhood and adolescence, homosexuality was not only criminalized but also largely exiled from the collective and individual consciousness. Thus, when I was growing up, my erotic desires were not the "bad me" but rather the "not me."

Even though I have been out of the closet for more than twenty years, I still enjoy passing for a straight man and on occasion fear being rejected for my gayness. Thus, as Ana astutely observed, in some of our enactments, I was in fact communicating to her "*I* refuse to be defined by my sexual orientation. *You* are the queer one." Yet, at the same time, I begrudgingly appreciated her nudging me to look into myself, to reflect on my own unfinished business: "What kind of gay man am I? What role do my sexual orientation and identity play in my clinical work"?

"Working Through"

Our psychotherapeutic relationship remained rocky for about a year. It seemed that there was nothing I could say to influence Ana's opinion of me. Even disclosing that I was in fact married to a man did not help. Ana was convinced that I referred to my husband as "she," which only contributed to her confusion and distrust. Not knowing what else to do, I was preparing myself for a premature termination of a failed treatment. However, according to Ana, she never seriously considered quitting. Despite being very busy with her research, she religiously attended our weekly therapy sessions.

While unpleasant, psychotherapy was actually benefiting her. She was productive and less anxious. She and her boyfriend effectively worked through their struggles with sexual intimacy and his emotional dependence on her. On some level, Ana must have felt relieved that I was containing the unwanted, anxiety-provoking as well as the guilt-inducing parts of her self – her "inferior me" and her "superior me." And Ana's consistency helped me calm down and look at myself from her perspective. We both began to mentalize ourselves and the other, to tolerate uncertainty. According to Peter Fonagy (1999, accessed on-line):

> From the point of view of process aims, the therapist must permit such externalizations in order for the therapy to be tolerable to the patient and seek moments of movement, which may be short windows of time, when the patient is able to hear yet is still convinced of the success of the externalization. From a technical point of view this is the hardest phase, where many treatments fail. A simple verbalization of the process will not suffice. The analyst, his mind colonized by alien ideas, must find sufficient reflectiveness to perceive patients as they are, having distanced himself from an alien self-construction. Perhaps human generosity is the most pertinent therapeutic capacity at this phase.

I might have inadvertently modeled for Ana that it was relatively safe to come emotionally undone in our relationship, to appear unsophisticated, unsure, anxious, and even ashamed. I shared with Ana the contents of my mind, including my efforts to tolerate shame. Over time, Ana intuitively accepted my invitation to explore my affective states and reciprocated in kind. For example, I told Ana that I was afraid of not being gay enough for her, that she would leave therapy the same way she had "grown out" of her past romantic relationships and friendships. In return, Ana explored her ambivalent reaction to my self-disclosure. While she appreciated my honesty, she was also feeling vindicated, victorious, superior – and she felt guilty about it.

Before Ana and I began to play together in a metaphorical space between fantasy and reality (Winnicott, 1971), Ana tended to use me like a transitional object, a teddy bear: something to cuddle, hate, and mutilate, but not destroy. While I did not particularly enjoy being treated that way, I felt safe enough to continue, and I let Ana know that. In hindsight, in the words of Thomas Ogden (2004), I found a way "to use verbal symbols to speak with a voice that had lived within the intersubjective analytic third, had been changed by that experience, and was able to speak about it, in my own voice, as analyst to the analysand (who had also been a part of the experience of the third" (p. 169). Over time, our analytic relationship became what Adam Phillips (1988) calls a "transitional space of collaborative exchange." Not only would we share our perceptions of each other, but we also practiced getting to know ourselves through each other's eyes.

We often assume that we need to be self-aware in order to understand other people. Yet, to acknowledge and accept the dissociated parts of our own selves, we first need to encounter them in the other. To know myself, I need to get to know you. In fact, we often develop deep insights into lived experiences that are different from our own (Phillips, 2012). To paraphrase Hilton Als (2013), delving into each other's "otherness" enabled me and Ana to articulate our own feelings of difference to ourselves and to each other.

One day, Ana came to my office feeling upset about a particularly unbecoming haircut. Although other female patients had previously taught me to keep any critical observations about women's hair to myself, that particular day their admonishments proved to be of little help. My smirk failed to escape Ana's radar, and she experienced my tepid attempt at empathy as smug and withholding. Yet, when I eventually fessed up to my critical, mean streak, she sighed with relief.

After a series of grueling job interviews, Ana received a tenure-track position at a prestigious university. While terribly excited, she was also worried that other people would envy her success and treat her differently. However, when I confessed to Ana that I was in fact one of those people who felt envious of her, she chuckled with pleasure. As we continued to process our emotional exchanges, "events in therapy spread, expanding concentric circles of inquiry" (Levenson, 1983, p. 103).

The attachment bond between Ana and me survived many ruptures and went through many repairs. Through the ordeal of intersubjective collisions and negotiations (Bromberg, 2011), both of us struggled to modulate our negative affect and tolerate relational stress. As we continued to reflect on our previously dissociated, mutually enacted "bad me" self-states in the "here and now," our capacity to tolerate and mentalize the meaning of our emotions slowly expanded.

Over time, our exchanges became more spontaneous and playful. The one-dimensional accounts of oneself and of the other slowly yielded to more creative and multifaceted versions of who she and I could be. Sometimes we were engaged in parallel play, but at other times we played together. For example, I once told Ana that while I do look more like Kevin Spacey than a young black woman, I occasionally fantasize about impersonating Josephine Baker and sing her famous "J'ai deux amours" in the privacy of my car. Ana found my self-disclosure amusing and promised to take pictures of my drag debut. While sharing my fantasies with Ana made me feel vulnerable and exposed, engaging her in this playful mixing of fantasy and reality was also exciting and freeing (Dimen, 2002).

During our conversation about my Josephine Baker fantasy, Ana introduced me to Anne Anlin Cheng's (2011) fascinating analysis of the interactions among race, gender, and sexuality in Modernist Primitivism. Cheng maintains that the aesthetics of Modernist artists, architects, photographers, and movie directors were influenced by their artistic and personal encounters with racial others (both real and imagined). In particular, she explores the reversals of the subject and object of gaze in Josephine Baker's sexualized, racialized theater and screen performances. Cheng contends that Baker toyed with her audience's sexual and racial fantasies, raising questions about the spectators' own ambivalence about "primitive" and "civilized," black and white, masculine and feminine.

In the playful inversion of the subject and object of gaze between me and Ana, it was I, a white man, who would be impersonating a black female performer, while Ana, a woman of color, would be watching my performance and taking photos. For Ana and me, it was a way of suspending and subverting (however temporarily) the familiar boundaries around our gendered and racialized sexual identities. In Cheng's account, "the staging of the racial fetish throws into relief rather than appeases the problematic distinction of segregating blackness from whiteness, cover from exposure, masculinity from femininity, civilization from brutality" (p. 48).

These exchanges also expanded our ability to imagine how we see the other person seeing us. Spurred by curiosity, Ana and I spent many sessions exploring her and my areas of defensive not knowing. On my end, I worked to bring together my various attitudes towards Ana. I reminded myself that while she often used other people's vulnerabilities as ammunition, there were other times when she genuinely cared about the well-being of the people around her. Through these explorations, I came to know her as a unique, complex, interesting woman, rather than filing her away in my mind as a neurotic person with low self-esteem.

Our relationship got unstuck when we began exploring together our vulnerabilities and emotional reactions. Along the way, we mustered the courage to hold on to our respective selves, while at the same time being open to the other's perceptions. It was not easy. Ana was often reluctant to give me negative feedback out of fear of appearing like a mean woman who enjoyed hurting my feelings. At the same time, she did not want to look weak, vulnerable, and inferior. For example, she felt that tearing up in front of me would be too embarrassing. It took us several years to become more comfortable with sharing with each other our hurt, critical, and competitive sides.

Eventually, we learned to collaborate, to be curious and less dissociated together. In particular, we focused on understanding the moment-to-moment changes in our emotional experience of each other. We also discussed the similarities and differences between Ana's relationships with her parents and friends and her interactions with me. For instance, I was both similar to and different from her mother, father, and her gay Jewish friends. Like her mother, I erroneously believed that Ana was incapable of paying her bills on time and ignored the frequent delays in her payments for psychotherapy. Like her father, I was so proud of our work together that I frequently presented it in my group supervision.

Over time, our shared language became more metaphoric, less concrete. Ana and I started to play with the notion that I could, in certain contexts, carry myself like a straight man while remaining gay at the same time. In jest, Ana began to refer to her boyfriend as the "gayest straight man." More importantly, we started to look at ourselves not as *either* gay or straight, but as "queer," not as either superior or inferior, but as flawed *and yet* likable. In that process, Ana and I learned that heterosexuality and homosexuality, body and mind, superiority and inferiority are "but different moments of the self, the passage between which might be regarded as pleasurable, even though when we leave the preferred polarity we are extraordinarily uncomfortable" (Dimen, 2002, p. 57).

Ana gradually learned to tolerate her ambivalent feelings about other people's actions and developed more nuanced representations of their personalities. For example, she began to view her mother not only as anxious and annoying, but also as resilient and resourceful. Similarly, Ana learned that her father was not only selfish and manipulative, but also isolated and suffering. Moreover, Ana gave herself permission to feel both love *and* resentment, respect *and* disappointment, towards her parents, friends, and her partner. Over time, Ana started to question her view of herself as a "brain in a jar" and became more tolerant of what she calls "life's mess," (i.e., ambivalence and uncertainty). Gradually, Ana developed a more accepting view of her strengths and weaknesses.

In the present, while she still tries to plan every part of her life, Ana appears less anxious, less rigid, and more flexible. Although Ana continues to work very hard, she no longer neglects her relationships and has a better work-life balance. She feels less competitive with her academic peers and even opened up to some of them about her struggles. And she treats Matt both as her best friend and a lover. As a result, she seems less afraid of ending up successful but alone. During one of our last sessions, Ana and I had the following conversation:

Ana: "You and I have been working together for four years. It's crazy! You know, very few people know me as well as you do."

Therapist: "There are parts of you that you have shared with me, that I know quite well. Yet, there are other sides of you that I still don't know at all."

Ana: "I feel that you know the part that I am ashamed about: my tendency to manipulate people and situations to my advantage."

Therapist: "Well, thanks to you, I have become queerer."

Conclusion

As Ana and I explored both her confusion about my sexual orientation and my defensive reactions, we began to question her and my habitual ways of viewing people as either gay or straight, privileged or marginalized, inferior or superior. Our curiosity, self-confrontation, and self-disclosure eventually challenged narrative rigidity and gradually led to relational growth in both participants. By accepting and exploring our conflicted feelings about each other, Ana and I slowly acknowledged the previously disowned, elusive parts of ourselves. Over time, our modes of thinking and relating became more spontaneous, playful, and joyful.

References

Als, H. (2013). *White girls*. San Francisco, CA: McSweeney's.
Benjamin, J. (2004). Beyond doer and done to: An intersubjective view of thirdness. *Psychoanalytic Quarterly*, *73*, 5–46.
Blechner, M. J. (2009). *Sex changes: Transformations in society and psychoanalysis*. New York, NY: Routledge.
Bromberg, P. (1998). *Standing in the spaces: Essays on clinical process, trauma, and dissociation*. New York, NY: Psychology Press.
Bromberg, P. (2006). *Awakening the dreamer: Clinical journeys*. New York, NY: Routledge.
Bromberg, P. (2011). *The shadow of the tsunami and the growth of the relational mind*. New York, NY: Routledge.
Butler, J. (1990). *Gender trouble: Feminism and the subversion of identity*. New York, NY: Routledge.
Campbell, D. B. (2011). Oppression of the different: Impact and treatment. *International Journal of Applied Psychoanalytic Studies*, *8*(1), 28–47.
Cheng, A. A. (2011). *Second skin: Josephine Baker and the modern surface*. New York, NY: Oxford University Press.
Cho, S., Crenshaw, K. W., & McCall, L. (2013). Toward a field of intersectionality studies: Theory, applications, and praxis. *Signs*, *38*(4), 785–810.
Collins, P. H. (2005). *Black sexual politics*. New York, NY: Routledge.
Collins, P. H. (2008). Reply to commentaries: Black sexual politics revisited. *Studies in Gender and Sexuality*, *9*(1), 68–85.
Corbett, K., Dimen, M., Goldner, V., & Harris, A. (2014). Talking sex, talking gender – a roundtable. *Studies in Gender and Sexuality*, *15*(4), 295–317.
Crenshaw, K. W. (1989). Demarginalizing the intersection of race and sex: A Black feminist critique of antidiscrimination doctrine, feminist theory and antiracist politics. *University of Chicago Legal Forum*, 139–167.

Crenshaw, K. W. (1991). Mapping the margins: Intersectionality, identity politics, and violence against women of color. *Stanford Law Review*, *43*(6), 1241–1299.
Davies, J. M. (2004). Whose bad objects are we anyway? Repetition and our elusive love affair with evil. *Psychoanalytic Dialogues*, *14*, 711–732.
Dimen, M. (2002). Deconstructing difference: Gender, splitting, and transitional space. In M. Dimen & V. Goldner (Eds.), *Gender in psychoanalytic space: Between clinic and culture* (pp. 40–61). New York, NY: Other Press.
Dimen, M. (2011). The mystery of hysteria and the crossroads of power: Commentary on paper by Sam Gerson. *Psychoanalytic Dialogues*, *21*(5), 531–537.
Drescher, J. (2007). From bisexuality to intersexuality. *Contemporary Psychoanalysis*, *43*(2), 204–228.
Fiscalini, J. (2004). *Coparticipant psychoanalysis: Toward a new theory of clinical inquiry*. New York, NY: Columbia University Press.
Fonagy, P. (1999, April 16). *The process of change and the change of processes: What can change in a "good" analysis*. Keynote Address to the Spring Meeting of Division 39 of the American Psychological Association, New York. Retrieved from https://mentalizacion.com.ar/images/notas/The%20process%20of%20change%20and%20the%20change%20o%20processes.htm
Fonagy, P., Gergely, G., Jurist, E., & Target, M. (2002). *Affect regulation, mentalization, and the development of the self*. New York, NY: Other Press.
Foucault, M. (1990). *The history of sexuality*. New York, NY: Vintage Books.
Goldberg, C. (2002). An exploration of the analyst's impeded curiosity. *Contemporary Psychoanalysis*, *38*, 141–151.
Hoffman, I. Z. (1998). *Ritual and spontaneity in the psychoanalytic process: A dialectical-constructivist view*. Hillsdale, NJ: The Analytic Press.
Layton, L. (2002). Gendered subjects, gendered agents: Toward an integration of postmodern theory and relational analytic practice. In M. Dimen & V. Goldner (Eds.), *Gender in psychoanalytic space: Between clinic and culture* (pp. 40–61). New York, NY: Other Press.
Leary, K. (2002). Race in psychoanalytic space. In M. Dimen & V. Goldner (Eds.), *Gender in psychoanalytic space: Between clinic and culture* (pp. 40–61). New York, NY: Other Press.
Levenson, E. (1983). *The ambiguity of change: An inquiry into the nature of psychoanalytic reality*. New York, NY: Basic Books.
Levenson, E. (2017). *The purloined self: Interpersonal perspectives in psychoanalysis*. New York, NY: Routledge.
Levenson, E. (2018). *Interpersonal psychoanalysis and the enigma of consciousness*. New York, NY: Routledge.
Meares, R. (1993). *The metaphor of play: Disruption and restoration in the borderline experience*. Lanham, MD: Jason Aronson, Inc.
Mitchell, S. A. (1993). *Hope and dread in psychoanalysis*. New York, NY: Basic Books.
Mitchell, S. A. (2002). *Can love last: The fate of romance over time*. New York, NY: Norton.

Ogden, T. H. (2004). The analytic third: Implications for psychoanalytic theory and technique. *Psychoanalytic Quarterly*, *73*, 167–195.
Perel, E. (2007). *Mating in captivity: Unlocking erotic intelligence*. New York: Harper.
Phillips, A. (1988). *Winnicott*. Cambridge, MA: Harvard University Press.
Phillips, A. (2012). *Missing out: In praise of the unlived life*. New York, NY: Picador.
Schnarch, D. (2009). *Intimacy and desire: Awaken the passion in your relationship*. New York, NY: Beaufort Books.
Sedgwick, E. K. (1993). *Tendencies*. Durham, NC: Duke University Press.
Sedgwick, E. K. (2003). *Touching feeling: Affect, pedagogy, performativity*. Durham, NC: Duke University Press.
Sommerville, S. B. (2000). *Queering the color line: Race and the invention of homosexuality in American culture*. Durham, NC: Duke University Press.
Spade, D. (2013). Intersectional resistance and law reform. *Signs*, *38*(4), 1031–1055.
Stern, D. B. (2003). *Unformulated experience: From dissociation to imagination in psychoanalysis*. New York, NY: Routledge.
Stern, D. B. (2010). *Partners in thought: Working with unformulated experience, dissociation, and enactment*. New York, NY: Routledge.
Stern, D. B. (2015). *Relational freedom: Emergent properties of the interpersonal field*. New York, NY: Routledge.
Stern, D. B. (2017). Interpersonal psychoanalysis: History and current status. *Contemporary Psychoanalysis*, *53*, 69–95.
Sue, G. W. (2010). *Microagressions in everyday life: Race, gender, and sexual orientation*. New York, NY: Wiley.
Verloo, M. (2013). Intersectional and cross-movement politics and policies: Reflections on current practices and debates. *Signs*, *38*(4), 893–915.
Wachtel, P. (2008). *Relational theory and the practice of psychotherapy*. New York, NY: The Guilford Press.
Winnicott, D. W. (1971). *Playing and reality*. London: Tavistock.

Chapter 2

Minding the gap

Intersections among gender, race and class in work with gender-variant children

Avgi Saketopoulou

I have barely stepped onto the inpatient unit to pick up DeShawn for our first therapy session when I see him running towards me. His sprint is interrupted by his body forcefully slamming into mine. He reaches up, grabs as much of my hair as he possibly can, and pulls it violently with all the strength his 9-year-old body can muster. I instantly tear up from the pain. Courtesy of this traumatic moment, time stops. I hear him scream, 'I swear, I'll pull all your hair out.' Reflexively I crouch down to his height to lessen the pain. I can neither think nor speak, an opportune moment for him to grab more of my hair. This draws me even closer and now our noses nearly touch. As he yells in my face, I can almost taste the smell of his breath. I feel the heat radiating from his body. Droplets of his sweat and saliva land on my skin as he is thrashing about. Somehow I recover (some of) my ability to think. 'I know you want your own long hair; I know you are angry and scared,' I say. My interpretation releases neither DeShawn from his rage nor my hair from his grip; he's still yanking, I'm still hurting, we are still painfully entangled. I call for help. As staff gets him to let go, a thick bunch of my hair is clasped in his small fists. He walks away threatening, 'Don't you ever come near me again; I'll pull it every fucking time.'

DeShawn is 10 and black American[1] and grew up in a poor family where no one had finished school. He and I worked together in various capacities for three years. I am 34, a white immigrant who grew up in Greece when it was still a monoracial culture, and come from a mixed-class background.

My work with DeShawn informs the thesis of this paper: that in clinical work with transgender (and otherwise queer)[2] patients, considerations of race and class are not only important facets of the work: they *are* the work. Contemporary theory has deconstructed essentialist conceptions of race and gender challenging the idea that female/male and black/white are neatly separated categories (Altman, 2000; Bornstein, 1995; Butler, 1990; Corbett, 1996, 2009; Dimen, 1991, 2007; Dimen & Goldner, 2005; Fausto-Sterling, 2000; Feinberg, 1996; Gillman, 1993; Goldner, 1991, 2003; Halberstam, 1998; Harris, 2005; Kovel, 2000; Straker, 2004; Stryker & Whittle, 2006; Suchet, 2004a, 2007). This has cracked open a Pandora's box of meanings that have been as decentering as they have been exciting. However, a clinical theory of trans experience requires that we address the emotional dimensions of gender fluidity in more nuanced ways than our current thinking permits. Existing theorizing tends to be problematic because it assumes either that gender atypicality is inherently pathological (Chiland, 2000; Coates, 1990; Green, 2000) or neglects the fact that gender in *both* its normative and non-normative iterations can become an expression of psychic pain.

The latter is a particularly thorny issue for psychoanalysts because of the blood that stains our clinical hands throughout a long history of pathologizing homosexuality and other variant identities (Blechner, 2009; Mitchell, 1981). In working with trans, the simmering fear of repeating the offense dampens the degree to which we are willing to reflect on whether/how we can distinguish gender variance from the emotional distress that traffics in gender. Further complicating these distinctions is that stigmatization and marginalization of trans experience comes with its own psychiatric costs that include depression (Cohen-Kettenis, Owen, Kaijser, Bradley, & Zucker, 2003; Huegel, 2003; Turban & Ehrensaft, 2018), substance abuse (Burgess, 1999), anxiety disorders (Durwood, McLaughlin, & Olson et al., 2015a; Landolt, Bartholomew, Saffrey, Oram, & Perman, 2004; Olson et al., 2015b; Wallien, van Goozen, & Cohen-Kettenis, 2007), and suicidality (Olson 2016; Steensma et al., 2014; Spack, 2005) and that are often erroneously attributed to the trans experience itself.

While some trans individuals' gender embodiment does not require recourse to medical intervention, others feel that some or substantial bodily alteration is necessary to align inner experience with outward presentation. Installed in a gatekeeping role, clinicians are asked to determine which trans subjects are eligible and emotionally ready for medical/surgical procedures. Despite the fact that rates of hormonal detransitioning and post-operative genital reconstruction surgery regret are low (respectively: Turban & Keuroghlian, 2018, Turban, Carswell & Keuroghlian, 2018; and Carroll, 1999; Kuiper & Cohen-Kettenis, 1998; Rachlin, 2002; Hembree et al., 2017), and that the two existing published reports of anecdotal cases of hormonal detransitioning both indicate that the individuals feel they benefitted from having been allowed to explore their gender through hormones (Turban & Keuroghlian, 2018; Turban, Carswell & Keuroghlian, 2018) the possibility captures our worst fears, fueling the mistaken impression of trans experience as a footprint of pathology. This impression draws on gender atypicality as a uniform category rather than as a set of lived experiences that are often expressions of variability and that can, in some cases, like all registers of human experience, be annexed by emotional pain. We lack and are in need of clinical theory that minds the gap between the pathologizing of transgender identities and political trans activism that fails to inquire about gender's psychic meanings.

I have come to think of DeShawn as a casualty of this particular gap, a casualty of our yet limited understanding of *both* the complexities *and* the complications of gender, of the fact that there is not one but many gender fluidities. This has significant implications in work with gender-variant children; though surgical decisions are postponed until adulthood with genderfluid kids, not being able to navigate the space 'between phobia and advocacy' (Corbett, 2008, p. 849) can be as problematic. Hormone-blocking protocols that have been applied and researched in Europe (Hembree, et al., 2017; Smith, van Goozen, & Cohen-Kettenis, 2001) are now also available in the United States, making medical interventions with transgender children a viable option. Alternatively, erring on the side of caution by advising parents to defer or altogether discourage transitioning is also accompanied by serious emotional repercussions on psychic development, ranging from a retreat into a false self and its dissociative aides (Lev, 2004) to suicidality (Cooper, 1999; Spack, 2005).

To straddle the proverbial fence and straddle it well, we need to inhabit a both/and position. We must consider *both* gender's reduction to rigid, binary male/female formations as pathological (Dimen, 2007; Goldner, 1991; Harris, 2005) *and* recognize that gender can, at times, be an expression of distress. But how are we to know when gender acts as proxy for psychopathology? If Foucault (1977) has taught us anything about discursive power, it is to be suspicious of such questions and mindful as to who asks them. In this case, the problem lies with the questions themselves not only because in our postmodern times we are more aware of the regulatory power of psychiatry, but also because they mislead us into thinking that gender, typical and atypical, can be conceived as a singular category.

Rather, we are better off approaching gender as a category of experience that can be appropriated by multiple psychic ends and that is permeable to varied identity categories (Harris, 2008). Of these, I believe that race and class as they clash onto and melt into each other, hold *a privileged position* vis-a-vis gender constitution. I rely on material from DeShawn's treatment to clinically illustrate how gender cannot be thought of monocausally, how race is woven into its fabric, and how both can be *appropriated by* and *folded into* mental illness. Drawing on theories of intersectionality from black feminist sociology (Collins, 2000, 2005), I hope to interrogate current psychoanalytical practices that conceptualize identity as the accretion of distinct constituents developing in parallel with and independently of one another, and to question the usefulness of notions of the self as constituted of clearly defined/clearly separated, layers of psychic meaning and experience (see also Brown, 2005).

DeShawn belongs to the small minority of transgender children who are also afflicted with severe psychopathology, a statistical epiphenomenon of how infrequently psychosis is encountered in childhood (an estimated 1:10,000, Remschmidt, 2001; Morgan, 2009). Genderfluid kids are impacted to varying degrees by social rejection in response to their gender unintelligibility. This is more pronounced for girlyboys than it is for masculine girls as caretakers are more receptive to the lacing of femaleness with masculinity, often perceived as a sign of precociousness, than male effeminacy which tends to be perceived as damaged masculinity (on how this shifts as girls enter adolescence, see Halberstam, 2004). I have, however, chosen to use my work with DeShawn as opposed to work with more psychically intact patients because it captures in especially poignant ways the interplay between gender and race[3] and because the complexities that arise in considering gender fluidity as it co-occurs with disability are largely neglected in the literature. Taking on these complexities requires as much of a focus on the cultural economies on race and class in the clinical milieu where I worked with DeShawn as it does on the individual work itself. Let me then begin by describing the setting where he was growing up and being treated.

Cultural and clinical setting

I met DeShawn on an inpatient unit that serves an inner-city child population of mostly black and Hispanic 5- to 10-year-olds that is often neglected in the analytical literature (Altman, 2009). Our patients usually come from homes ravaged by poverty, a lack of education and unemployment and often bear the marks of neglect, physical violence and sexual intrusions by parental figures who are themselves hemorrhaging from early deprivation and maltreatment. Children are developmentally unequipped to manage such levels of psychic pain and as a result trauma goes unmentalized (Fonagy & Target, 1996). These primitive internal states coalesce around affective holograms (Ferro, 2006), which have often left me in horror: a child hallucinating a blood-soaked Holy Mary, a naked patient rubbing her genitals against a door, a boy barking like the dog he is convinced he is, a 7-year-old scratching his face, leaving trails of blood-soiling clothes and psyche alike. The severity of these illnesses makes press reports questioning the existence of child psychiatric disorders and challenging psychotropic medication use seem ignorant and naïve. Stabilizing these patients requires months, even years, of their early lives spent in the hospital.

As a result, clinicians and unit staff become real parental figures as much as they are transferentially imbued with such roles. Staff spend several hours a day with each child waking them up, helping them get dressed, accompanying them to the school (located within the hospital), eating meals with them, tucking them in at night. These relationships are steeped in the nuances of early attachment; love, hatred, longing, envy, idealization, grief, disappointment. Bonds that develop among staff are similarly powerful, forming a community that coheres around clinical care and its traumata. Race and class mark a divide: clinicians are mostly white, nursing staff almost exclusively not and staff's class and racial backgrounds are more proximal to that of the patients'. These psychic fault lines lend themselves to identificatory and counter-identificatory processes that figure prominently in the patients' internal lives and create complicated dynamics that, as I discuss, permit some interventions and foreclose others.

However cursory, contact with this world of raw affects and the violent projective and introjective processes they engender is inherently traumatic. In the course of my work, I've found my ability to maintain the links between my thoughts to be constantly under attack (Bion, 1967) and have had to actively resist the mutiny of my own distancing defenses. To prevent such anxieties from stultifying this paper, I have chosen to avoid the standard authorial format of presenting separately material from different registers. Instead, I have braided together the strands of clinical material relevant to this paper with theory, history and research.

DeShawn; first introductions

DeShawn was admitted to our unit when he was 7 with a diagnosis of schizoaffective disorder, multiple hospitalizations starting at age 4 and only partial responsiveness to antipsychotics. Biologically encumbered with serious mental illness on both sides of his family, he had tried to kill his adult sister, stabbed a peer, was threatening suicide and was severely thought disordered. DeShawn's hypersexual behaviors were equally disturbing. When manic he would implore male staff to 'fuck me', often screaming, 'I'm going to suck your dick'. Preying on younger, developmentally delayed male patients whose genitals he'd try to touch, he required constant supervision. Multiple trials of psychotropics proved him impossible to stabilize and when he did respond, medical complications required that his medications be discontinued. Efforts to help him transition to structured settings outside the hospital failed, requiring numerous readmissions.

Sprinkled in this weighty clinical record were also derisive references to his cross-gender identifications as 'sissy-like behaviors'. DeShawn had wanted to be a girl from as early as his mother, Ms. H, could remember.[4] On the unit, he walked and gestured in ways hailed as effeminate. Most of the nursing staff and clinicians felt disturbed by his presentation; their transphobic concerns were amplified by their genuine wish to protect him from being bullied and teased by his peers. In a society that adheres to rigid taxonomies of gender, a genderfluid presentation poses serious risks to physical safety (Walton, 2005). Even for parents who are accepting of their children's variance, bullying and physical abuse in school are serious concerns that need to be weighed carefully in making decisions about use of pronouns, dress and overall transitioning (Brill & Pepper, 2008). In the hope, thus, of encouraging masculine identifications and 'correcting' his gender, staff prevented DeShawn from frequenting the girls' areas and ensured that he was cared for by male aides.

Staff's viral approach to gender, as something DeShawn would hopefully 'catch' if sufficiently exposed to males, was proposed by Greenson (1966) and Stoller (1966, 1968). These psychoanalysts attributed boyhood femininity to difficulties dis-identifying from the mother and with 'excessive' maternal contact.[5] We know today that clinical interventions based on this rationale are notoriously unsuccessful in converting gender experience (Pickstone-Taylor, 2003). Aside from being misguided though, for DeShawn, paired with admonitions that he 'be a man', the feelings of shame and self-hatred they engendered got stacked onto preexisting layers of low self-esteem and negative self-perceptions that derived from his psychiatric illness and repeated hospitalizations. Like other effeminate boys who respond to such pressures by encasing their true selves in the protective shield of a false presentation (Menvielle, 1998; Rowland & Incrocci, 2008), DeShawn also struggled with how he was being perceived. Often humiliated and attacked by peers he would withdraw to his room to play by himself.

To make matters worse, staff otherwise accustomed to working with sexually intrusive patients recoiled from DeShawn's effeminacy and homoeroticism. Whereas they physically soothed other hyper-sexual children when they were upset, they hesitated to touch DeShawn, populating his inner life with rejecting objects and representations of himself as disgusting and abject. To ensure the desperately longed-for physical contact, DeShawn responded by dramatically escalating his aggression, unconsciously provoking intrusive physical interventions. In turn, these lent reality to his internal experience of feeling assaulted and left staff feeling emotionally drained.

Information about DeShawn's early history had been sparse or, to be more precise, the little that was known was fragmented. There was no known physical or sexual abuse, but I otherwise had little information about his earlier life. When Ms. H was 10, there had been a murder in the family, the circumstances of which were unclear. Ms. H had suffered a serious medical illness early in DeShawn's life from which she was now seemingly recovered. His father's whereabouts, and maybe his identity too, were unknown. Beyond a general sense of his early years being steeped in intergenerational trauma and emotional chaos, this information lent itself to conjecture but provided limited substantial help.

Ms. H would visit her son weekly but was too overwhelmed by her own life to participate in his treatment. More than anything, she'd comment on his effeminacy. Typical of parents of gender-variant boys (Pleak, 1999) she hoped that her son would develop into a gay man, casually commenting, 'He can be a faggot all he wants, but he ain't wearing any of *my* dresses.' While studies had previously suggested that atypically gendered children mostly grow up to be gay rather than transgender adults (Green, 1987; Zucker & Bradley, 1995), suggesting that effeminacy may mark one particular type of homosexual boyhood (see also Corbett, 2009). This raised questions about whether our field's clinical focus on fluidly gendered children may serve as an indirect way of psychiatrically targeting homosexuality (Burgess, 1999; Leli & Drescher, 2004; Menvielle, 1998). As Sedgwick (1991) noted bolstering this notion, the diagnosis of 'gender identity disorder' was introduced in the 1987 edition of the *Diagnostic Statistical Manual of Mental Disorders*, the first from which homosexuality was purged as a psychiatric category. We are today, however, in the position to better assess that these early studies suffered from serious methodological difficulties that put the finding (that most atypically gendered kids grow up to become gay adults) under considerable pressure (Olson, 2016; Turban, Carswell, & Keuroglian, 2018; Turban & Keuroghlian, 2018).

Gender variance in the clinical milieu

The question of how to understand DeShawn's effeminacy arose early in his hospitalization. Following a long tradition of dismissing trans experience as delusional and pathognomonic of schizophrenia (Caldwell & Keshavan, 1991; Laufer, 1991; Siomopoulos, 1974), clinicians' countertransferential anxieties about DeShawn's gender were expiated by attributing it to his psychosis. DeShawn was seen as a boy who wanted to be a girl because he was a *disturbed* boy.[6] His psychosis made him dismissible, discounting his right to a serious consideration of his gendered experience (McRuer, 2006; Siebers, 2009). Defensive mechanisms he mobilized to protect himself from the barrage of external pressures complicated the clinical picture and were misattributed to his effeminacy rather than to the impact of its suppression. Such conceptualizations persisted despite the fact that, even when psychotic symptoms yielded to psychotropic intervention, his cross-gender identifications remained unaffected.

The experiential gap between one's gender fluidity and the rigid cultural regulation of gendered behavior can be profoundly disorienting (Di Ceglie, 1998). A robustly constituted ego may be able to enlist the psychic derivatives of such discrepancies in a variety of successful ego adaptations (e.g. activism; see Muñoz, 1999). However, for an ego that is constitutionally porous to psychotic processes or that of a child's which is called upon to also tackle multiple developmental challenges, withstanding and creatively refashioning the pressures of gender normative expectations may be impossible. Under those circumstances, 'the person with a shameful differentness can break with what's called reality' (Goffman, 1963, p. 10) and psychosis may come to mark the only psychic space within which these misalignments can be tolerated. For such patients, encouraging the exploration of the meanings of gendered experience and offering the opportunity to metabolize affective reactions and unconscious fantasies becomes a matter of psychic life or death, psychosis and its containment.

Bringing to the clinical table both psychiatric vulnerability and a developing ego well below his chronological age, DeShawn's functioning was further compromised by the excess in the familial trauma of murder, his mother's medical illness, his father's absence and multiple disrupted attachments. In this context I felt that deeming his gender a manifestation of illness did more than just marginalize him: it *fenced him into his psychosis*. Out of concern that I'd be seeking to explore rather than 'fix' his gender and the fear that my feminine appearance would intensify his longings, DeShawn had by this time worked with almost every other clinician and trainee on the unit before being assigned to me despite my experience with genderfluid children. I had had a hard time watching clinicians agonize over whether he should be allowed to play with dolls, whether it was acceptable to let him talk about wanting to be a girl for fear that 'it would encourage his belief' or 'make him more hypersexual'. Therefore, when he'd seek me out on the unit long before I started treating him individually, I'd gladly engage with him around his interests in dolls and makeup. He had many questions – how did it feel to have my hair brush against my shoulders? How did I learn to walk in heels? How did I coordinate colors?

The bond that developed through these interactions was strong and intimate. When he became thought disordered and self-abusive upon being shamed for his effeminacy, he'd seek me out. Wrapping his arms around my waist, he'd press his head against my belly and cry inconsolably with an abandon children have not yet learned to suppress. My hair figured prominently in this process. Amidst his tears he'd beg, 'please, let me touch it', clasping strands of it between his hands. The vibrations of his small, sobbing body gently tugging on my hair would transcribe his emotional experience into a somatic one of my own. Sometimes he'd weep '*please please*' and before I could stop him he'd stuff my hair into his mouth with the urgency of a famished infant ravenously reaching for the nipple.

I understood these intense moments as primitive communications of tangled knots of affect that DeShawn was unable to process and, much less, verbalize. The regressive quality of his dependency spoke as much to the grief and longing that his lengthy separation from his family evoked, as it did to what I was now convinced must have been Ms. H's limited emotional availability from early on his life. I viewed the despair with which he'd throw himself on my lap soaking my clothes in his tears, as a reflection of how little emotional containment he'd had. I imagined Ms. H in his early years, overwhelmed by her own unmentalized trauma and the tremendous undertaking that attending to her ill son must have been, helplessly retreating from him when he'd need her, letting him soak in a pool of escalating affects he was unable to regulate. As such while staff's rejections were in themselves traumatic, they also transferentially activated these early experiences of neglect and emotional abandonment. My hair which evoked so much yearning, envy and pain not only represented his fantasy of an uncomplicated, 'natural' femininity which he was convinced I embodied, but also captured his need for an idealized mother who could withstand the hurricane of his primitive experience and help him modulate it, a mother who would want and be able to know him for who he was.

I wanted to do all that for DeShawn and, yet, his pain and anguish were often hard to bear. Sometimes I felt so spent I had to guiltily take breaks off the unit. Between his intensity and staff's strong reactions to him, my exhaustion swelled. For months I was visited by terrifying nightmares; this insufficiently processed emotional material, what Ferro (1999) calls 'balpha elements', was evidence of my inability to detoxify DeShawn's evacuated primitive mental states, unwelcome traces of my own anxieties about whether I'd be able to negotiate the complexities of his treatment. At the same time, I was concerned for the fate of his affects were they to remain unmetabolized, as I had come to see his physical aggression, predatory sexual behaviors, and thought disorder as undigested bits of experience that morphed into psychic objects that could not be processed and which needed to be urgently and forcefully evacuated (Bion, 1967). For them to be thinkable, for DeShawn to no longer need to violently expel them, they would need to be alphabetized and made tolerable (Ferro, 2005). But how could I detoxify them when I also felt hostage by them?

Lessons from the clinical front

The contrast between DeShawn's regressively desirous relationship to my hair and the barbarism with which he'd pulled it had left me feeling shocked, hurt and rejected. It was, thus, with some apprehension that a few minutes after he'd pulled my hair I took him off the unit, agreeing to his insistence that we not cancel our first session.

Walking to my office DeShawn asks to hold my hand, an attempt at reparation. Unlike prepubertal boys who retreat from the indignities of needing physical contact, DeShawn is starved for it. As we are walking down the corridor with his hand in mine, he tells me casually about his day. I'll later notice that he lets go of my hand around staff; right now I'm just relieved that a point of connection can be still be found. I miss this signifier of a social awareness that is saturated with meaning of which I am yet unaware.

When we arrive at my office, he ravenously rummages through bags of toys. In contrast to descriptions of gender-variant boys' play as 'compulsive, joyless' (Coates & Moore, 1998, p. 53), DeShawn's is anything but stilted. He intently sets aside several black dolls before he finds a white one with long, luscious, silky hair. He places her on top of a fan and giggles joyfully as he watches the transformation of a still, lifeless toy into a girl whose tresses are now playfully getting tangled in the wind. His pleasure is contagious, and it catches me in its draft as I watch him enjoy the freedom of playing with a doll. These moments are not only gendered, they are also racially marked. DeShawn is happy to play but not any doll will do. Over time he will often enact the same sequence, always consistent in his choice of the white doll.

Registers of meaning are multiple and multiply layered. I ask myself, is this driven by his relationship to me? Has DeShawn conflated my comfort with his gender fluidity with my white skin and staff's discomfort with their being black? I wonder if his insistence on the white doll may be a result of an identificatory process, a transferentially saturated choice made because DeShawn has come to feel that it is skin color that determines whether he'll be accepted. In other words, if he's going to be playing with dolls, does he feel it's easier to do so in white company?

Or, might it be that gender is being appropriated by racial self-hatred? I think of Kenneth Clark's research and his then-surprising-now-familiar finding that black schoolchildren preferred white to black dolls (see Klueger, 2004). 'Inherited across time', Cheng (2001) wrote, 'this wound endures not only in the individual psyche, but in the American national psyche as well' (p. x). And endure it does in DeShawn's play as it becomes the dominant theme in our work. Does that indicate a hatred of his black skin, one that metamorphoses into wanting to be a white girl? If Freud's dictum that anatomy is destiny is no longer true in a time where genitals can be surgically altered, can gender offer itself as an alternative to race?

Conversely, I also wonder, has DeShawn folded race *into* gender? I linger on the long history of black women struggling with the length and texture of their hair (Banks, 2000), of the bleaching agents used to lighten their complexions, of Madam Walker who built her empire on the proceeds of her hair-straightening pomades to become the first black female millionaire (Rooks, 1996). As a black boy growing up with this particular brand of racial discourse, could DeShawn be experiencing femininity as being *at odds with* his blackness? If ideals of femininity are hued in white, does gender subordinate race, encoding it differently for white than for black Americans? How does race do gender?

Under the weight of these questions, considering race and racial difference in work with non-white transgender patients carries different meanings than when working with white gender-variant children or with black normatively gendered youth. In the latter, considerations of race tend to exclude how racial affiliation complicates and is complicated by gender. DeShawn, however, was not yet ready to follow me into this labyrinth. When I'd try to bring up race, he'd outright ignore me and when I failed to take the hint, he'd offer supervision, instructing me to 'shut up'.[7] Though rebutted, my questions indicated to him my willingness to take on race; my technical choice was to wait and listen. The shift came, as it does in child work, in the form of play.

DeShawn picks off my toy shelf a big, stuffed teddy bear wearing a pink wig, that's been sitting on my shelf all along but which he has previously never touched. He tries the wig on. Looking at himself in the mirror he says proudly, 'I'm beautiful.' He seems genuinely pleased with himself and in this moment that he is admiring his reflection in the mirror he is no longer the insecurely effeminate gender-variant boy I've known; his girliness has now become something to delight over. A new image of him enters my mind – I visualize him as an adult. A vibrant, radiant performer he's onstage singing, 'I will survive', the audience beneath him cheering him on: drag queen extraordinaire! My reverie, the product of our intersubjective process (Ogden, 1998), captures a creative, resilient part of DeShawn. For the first time, I'm picturing him happy and outside institutional walls. This moment does not rest on splits and dichotomies, dissociation and repression. The importance of this moment does not hinge on whether DeShawn will indeed grow up to be a drag performer;

this is not about how his atypical gender will carry him into adulthood. What matters is that hope, happiness, a community where DeShawn can be accepted, loved, even admired has been possible to imagine. 'You are *so* beautiful' I tell him, moved; he stares at himself in the mirror, smiling with pleasure.

Race has been so far too radioactive to handle in the immediacy of the transference. I hope that this moment which has afforded us a different angle into his experience can help bear the weight of a discussion around race. I hope that the projective barrier can hold the tension. I point to a black doll he's cast aside earlier in our session. 'What does she think of all this?' I ask. He shrugs. A pause. I wait. 'I'm sorry I pulled your hair that day,' he says. I'm caught off guard. He's apologized before but always mechanically, never with time to talk about it. I wonder, why now? Why after I ask about the black doll? 'I think about it too,' I tell him, careful to navigate the fragile space between acknowledging his aggression and shaming him for it. 'Do you know why you were so upset that day?' He nods. Another, long pause. Then, 'That was the day I got my haircut, you know?'

No. I had not known. DeShawn had fought hard to be allowed to grow his hair. His interest in it had gone through multiple iterations since his admission. Early ones involved a troll doll whose kinky hair he'd violently tear from its plastic head. His brutality was followed by reparative attempts, as compulsive as they were dismal, to glue it back on. The result was grotesque, and he soon abandoned this play. He had then shifted to constructing makeshift wigs. He'd staple paper in a circle and would then attach to its periphery long pieces of string. When worn over his head, the string mimicked strands of hair brushing against his shoulders. His elation had equaled only staff's upset. Only with its gendered meanings smothered by referring to it as a 'headband' was DeShawn allowed to wear it.

However, when he started playing with the 'hair', tucking it behind his ears in girlish mannerisms, staff and teachers had had it. Grabbed off his head, the wig would be taken from him and thrown out. Or somehow, somewhere between bedtime and the next morning it would mysteriously disappear. No one 'knew' what had happened to it. No sooner had a new one been constructed then it would again go missing. In an effort to restore some semblance of control, DeShawn started compulsively destroying his wigs, biting staff and becoming self-abusive. The unit was in disarray.

I spoke to the clinical team, insisted on special trainings for both staff and clinicians. We discussed DeShawn's gender, and I approached those working directly with him to talk more about their frustrations. Slowly, some came to me with questions: 'Why can't he just be normal?' 'Is he gay?' 'Why not just stop this nonsense?' Slowly, these questions gave way to private confessions about underlying anxieties that his gender transgressions had stirred up; someone's brother who'd recently come out, a male cousin caught wearing a dress, an unmarried aunt living with a female 'friend'. Heartened though I was by this interest it had little impact on staff's tolerance of DeShawn's effeminacy. In the absence of being emotionally processed, it remained concrete information, barren knowledge (Bion's, 1962) and it could not be productively used.

It was then that DeShawn shifted everything by coming up with an ingenious solution. Casting 'wig' and 'headband' aside, he began referring to his stringed strands as 'dreadlocks'. In its linguistic drag the wig was freed from its feminine inscriptions and now became acceptable. For the first time it survived the night and he was allowed to wear it on the unit and in school. Staff now agreed to a request he had made often before and which had always been previously rejected: He was allowed to grow his hair and to have it braided. DeShawn's rage subsided, and things began to calm down. And while his psychosis did not resolve, he became less thought disordered, his communications began making more sense and his aggressive outbursts diminished in frequency and intensity.

Somehow, however, DeShawn never did grow out his hair. When I'd asked him about it, he'd dismissed my questions but at this moment he was ready to talk about it. 'How come you got the haircut?' I asked. DeShawn said plainly, 'Paul said that I gotta keep it real, I gotta be a man.' Paul had worked with DeShawn for years and felt strongly about the importance of 'protecting' my patient's masculinity. His explicit commitment to 'make a man out of him' had routinely overridden any concerns about feelings of rejection they engendered in DeShawn. 'You didn't want to disappoint him,' I said sadly. 'No!' DeShawn corrected me, '*I*' – he emphasized the *I* – '*I* gotta keep it real.'

In DeShawn's crisp response, I now heard something new. I had till now been thinking of his interest in the white dolls' and my hair as gender based, with race implicated only insofar as it was caught in femininity's white web. Condensed in Paul's statement, however, the sentence that DeShawn so clearly recalled was a gender imperative spoken in ebonics.

The kind of 'man' that Paul implored my patient to be wasn't merely rigidly gendered – it was raced. What made DeShawn's dreadlock wig acceptable was not only that it had been purged of feminine markers but also that, perhaps more importantly, dreadlocks safeguarded DeShawn's blackness. It proved not merely that a black man with long hair can still be a man, but that *he can still be black.* What had been at stake here was not masculinity but racial identification, and it was because of that why discussions with staff had amounted to 'barren knowledge'.

DeShawn may have shrugged a dismissive 'I don't know' when I'd asked him about the linguistic shift from 'wig' to 'dreadlocks' but he had on some level been keenly aware of and responsive to the racial anxieties underlying staff's fears, racial anxieties that he likely also shared. I now saw how my previous attention to homophobia and transphobia and my consideration of his race as an independent identity strand to be kept in mind had blinded me to considering the intersections between and co-constitution of those different elements, that it had blinded me to *the racial demands on DeShawn's gender*. Caught up in a discourse which treats masculinity as white culture's most prized possession, I had missed that *for black boys racial identification trumps gender anytime*. 'The specter of the fag' Pascoe (2007) found in her research in American high schools 'is tightly raced' (p. 97). Where white teenage boys taunt one another for being 'a faggot', for black adolescents the offense is 'acting white'. Further, race and class mediate perception of gender transgressions. Consider, for instance, the fact that interest in one's hair, clothing and shoes is an indisputably masculine preoccupation among black adolescents but marks effeminacy in white teenagers (Perry, 2002).

If for the (largely white) clinicians, questions about DeShawn's gender revolved around its relation to his psychosis, for the non-white staff it could not be extricated from a racial matrix. Embedded in a historical discourse on attacks on black masculinity, ranging from actual castrations (see Dray, 2003) to the more symbolic emasculation of black men who were denied access to paternity rights and male entitlements by their white slave owners (Ferguson, 2005a; hooks, 2004), the notion of approaching DeShawn's gender atypicality as nonpathological was seen as akin to a form of black male emasculation. In this cultural milieu, my being white subjugated my views on his effeminacy to the trope of black male emasculation, intensifying the perception of a threat to his black identity and diluting the usefulness of my interventions on the unit level. My previous, casual observation that DeShawn would let go of my hand when we'd be around staff, now made more sense.

I started researching the historical origins of the investment in normative iterations of identity among black Americans. In discussing the economics of reproduction in colonial times, Collins (2005) describes how slaves were encouraged to have as many children as possible to enhance wealth and power for their owners. Affording 'breeder women' the protections of not being sold, this consolidated the survival value of heterosexuality (Cole & Guy-Sheftal, 2003). When the 1863 American Freedman's Inquiry Commission sought to situate newly emancipated slaves in the state system, it deemed unions outside matrimonial walls as emblematic of the 'uncivilized, degraded . . . ways of the slaves' (Ferguson, 2004, p. 86). For former slaves, therefore, American citizenship was made contingent on heterosexual marriage. Those who refused to comply were severely sanctioned.[8]

The erasure of homosexuality was thus to be counted among the costs for black Americans' inclusion in the white, dominant culture. Homosexual deviations jeopardized not only the social standing of transgressors but also endangered the status of the entire race. 'African Americans', Richardson wrote, 'have often looked to heterosexual marriage to afford us respectability' (Bailey, Kandaswamy, & Richardson, 2008, pp. 113–114). This whitewashed homosexuality gave birth to the notion that those who are gay cannot possibly be authentically black (West, 1993).[9] This assimilationist violence extended beyond the brutalities of cultural erasure to the violence perpetrated on the black men whose non-normativity threatened to forestall the race's upward mobility, melting race into class (Kennedy, 2008; see also Sycamore, 2004). Thus, although the notion that homosexuality compromises masculinity does not adhere to race, in black American culture homosexuality carries the additional burden of imperiling racial membership (Ferguson, 2005b). 'Homosexuality,' said Julien (1989/2007) in his famous *Looking for Langston*, 'is *a sin against the race*.' Things were now making more sense: Unlike white girly-boys I'd worked with, DeShawn was dealing not just with straight-up homo/transphobia but also with its racially queered equivalent, saturated in intergenerationally transmitted anxieties about preserving black identity.

In thinking about the intersectional identities of minoritarian subjects at a time that the term *intersectionality* had not yet developed the traction that it has in our discourse today, the queer theorist Jose Muñoz wrote:

> I always marvel at the ways in which nonwhite children survive a white supremacist US culture that preys on them. I am equally in awe of the ways in which queer children navigate a homophobic public sphere that would rather they did not exist. The [psychic] survival of children who are both queer and racially identified [as nonwhite] is nothing short of staggering.
>
> (1999, p. 37)

Muñoz's language is blunt, lacerating: it is this precarity of psychic survival that we are confronted with as clinicians in working with patients like DeShawn, patients who navigate worlds that would rather they not exist. These worlds are not only the cultural worlds undergirded by white supremacy, classism and heteronormativity; they are also largely – and with only few exceptions, even to this day – the worlds offered to us as therapists by our theoretical frameworks and our clinical techniques. Our theories of therapeutic action and our models for understanding racialized gendered embodiment are refracted through the enduring difficulties of psychoanalysis to think of race with gender and with class; to think through history and its reverberating impact; to think about the psychic tangles of how these materialize in a single individual. This is especially urgent when it comes to working with children, further raising the stakes for the lived implications for our metapsychology.

On not concluding

I wish that I could go on from here to describe how this rigorous intellectual and clinical journey led to a major shift in technique that then changed my patient's life. I have always been envious, and perhaps because of that somewhat mistrustful, of clinical narratives where an analyst's new insight bends the therapeutic rainbow to that coveted pot of clinical gold, that aha moment that breeds radical experiential and behavioral change. To the contrary, there was nothing spectacular in how these thoughts influenced my work as they slowly worked their way into my treatment of DeShawn.

Having a way of linguistically representing and, thus, of being able to think of the continuities between race and gender, having found my way into the clinical iteration and lived experience of identity as intersectional, my receptivity to DeShawn's material began to gradually shift. I found myself entertaining questions that pertained less to his gendered and racial experience as based on static, distinct and monolithic systems but that, rather, allowed them to be intricately knotted together. But of this, I said very little if anything at all. Mostly, I became better able to nod encouragingly as he'd turn to me anxiously when his play would venture into what I now recognized as racio-gendered territory. Where I'd have previously jumped into his play to verbalize my sense of what he was struggling with, framing it as distinctively raced or gendered, I now stopped disrupting him from playing, playing out, and dwelling on their tangled meanings. DeShawn's play flourished and a wider variety of enacted scenarios began emerging, a newly found flexibility in his emotional range.

Sadly, I did not have the opportunity to continue to work with DeShawn much longer. Two months after these issues had started becoming clear to me, I left the hospital and I left DeShawn. I've managed my guilt by taking solace in the fact that what I learned through him stays with me, permeating my clinical thinking with my other patients. That one category of difference can be cloaked in another's garb, the mechanism by which one category can offer itself as a viable alternative to negotiating trauma and psychic pain originating in another, has been possible to see with increasing frequency in my work with gender and sexual variance. Is it too much to hope that work which bears the tensions of these complexities might help disrupt the kind of developmental trajectory that fuel well-founded concerns about how to work with non-normatively gendered patients? Is it possible to consider this kind of clinical work without collapsing all non-normative phenomena into potential catastrophes that need to be averted? How do we mind the gap?

Worrying is endemic to child work. But when we work with genderfluid children, worry increases exponentially. Contrary to clinical issues where we can, for the most part, map a topography of possible adaptations our patients can make to the external world, treating atypically gendered children at this point in time carries the additional burden of trying to imagine a world that does not yet exist. What does this future that we are asked to envision hold for fluidly gendered kids? What does the future hold specifically for someone like DeShawn who lacks the protections afforded those with the cultural capital of class (see also Munt, 2009)? Will he be happy as a cross-dresser, a transwoman, a gay man, a drag queen? Will he be living in a hospital, in a community, in jail, in the streets? Is he awaited by a life of happiness, rejection, creativity, hope, despair? Observing how his race, his class, and his gender loop together offers no answers. Rather, it queers the discourse, breeding further questions still. Was DeShawn a boy who wanted to be a girl, but felt that being black limited how feminine he could eventually succeed in being? Did feeling feminine locate him outside his racial identity because not being a typical boy compromised his blackness? Was he a black boy struggling with racial self-hatred who used gender to negotiate skin color? As asking these questions becomes possible for us, it may also become possible for DeShawn, and he may one day be able to make his own decisions.

Space limitations don't permit me to follow in this paper the labyrinthian trails of several other important aspects of DeShawn's psychic make-up that arose in the course of our work. What about the place of eroticism, the maternal erotic transference (Wrye & Welles, 1998) in his intense engagement with my white, female body? How about his attraction to males, of which I've only said little and which was exclusively interracial? Is there a link between the transgressions of homoeroticism and those of miscegenation (Cheng, 2001)? Would it (not) be stereotype to assume that the allure white men held for DeShawn reflects self-loathing, as the popular claim goes (Craig-Henderson, 2006) and others challenge (Fisher, 1996; Mercer & Julien, 1988; Reid-Pharr, 2001)? Would those possibilities as readily enter our minds if DeShawn had been white and desired cross-racially? Or would we then turn our attention to the black subject, now object, of desire as fetish (hooks, 2004; Poulson-Bryant, 2005)? Does the notion that a non-white subject has absorbed racial fantasy (LaFarriere, 2010) necessarily have to submit to the trope of stereotype (Cheng, 2001)?

How about the way in which my own subjectivity framed this work? What does it mean for me as a white person to be wondering about these issues? How does it relate to the fact that as a foreigner who was raised in Greece when it was still an exclusively white culture, my whiteness has different meanings than that of my white American colleagues (Crouch, 1995; Suchet, 2004b)? Does that (in)validate the questions I ask? The ones that elude me? How are my questions as a cis woman different from otherwise sexed others, and which important ones does my gender and the way I inhabit it preclude? How about my class privilege and the fact that, unlike DeShawn, whose aspiration is to work at McDonald's, I can enjoy the luxury of being able to reflect on our work and process its emotional impact and its psychic toll by writing about it? What about you? How does *your* gender, *your* racial identity, *your* class background sculpt your understanding of DeShawn? Who gets to ask what and how dismissible do our subject positions make us anyway?

The most apt commentary on these questions is, perhaps, that of 9-year-old Doshanda, DeShawn's hated rival and ardent attacker who would appear, whenever he wore his wig, as if out of nowhere to inflict psychic pain and physical injury. When I asked her what she found so upsetting about him, she was disarmingly direct and disturbingly clear: 'he makes my brain hurt,' she replied. Her statement made immediate, visceral sense. My brain had also hurt as I tried to disentangle the different discursive threads in working with DeShawn, and maybe yours has as well as you've been reading through this paper. Still, Doshanda's succinct response stays in my mind as the most comprehensive, most succinct explication of homophobia and transphobia I've heard.

When I announced that I was leaving the hospital, staff was worried: 'What's going to happen to DeShawn?' Deciding to leave the hospital had been especially hard because I specifically did not want to end my work with him. Plus, I dreaded having to tell him. When I did, he bit and kicked me; he pulled my hair, then begged me to stay. A few weeks later in the community meeting where I was saying good-bye, DeShawn was floridly psychotic: hallucinating, giggling, talking to himself. Hearing patients and staff express their sadness, I teared up. For DeShawn, it was too much. Wrapping his face in a curtain his speech became unintelligible before he was eventually able to tell me: 'it pisses me off that you're crying; just stop it!' I later found him in his room sobbing. He pleaded with me, for yet another time, not to leave him. When he calmed down, he asked me if I'd get him a tissue. 'How about we get one together?' I offered, not wanting to leave him alone. 'No,' he said, 'I don't want others to see me cry and think I'm a fruit.' There he was, my 10-year-old patient, a child assigned-male-at-birth who had by now been wearing a wig for several months, worrying that it would be his tears that would mark him as queer. That image in its poignancy and absurdity, in the depth of his shame and the extent of his need, captures the complexity of who I knew DeShawn to be. Six months later, together with his new therapist, he made some drawings that he asked her to send me. In bright red and gold glitter he wrote, 'I very miss you. I'm sorry I pulled your hair. Do you love me?'

Notes

1 Racial identities mediated by ethnicity, immigration and the particular brands of imperialism that stain them do not carry uniform meanings. Rather, they are steeped in taxonomies of history and ideology that are contingent on cultural, geographical and chronological locale. Consequently, African, West Indian and American blacks all carry and experience their racial identities differently; this paper deals specifically with black American identities.
2 I use the term 'queer' here to encompass variant identities that resist culture's normative regulation of gender and sexuality and that include genderfluid experience (masculine women, effeminate men, drag queens and kings, transmen and transwomen), and variant sexual orientations (gay, lesbian, bisexual and leather).
3 The focus of this essay is to theorize the links among gender, race and class and, as such, a discussion of other aspects of my work with DeShawn, and technique issues arising in work with this population are beyond its scope.
4 Despite his feminine identifications, DeShawn felt strongly about and insisted on the use of male pronouns.
5 This model of gender contagiousness is not an exclusive property of the 1960s and '70s; see Nicolosi and Nicolosi (2002) who advise that effeminate boys shower with their fathers to help foster a "relaxed, anatomically based identity and dispel the erotization of male anatomy which may accompany concealment" (p. 82).
6 It is, of course, impossible to miss the sexist implications of such formulations.
7 I am here drawing on Bion's (1994) idea of the patient as 'our best colleague'. See also Ferro (1999) for discussions on using child patients' verbal and nonverbal responses as supervisory input.
8 Other minorities have similarly suffered heteronormative impositions to gain American citizenship (Gopinath, 2005). See also Puar (2007) for a discussion of a related and very interesting discussion of how non-normativity has more recently and in the context of the War on Terror, been appropriated by projects of American citizenship.
9 Cohen (1999) uses the term *advanced marginalization* to describe how minority groups trying to establish their legitimacy within a majority culture erase their non-normative members. Examples abound: The gay movement, for instance, notoriously marginalized transgender individuals (Serano, 2007; Sycamore, 2008) and leather sexuality (Samois, 1981) in its efforts to secure homonormative rights for its members.

References

Altman, N. (2000). Black and white thinking: A psychoanalyst reconsiders race. *Psychoanalytic Dialogues, 10*(4), 589–605.

Altman, N. (2009). *The analyst in the inner city: Race, class and culture through a psychoanalytic lens*. New York, NY: Routledge.

Banks, I. (2000). *Hair matters: Beauty, power, and Black women's consciousness*. New York, NY: New York University Press.
Bion, W. R. (1962). *Learning from experience*. London: Karnac Books.
Bion, W. R. (1967). *Second thoughts*. London: Karnac Books.
Bion, W. R. (1994). *Clinical seminars and other works*. London: Karnac Books.
Blechner, M. J. (2009). *Sex changes: Transformations in society and psychoanalysis*. New York, NY: Routledge, Taylor & Francis.
Bornstein, K. (1995). *Gender outlaw: On men, women, and the rest of us*. New York, NY: Vintage Books.
Brill, S., & Pepper, R. (2008). *The transgender child: A handbook for families and professionals*. San Francisco, CA: Cleis Press, Inc.
Brown, W. (2005). *Edgework: Critical essays on knowledge and politics*. Princeton, NJ: Princeton University Press.
Burgess, C. (1999). Internal and external stress factors associated with the identity development of transgendered youth. In G. P. Mallon (Ed.), *Social services with transgendered youth* (pp. 35–47). New York, NY: Hawthorne Press.
Butler, J. (1990). *Gender trouble: Feminism and the subversion of identity*. London: Routledge.
Caldwell, C., & Keshavan, M. S. (1991). Schizophrenia with secondary transsexualism. *Canadian Journal of Psychiatry*, *36*, 300–301.
Carroll, R. (1999). Outcomes of treatment for gender dysphoria. *Journal of Sex Education and Therapy*, *24*, 128–136.
Cheng, A. A. (2001). *The melancholy of race: Psychoanalysis, assimilation, and hidden grief*. New York, NY: Oxford University Press.
Chiland, C. (2000). The psychoanalyst and the transsexual patient. *International Journal of Psychoanalysis*, *81*, 21–35.
Coates, S. W. (1990). Ontogenesis of boyhood gender identity disorder. *The Journal of the American Academy of Psychoanalysis and Dynamic Psychiatry*, *18*, 414–438.
Coates, S. W., & Moore, M. S. (1998). The complexity of early trauma: Representation and transformation. In D. Di Ceglie (Ed.), *A stranger in my own body: Atypical gender identity development and mental health* (pp. 39–62). London: Karnac Books.
Cohen, C. J. (1999). *The boundaries of blackness: AIDS and the breakdown of black politics*. Chicago: University of Chicago Press.
Cohen-Kettenis, P. T., Owen, A., Kaijser, V. G., Bradley, S. J., & Zucker, K. J. (2003). Demographic characteristics, social competence, and behavior problems in child with gender identity disorder: A cross-national, cross-clinic comparative analysis. *Journal of Abnormal Child Psychology*, *31*, 41–53.
Cole, J. B., & Guy-Sheftal, B. (2003). *Gender talk: The struggle for women's equality in African American communities*. New York, NY: Ballantine.
Collins, P. H. (2000). Gender, black feminism, and black political economy. *Annals of the American Academy of Political and Social Science*, *568*, 41–53.

Collins, P. H. (2005). *Black sexual politics: African Americans, gender and the new racism*. New York, NY: Routledge.
Cooper, K. (1999). Practice with transgendered youth and their families. In G. P. Mallon (Ed.), *Social services with transgendered youth* (pp. 111–129). New York, NY: Hawthorne Press.
Corbett, K. (1996). Homosexual boyhood: Notes on girlyboys. *Gender and Psychoanalysis*, *1*, 429–461.
Corbett, K. (2008). Gender now. *Psychoanalytic Dialogues*, *18*(6), 838–856.
Corbett, K. (2009). *Boyhoods: Rethinking masculinities*. New Haven, CT: Yale University Press.
Craig-Henderson, K. M. (2006). *Black men in interracial relationships: What's love got to do with it*. Piscataway, NJ: Transaction Books.
Crouch, S. (1995). *The all-American skin game, or, the decoy of race*. New York, NY: Vintage Books.
Di Ceglie, D. (Ed.). (1998). *A stranger in my own body: Atypical gender identity development and mental health*. London: Karnac Books.
Dimen, M. (1991). Deconstructing difference: Gender, splitting and transitional space. *Psychoanalytic Dialogues*, *1*, 335–352.
Dimen, M. (2007). Ma vie en rose: A meditation. In M. Suchet, A. Harris, & L. Aron (Eds.), *Relational psychoanalysis, vol. III: New voices* (pp. 53–60). Mahwah, NJ: The Analytic Press.
Dimen, M., & Goldner, V. (2005). Gender and sexuality. In A. Cooper, G. Gabbard, & E. Person (Eds.), *The American Psychiatric Association publishing textbook of psychoanalysis* (pp. 93–114). Washington, DC: American Psychiatric Publishing.
Dray, P. (2003). *At the hands of persons unknown: The lynching of Black America*. New York, NY: Modern Library Paperback.
Durwood, L., McLaughlin, K. A., & Olson, K. R. (2017). Mental health and self-worth in socially transitioned transgender youth. *Journal of the American Academy of Child and Adolescent Psychiatry*, 56, 116–123.
Fausto-Sterling, A. (2000). *Sexing the body: Gender politics and the construction of sexuality*. New York, NY: Basic Books.
Feinberg, L. (1996). *Transgender warriors: Making history from Joan of Arc to Dennis Rodman*. Boston: Beacon Press.
Ferguson, R. A. (2004). *Aberrations in Black: Toward a queer of color critique*. Minneapolis: University of Minnesota Press.
Ferguson, R. A. (2005a). Of our normative strivings: African American studies and the histories of sexuality. *Social Text*, *23*(3–4), 25–100.
Ferguson, R. A. (2005b). Race-ing homonormativity: Citizenship, sociology, and gay identity. In E. P. Johnson & M. G. Henderson (Eds.), *Black queer studies: An anthology* (pp. 52–67). Durham, NC: Duke University Press.
Ferro, A. (1999). *The bi-personal field: Experiences in child analysis*. London: Routledge (The New Library of Psychoanalysis; P. Slotkin, trans.).

Ferro, A. (2005). *Seeds of illness, seeds of recovery: The genesis of suffering and the role of psychoanalysis*. London: Routledge (The New Library of Psychoanalysis; P. Slotkin, trans.).
Ferro, A. (2006). *Psychoanalysis as therapy and as storytelling*. London: Routledge (The New Library of Psychoanalysis; P. Slotkin, trans.).
Fisher, G. (1996). *Gary in your pocket: Stories and notebooks of Gary Fisher*. Durham, NC: Duke University Press.
Fonagy, P., & Target, M. (1996). Playing with reality: I. Theory of mind and the normal development of psychic reality. *International Journal of Psychoanalysis, 77*, 217–233.
Foucault, M. (1977). *The history of sexuality* (vol. I). London: Routledge.
Gillman, S. L. (1993). *Freud, race and gender*. Princeton, NJ: Princeton University Press.
Goffman, E. (1963). *Stigma: Notes on the management of spoiled identity*. New York, NY: Simon & Schuster, Inc.
Goldner, V. (2003). Ironic gender/authentic sex. *Studies in Gender and Sexuality, 4*, 113–139.
Goldner, V. (1991). Toward a critical relational theory of gender. *Psychoanalytic Dialogues, 1*, 249–272.
Gopinath, G. (2005). *Impossible desires: Queer diasporas and South Asian public cultures*. Durham: Duke University Press.
Green, R. (1987). *The sissy boy syndrome: The development of homosexuality*. New Haven, CT: Yale University Press.
Green, R. (2000). Family cooccurrence of "gender dysphoria": Ten sibling or parent-child pairs. *Archives of Sexual Behavior, 29*(5), 499–507.
Greenson, R. (1966). A transvestite boy and a hypothesis. *International Journal of Psychoanalysis, 47*, 396–403.
Halberstam, J. (1998). *Female masculinity*. Durham, NC: Duke University Press.
Halberstam, J. (2004). Oh bondage up yours! Female masculinity and the tomboy. In S. Bruhm & N. Harley (Eds.), *Curiouser: On the queerness of children* (pp. 191–212). Minneapolis: University of Minnesota Press.
Harris, A. (2005). Gender in linear and nonlinear history. *Journal of the American Psychoanalytic Association, 53*, 1079–1095.
Harris, A. (2008). *Gender as soft assembly*. New York, NY: Relational Perspectives Book Series.
Hembree, W. C., Cohen-Kettenis, P. T., Gooren, L., Hannema, S. E., Meyer, W. J., Murad, M. H., & T'Sjoen, G. G. (2017). Endocrine treatment of gender-dysphoric/gender-incongruent persons: An endocrine society clinical practice guideline. *The Journal of Clinical Endocrinology & Metabolism, 102*, 1–35.
hooks, b. (2004). *We real cool: Black men and masculinity*. New York, NY: Routledge.
Huegel, K. (2003). *GLBTQ: The survival guide for queer and questioning teens*. Minneapolis: Free Spirit Publishing.
Julien, I. (Director). (1989/2007). *Looking for Langston* [DVD]. Strand Releasing.

Kennedy, R. (2008). *Sellout: The politics of racial betrayal*. New York, NY: Pantheon Books.
Klueger, R. (2004). *Simple justice: The history of Brown v. board of education and Black America's struggle for equality*. New York, NY: Vintage Books Edition.
Kovel, J. (2000). Reflections on white racism. *Psychoanalytic Dialogues, 10*, 639–655.
Kuiper, A. J., & Cohen-Kettenis, P. T. (1998). Gender role reversal among postoperative transsexuals. *International Journal of Transgenderism, 2*(3). Retrieved June 3, 2009, from www.symposion.com/ijt/ijtc0502.htm
LaFarriere, D. (2010). *How to make love to a negro without getting tired*. Montreal, Canada: Douglas & McIntyre.
Landolt, M. A., Bartholomew, K., Saffrey, C., Oram, D., & Perman, D. (2004). Gender nonconformity, childhood rejection, and adult attachment: A study of gay men. *Archives of Sexual Behavior, 33*(2), 117–128.
Laufer, E. M. (1991). Body image, sexuality and the psychotic core. *International Journal of Psychoanalysis, 72*, 63–71.
Leli, U., & Drescher, J. (Eds.). (2004). *Transgender subjectivities: A clinician's guide*. New York, NY: Harrington Park Press.
Lev, A. I. (2004). *Transgender emergence: Therapeutic guidelines for working with gender-variant people and their families*. New York, NY: The Haworth Clinical Practice Press.
McRuer, M. (2006). *Crip theory: Cultural signs of queerness and disability*. New York, NY: New York University Press.
Menvielle, E. J. (1998). Gender identity disorder: Letter to the editor. *Journal of the American Academy of Child and Adolescent Psychiatry, 37*(3), 243–244.
Mercer, K., & Julien, I. (1988). Race, sexual politics and black masculinity: A dossier. In R. Chapman & J. Rutherford (Eds.), *Male order: Unwrapping masculinity* (pp. 97–164). London: Lawrence and Wishart.
Mitchell, S. (1981). The psychoanalytic treatment of homosexuality: Some technical considerations. *International Review of Psychoanalysis, 8*, 63–80.
Morgan, S. (2009). Childhood psychosis. In G. Hall, F. Hivernel, & S. Morgan (Ed.), *Theory and practice in child psychoanalysis: An introduction to the work of Françoise Dolto* (pp. 39–62). London: Karnac Books.
Muñoz, J. E. (1999). *Disidentifications: Queers of color and the performance of politics*. Minneapolis: University of Minnesota Press.
Munt, S. R. (2009). *Queer attachments: The cultural politics of shame*. London: Ashgate Publishing Limited.
Nicolosi, J., & Nicolosi, L. A. (2002). *A parent's guide to preventing homosexuality*. Dowers Grove: IVP Books.
Olson, K. R. (2016). Prepubescent transgender children: What we do and do not know. *Journal of the American Academy of Child and Adolescent Psychiatry, 55*, 155–156.
Olson, K. R., Key, A. C., & Eaton, N. R. (2015a). Gender cognition in transgender children. *Psychological Science, 26*, 467–474.

Olson, J., Schrager, S. M., Belzer, M., Simons, L. K., & Clark, L. F. (2015b). Baseline physiologic and psychosocial characteristics of transgender youth seeking care for gender dysphoria. *Journal of Adolescent Health*, *57*, 374–380.

Ogden, T. (1998). *Reverie and interpretation*. Northvale, NJ: Jason Aronson Press.

Pascoe, C. J. (2007). *Dude, you are a fag*. Berkeley, CA: University of California Press.

Perry, P. (2002). *Shades of White: White kids and racial identities in high school*. Durham, NC: Duke University Press.

Pickstone-Taylor, S. D. (2003). Children with gender non-conformity: Letter to the editor. *Journal of the American Academy for Child and Adolescent Psychiatry*, *42*(3), 266.

Pleak, R. R. (1999). Ethical issues in diagnosing and treating gender-dysphoric children and adolescents. In M. Rottnek (Ed.), *Sissies and tomboys: Gender nonconformity and homosexual boyhood* (pp. 34–51). New York, NY: New York University Press.

Poulson-Bryant, S. (2005). *Hung: A meditation on the measure of Black men in America*. New York, NY: Doubleday.

Puar, J. K. (2007). *Terrorist assemblages: Homonationalism in queer times*. Durham: Duke University Press.

Rachlin, K. (2002). Transgender individuals' experiences of psychotherapy. *International Journal of Transgenderism*, *6*, 1–33.

Reid-Pharr, R. F. (2001). *Black gay man: Essays*. New York, NY: New York University Press.

Remschmidt, H. (2001). *Schizophrenia in children and adolescents*. Cambridge: Cambridge University Press.

Rooks, N. M. (1996). *Hair raising: Beauty, culture, and African American women*. New Brunswick, NJ: Rutgers University Press.

Rowland, D. L., & Incrocci, L. (2008). *Handbook of sexual and gender identity disorders*. Hoboken, NJ: John Wiley & Sons, Inc.

SAMOIS. (1981). *Coming to power*. Palo Alto: Up Press.

Sedgwick, E. K. (1991). How to bring your kids up gay. *Social Text*, 9, 18–27.

Serano, J. (2007). *Whipping girl: A transsexual woman on sexism and the scapegoating of femininity*. Emeryville: Seal Press.

Siebers, T. (2009). Sex, shame and disability identity. In D. M. Halperin & V. Traub (Eds.), *Gay shame* (pp. 201–216). Chicago: University of Chicago Press.

Siomopoulos, V. (1974). Transsexualism: Disorder of gender identity, thought disorder or both? *Journal of the American Academy of Psychoanalysis*, *2*, 201–213.

Smith, Y., van Goozen, S., & Cohen-Kettenis, P. T. (2001). Adolescents with gender identity disorder who were accepted or rejected for sex-reassignment surgery: A prospective follow-up study. *Journal of the American Academy for Child and Adolescent Psychiatry*, *40*(4), 472–481.

Spack, N. (2005). *Transgenderism*. Retrieved August 5, 2008, 11:15am, from http://imatyfa.org/wp-content/uploads/2007/07/microsoft-word-doctor-spack-article.pdf

Steensma, T. D., Zucker, K. J., Kreukels, B. P., VanderLaan, D. P., Wood, H., Fuentes, A., & Cohen-Kettenis, P. T. (2014). Behavioral and emotional problems

on the Teacher's Report Form: A cross-national, cross-clinic comparative analysis of gender dysphoric children and adolescents. *Journal of Abnormal Child Psychology*, *42*, 635–647.
Stoller, R. J. (1966). The mother's contribution to infantile transvestic behavior. *International Journal of Psychoanalysis*, *47*, 384–395.
Stoller, R. J. (1968). *Sex and gender: On the development of masculinity and femininity*. New York, NY: Science House.
Straker, G. (2004). Race for cover: Castrated whiteness, perverse consequences. *Psychoanalytic Dialogues*, *14*, 405–422.
Stryker, S., & Whittle, S. (Eds.). (2006). *The transgender studies reader* (pp. 656–665). New York, NY: Routledge.
Suchet, M. (2004a). A relational encounter with race. *Psychoanalytic Dialogues*, *14*, 324–438.
Suchet, M. (2004b). Whiteness revisited: Reply to commentary. *Psychoanalytic Dialogues*, *14*, 453–456.
Suchet, M. (2007). Transitions. In M. Suchet, A. Harris, & L. Aron (Eds.), *Relational psychoanalysis, vol. III: New voices* (pp. 313–322). Hillsdale, NJ: The Analytic Press.
Sycamore, M. B. (2004). There's more to life than platinum: Challenging the tyranny of sweatshop-produced rainbow flags and participatory patriarchy. In M. B. Sycamore (Ed.), *That's revolting: Queer strategies for resisting assimilation* (pp. 1–10). Brooklyn: Soft Skull Press.
Sycamore, M. B. (Ed.). (2008). *That's revolting!: Queer strategies for resisting assimilation*. Berkeley: Soft Skull Press.
Turban, J. L., Carswell, J., & Keuroghlian, A. S. (2018). Understanding pediatric patients who discontinue gender-affirming hormonal interventions. *JAMA Pediatrics*, *173*(10), 903–904.
Turban, J. L., & Ehrensaft, D. (2018). Research review-Gender identity in youth: Treatment paradigms and controversies. *The Journal of Child Psychology and Psychiatry*, *59*(12), 1228–1243.
Turban, J. L., & Keuroghlian, A. S. (2018). Dynamic gender presentations: Understanding transition and de-transition among transgender youth. *Journal of the American Academy of Child and Adolescent Psychiatry*, *57*(7), 451–453.
Wallien, M. S. C., van Goozen, S. H. M., & Cohen-Kettenis, P. T. (2007). Physiological correlates of anxiety in children with gender identity disorder. *European Child and Adolescent Psychiatry*, *16*, 309–315.
Walton, G. (2005). Bullying and homophobia in Canadian schools: The politics of policies, programs and educational leadership. In J. Sears (Ed.), *Gay, lesbian, and transgender issues in education: Programs, policies and practices* (pp. 89–104). New York, NY: Harrington Park Press.
West, C. (1993). *Race matters*. Boston: Beacon Press.
Wrye, H. K., & Welles, J. K. (1998). *The narration of desire: Erotic transferences and countertransferences*. Hillsdale, NJ: The Analytic Press.
Zucker, K. J., & Bradley, S. J. (1995). *Gender identity disorder and psychosexual problems in children and adolescents*. New York, NY: Guilford Press.

Part II

Sexual exploitation of women

Chapter 3

Subordinated selves

Integrating intersectional oppression and the unconscious mind in prostitution discourse

Hannah Pocock

Introduction

Debates on prostitution carve a fault line among feminists, creating a schism between those who view prostitution as violence and those who see it as a form of work like any other. Both camps typically frame prostitution mainly in terms of gender relations; race and class enter the conversation only as footnotes to the primary focus on patriarchy as the system responsible for, or subverted through, prostitution[1] (Razack, 1998). Yet, white supremacy and capitalism are as much at play in prostitution as male hegemony. As a white, middle-class woman, I believe it is vital to interrogate how white, middle-class femininity is constituted by the subjugation of racialized and poor women. In my work as a psychotherapist, I have encountered minority women who understand their experiences in prostitution to be inextricably linked with their multiple marginalized identities. Their stories, however, are often obscured by the focus of prostitution debates on the single axis of gender. I do not write this chapter, though, to speak for women whose experiences are substantially different from my own. Instead, I hope to build on the growing body of intersectional literature that aims to re-center racialized and poor women in prostitution debates by examining how interlocking systems of oppression script black, brown, and poor female bodies for prostitution in the white imagination (Fellows & Razack, 1998; Razack, 1998), consigning them to exploitation so that others may "live lives of lesser violence" (Razack, 1998). The first section of this chapter outlines some of the Western feminist perspectives on prostitution, interrogating them through an intersectional lens to dismantle the purportedly "universal" female subject at the center of this discourse and expose how this universalizing focus obscures and silences racialized and poor women. Adding psychological nuance to this argument, I examine how oppression operates at the intrapsychic as well as societal levels, outlining the process by which white and class-privileged people project undesirable traits into racialized and poor women, with toxic consequences. Here, I reject the narrative that prostitution is a matter of agency, but not to argue that women in prostitution are passive victims. Rather, I suggest that external power structures and internalized power relations interact in ways that complicate the very notion of agency.

Contemporary psychoanalysis, informed by developments in traumatology and neuroscience, offers a useful lens for analyzing the interaction of structural oppression with the interpersonal trauma that so often precedes and accompanies prostitution. In the second section, I discuss how relational psychoanalytic models of trauma and dissociation provide a framework for understanding the impact of racial and relational traumas on the survivor's psyche and social world. I illustrate the implications of this framework for women in prostitution through a case analysis in the third section. This analysis examines how structural oppression and relational trauma in childhood laid the foundation for Shirelle's subsequent exploitation in prostitution, and how her experiences in prostitution reinforced dissociative structures of mind that used compliance as the only available means of survival. Finally, I offer suggestions for clinical practice that I hope may inspire psychoanalytic therapists to incorporate an embodied approach to treatment for women with prostitution histories, and for other trauma survivors. By bringing intersectional psychoanalytic perspectives into conversation with prostitution discourse at both the systemic and intrapsychic levels, I aim to pursue what Razack (1998) has termed "anti-subordination," both inside and outside the consulting room.

Multiple marginalities and disavowed selves: missing links in prostitution discourse

Feminist debates on prostitution

Razack (1998) notes that feminists tend to fall into two primary camps regarding prostitution: those who see prostitution primarily as work and those who see it primarily as violence. I review the commonly cited arguments of each school of thought, then note ways that each tends to relegate race, class, and the role of unconscious processes to the periphery of the debate.

Feminists who view prostitution as violence often argue that prostituted women are compelled into prostitution by social circumstances (systemic gender inequality, structural racism, poverty), and that these make meaningful consent to prostitute impossible (Giobbe, 1996; Kissil & Davey, 2010). Some argue that the inherent violence of prostitution lies in men's presumed "right" to purchase sexual access to women's bodies – an expression of patriarchal dominance (Dworkin, 1997; Erbe, 1984; Giobbe, 1990; Leidholdt, 2003; MacKinnon, 1993). Many in this camp argue that calling prostitution "sex work" masks the harm done to women in prostitution (e.g., frequent violence and rapes at the hands of pimps and johns) and obscures the psychological impact of commercialized sexual exploitation (Farley et al., 2004; Giobbe, 1990).

Conversely, proponents of prostitution as work argue that, while the choice to enter into prostitution may be constrained by social circumstances, it is nonetheless a matter of women's right to choose how they earn a living and what they do with their bodies (Doezema, 2000). Framing commercial sex as inherently exploitative, they argue, renders women as passive victims rather than active subjects and denigrates those women who have made the choice, however constrained, to enter the sex industry (Chuang, 2010). Many in this camp charge critics of prostitution with antisex moralizing and argue that prostitution subverts Victorian notions of "respectable" behavior often used to control women's sexuality (Chuang, 2010; Duncan, 1996; Hidalgo, 2006; Schweitzer, 2000; Shaver, 1994).

Yet, as Razack (1998) points out, "subversion . . . cannot be the basis of our politics unless we have worked out how various women are regulated differently" (p. 346). Both the prostitution-as-work and the prostitution-as-violence viewpoints lack intersectional and psychological dimension. Each fails to interrogate, for example, how white, middle-class women are "stakeholders in this game" (Razack, 1998, p. 354), benefiting from the existence of a class of women who absorb male violence. Those in the violence camp mention race and class simply as factors that make an existing situation worse. They point out that women of color experience higher levels of violence in prostitution (Vanwesenbeeck, 1994), or that racialized and poor women enter prostitution at earlier ages than their white counterparts (Clarke, Clarke, Roe-Sepowitz, & Fey, 2012; Kramer & Berg, 2003). As Crenshaw (1991) argues in *Mapping the Margins: Intersectionality, Identity Politics, and Violence Against Women of Color*, such tokenization of minority and poor women is inherently objectifying and voyeuristic, and as silencing as complete exclusion. This approach precludes the discussion of strategies and policies to effectively address minority women's needs because their experiences are held up "simply to magnify the problem rather than to humanize their experiences" (Crenshaw, 1991, p. 1261).

The argument for prostitution as primarily about agency or transgression, on the other hand, relies on a universal female subject who embodies white, Western, middle-class ideals of unfettered autonomy, while subverting patriarchal restrictions on female sexuality. Feminists in this camp, however, neglect to ask whom those restrictions were designed to protect and manage, or how different women's bodies are regulated differently in a white supremacist patriarchal society. A universal female sex-worker subject cannot adequately account for the ways in which racialized and poor women's bodies are marked as outside the moral social order and therefore seen as sexually violable. The following section applies an intersectional psychoanalytic lens to examine the raced, classed, and gendered assumptions that underpin the supposedly universal subject, and the collective projections required to maintain this myth.

The cult of autonomy and the myth of the universal female subject

The emphasis on dynamics of individual agency in prostitution discourse is grounded in Western ideals of individualism and self-control – ideals that are inherently gendered, raced, and classed. Benjamin (1988) has noted that the Western assumption of the primacy of individualism in human development is implicitly gendered. Rationality and autonomy (qualities attributed to the father in traditional psychoanalytic frameworks) are celebrated, while empathy, emotion, and other human capacities deemed feminine are devalued. Yet, when rational, autonomous action is considered the hallmark of selfhood, the gendered nature of these values is obscured. The unequal valuing of supposedly male and female qualities is replicated at the societal level, where rationality and the language of individual rights and responsibilities form the core of our political, educational, and legal systems. Nurturance and interdependence, on the other hand, are relegated to the private sphere. While these systems cloak themselves in the mantle of neutrality, Benjamin argues that it is precisely the disproportionate valuing of rationality and objective indifference to personal need that are the trademarks of male dominance (1988).

Autonomy and dependency are raced as well as gendered in Western society. Altman (2010) suggests that the idealization of freedom and agency implicit in the American Dream requires a denial of natural dependency needs in service of maintaining a sense of total self-reliance. Inasmuch as self-reliance is bound up in the construction of a "good" white American self, anything that threatens that self-image must be disavowed. Volkan and Sinclair (1997) suggest that the majority always seeks a minority group to serve as a "suitable target for externalization" of the majority group's anxieties. Thus, dependency needs, along with other intolerable aspects of experience, are projected into "bad" racialized others against whom whites measure their "goodness." When whites project dependency needs into black women, for example, they then denigrate those women as lazy and unwilling to support themselves, as in racialized stereotypes of the "welfare queen." (Aggression and lust, impulses incompatible with the purely rational, self-contained Western subject, are also socially projected into racialized and poor people, with particular implications for women of color and poor women. I discuss this process and its consequences in the following section.)

If the supposedly autonomous, rational subject is created by the disavowal of gendered and raced qualities such as emotion, empathy, and dependency needs, what are the implications for the purportedly universal female subject at the center of prostitution debates? Razack (1998) has noted that the relegation of race and class to the periphery of this discourse has allowed the formation of a "universal woman [who] embodies the characteristics of the most privileged women" (p. 340), thereby centering white, middle-class women's narratives in the analysis of a phenomenon that primarily impacts women with multiple marginalized identities. Further, by couching the discussion in terms of individual choice (a rational act), or individual coercion (a location of dependency), feminists on each side of the debate rely on the language of white male dominance to construct a universal woman who embodies only those traits deemed acceptable by the gendered logic of patriarchy. As such, the universal female subject at the heart of prostitution discourse bolsters white supremacist patriarchy even as she is purported to stand for the rights of all women.

If we acknowledge that the universal woman is not, in fact, universal, we must examine how the projective processes that create this illusion damage the actual subjects it obscures. The social projections required to create a "good" white American self lead to a culture in which the racialized others to whom "bad" qualities are attributed become viable targets for hatred and criminalization. Laws are passed, policies drafted, and diagnoses codified around the myth that aggression, lustfulness, and laziness are inherent to racialized and poor members of society, rather than reflecting disowned qualities and drives of the dominant group and the systems that sustain their dominance.

By imputing unacceptable attributes to racialized and poor others, whites create justification for maintaining power and control (Pinderhughes, 1989), while tacitly communicating beliefs about the inferiority of the other. In a process termed *internalized subordination*, these beliefs are taken in by members of oppressed groups to the detriment of self-concept (Akhtar, 2014; Holmes, 2006; Pinderhughes, 1989) and manifest along a continuum from self-doubt to self-hatred. Holmes (2006) has observed that this often takes the form of a "success neurosis," which leads people of color and poor people to internalize the message that their success is prohibited, damaging their "readiness to pursue that which one's society systematically opposes" (p. 219). Consequently minority individuals – often also deprived in reality of resources and networks that would prepare them for success – find their options circumscribed both by external reality and by the harmful effects of this introjected prohibition (Akhtar, 2014).

The unique impact of social projection and introjection on women of color and poor women is revealed when one examines these processes along the axis of gender as well as the axes of race and class. Racialized and poor women have long been targets, for example, for the projection of white society's unacceptable sexual desire. I discuss this particular projective-introjective process and its social, legal, and psychological ramifications next.

The "White Madonna"/"Black Whore" fallacy

Unequal valuing of women's bodies is at the heart of the racialized and classed dimensions of prostitution. Historically, arguments for protecting women from sexual violation have focused on property-like aspects of white, class-privileged women's chastity. "Sexual stratification" theory suggests that dominant-group men assume a right of sexual access to the most socially desirable women, usually members of socially privileged groups (R. Collins, 1971). Because of white men's property interest in the chastity of white, class-privileged women (the mechanism by which the privileged classes reproduce their own power), the purity of socially privileged women must be protected from violation by socially subordinate men. Alexander (1994) notes how colonial law reinforced this "cult of true womanhood" through criminalization of black male sexuality and legitimization of white men's rape of black women. Such laws neatly reified the concepts of the untouchable "white madonna" and the promiscuous "black whore" that persist today (Alexander, 1994).

The "white madonna" myth was further valorized with the emergence of the bourgeoisie in the late nineteenth century. Foucault (1978) argues that the bourgeois subject's claim to power lay in the sexual politics of respectability and self-control (in contrast to the supposedly degenerate poor and the profligate aristocracy). The well-ordered middle-class home exemplified these values and served as a bulwark against the creeping contamination of the slum, where women in prostitution absorbed what were thought to be "the distasteful but inevitable waste products of male lustfulness, leaving the middle-class household and middle-class ladies pure and unsullied" (Davidoff, 1995, p. 105). The myths of the degenerate sexuality of the poor and the purity of white womanhood were further entrenched.

White and class-privileged women have a vested interest in maintaining these myths to secure their position of relative dominance in the white supremacist hierarchy. Yet, this role creates a psychological conflict: to the extent that a white woman's limited power stems from her respectability, from her role as mother rather than sexual subject, her sexual desire threatens her tenuous grasp on that power. Desire must be projected outward. Gilman (1985) has suggested that projection of sexuality onto "dark" races has long allowed whites to simultaneously represent and deny their own desire. By locating wanton sexuality in black women, rather than themselves, white women resolve their cultural-intrapsychic dissonance – but at what cost? Their projection makes them complicit in the subjugation of women of color and simultaneously reinforces their own subordination to men of their race and class.

White men, too, must engage in a projective process to protect the "white madonna" mythology that provides for the reproduction of their supremacy. For white, class-privileged women to be pure and inviolable, they must be shielded from lustfulness and divorced from sexuality in the white male psyche. White men's desire, then, must be directed outside the domestic sphere – a task made possible by the existence of a group of women already presumed to be lascivious. In his account of racist attitudes in the American colonies, Jordan (2012) notes that white men's rape of enslaved women was routinely justified through descriptions of black women as lusty and passionate: "not only did the Negro woman's warmth constitute a logical explanation for the white man's infidelity, but, much more important, it helped shift responsibility from himself to her" (p. 151). White men, unable to fully acknowledge their own lust for fear of upending the racial hierarchy that positions rational (white) subjects over passionate and unruly (black) objects, disavow their sexual desire and project it into black women. With lust thus relocated, white men's sexual domination over black women is justified, white and class-privileged women remain de-sexed, and existing racial and gender hierarchies are reinforced.

Institutional efforts at regulating female sexuality have long relied on the stereotypes of chaste white women and sexually deviant black women. Early rape legislation emphasized proof of an accuser's chastity as the primary determinant of her victimhood, yet some states explained to juries that black women, unlike white women, were not presumed to be chaste (Crenshaw, 1989). Hypersexualization of black women by whites appears in landmark works of Western thought from the colonial age to the present. One need only look to Freud's "dark continent" of female sexuality to observe the association of sexually active women with black colonial Africa and its supposed sexual exoticism and pathology (as cited in Gilman, 1985, p. 238). The link between degenerate sexuality and blackness is so entrenched in dominant narratives that black women have long been conflated with prostituted women in the white imagination. Nineteenth-century eugenicists merged perceptions of prostituted women and black women to the point that popular and pseudo-scientific depictions of prostituted women portrayed them with physiological traits that had long been attributed only to the supposedly primitive and hypersexual black woman, such as elongated labia majora, large buttocks, and supposedly "masculine" jaws and facial features (Gilman, 1985; Razack, 1998).

The conflation of prostitution with blackness also racializes and sexualizes poor women, who themselves exist outside the margins of virtuous middle-class respectability and occupy instead the perceived degeneracy and disorder of the slum (Razack, 1998). There, even white bodies can slip toward blackness by association with sexuality and filth (Goldberg, 1993; Razack, 1998; Roberts, 1994). As Razack points out, a woman walking in a suburban neighborhood will rarely be assumed to be selling sex, while a woman walking in a poor area is much more likely to be read as a "prostitute" simply because she is located in a space where sexual availability is assumed (Razack, 1998).

Regardless of location, women of color rarely "leave the space of prostitution in the white imagination; it is a space worn on the body" (Razack, 1998, p. 356). A recent news story exemplifies the power of the white imagination: A young black actress was detained by Los Angeles police after being "mistaken for a prostitute" while kissing her white boyfriend in public (Boren, 2014). Simply being black and female marked her as outside the moral order and scripted her as "a prostitute" in the eyes of the dominant culture. Christen Smith (2014) echoes Razack's argument that black women, by virtue of their combined race and gender, "are seen as violable in part because black femaleness is always already marked as outside the social contract and thus, by extension, outside the moral social order" (2014, p. 108). When all racialized and poor female bodies occupy the space of prostitution in the white imagination, and all prostituted female bodies take on the characteristics of racial "others," membership in either group becomes a proxy for membership in the other.

Invisibility of violence against racialized and poor women

Unequal valuing of women's bodies has profound ramifications. Valerie Smith argues that

> [t]o the extent that rape is constructed as a crime against the property of privileged white men, crimes against less valuable women – women of color, working-class women, and lesbians, for example – mean less or mean differently than those against white women from the middle and upper classes.
>
> (1990, pp. 275–276)

Studies have found, for example, that prosecutors are less likely to press rape charges when the victim is a black woman, for fear that juries' biases will result in non-conviction (Pokorak, 2006). When charges are pressed and convictions reached, black men accused of raping black women receive the most lenient treatment, while black men accused of raping white women are punished most harshly (Lafree, 1989). Yet anti-racist activists often fail to address how the violation of black women is obscured by the legal system's focus on punishing black men for transgressing the presumed sexual property rights of patriarchal elites. Feminist movements, on the other hand, have traditionally failed to interrogate how this system benefits white women at the expense of women of color.

Many have also noted the tendency of criminal justice institutions to dismiss the complaints of prostituted women, particularly those who are women of color, homeless, or struggle with substance abuse (Cooper, 1990; Herndon, 1990; LaFree, 1989; Richie, 2012). Many states even allow the admission of prostitution history as evidence of the complainant's "unchaste" tendencies in rape trials (Portlock, 2007). Portlock (2007) emphasizes the racial implications of these laws, because of the overrepresentation of women of color in the types of prostitution (such as street prostitution and prostitution in drug houses) that present the highest risk of sexual violence. Studies show high rates of violence against women in prostitution, including rape, murder, and violent assault (Farley, Baral, Kiremire, & Sezgin, 1998; Farley et al., 2004; Silbert & Pines, 1982; Suresh, Furr, & Srikrishnan, 2009; Hong et al., 2013), yet accounts of violence against prostituted women are commonly questioned, discredited, or chalked up to exaggeration (Chuang, 2010; Doezema, 2000; Weitzer, 2011).

The racialized and poor women who bear the brunt of this violence rarely appear in accounts of chosen, professional prostitution. These accounts, as Razack (1998) points out, speak only with the voice of those who have the true option to prostitute or not to prostitute – women who are privileged but for their gender. White, class-privileged sex workers who present their stories as the universal experience of prostitution largely fail to represent the lived realities of prostituted women whose experiences are substantially different from their own. Those with multiple subordinated identities are silenced by the interactions of race, class, and gender oppression, which diminishes their bargaining power both in commercial sexual transactions and in academic discourse. The real subjugation of racialized and poor women in prostitution is kept invisible.

To truly challenge the assumptions that create and reinforce hierarchical relationships among women in prostitution, we must abandon the thinking that consigns some to prostitution, so that others may live relatively free of violence. The debate must shift away from the neoliberal focus on individual choice, which de-politicizes prostitution, unmoors gender and race theory from their commitments to social justice, and distracts from radical critiques of the power relations that sustain and are sustained by prostitution. The idea that individual agency is the solution to all societal ills undercuts the political solidarity that underpins struggles for feminist and racial justice (Mohanty, 2013). In the case of prostitution, it pits class- and race-privileged "sex workers" against those whose bodies are scripted for prostitution, by denying the role in their lives of interlocking systemic oppressions. To address the issue of prostitution in a way that is liberatory for *all women*, we must move toward an intersectional analysis and critique of the forces of power that define, rank, and oppress women according to race, class, and gender hierarchies. The question of whose voices make up the coalitions that address such violence is not a petty question. As Crenshaw (1991, p. 1265) reminds us: "[i]n the context of violence, it is sometimes a deadly serious matter of who will survive – and who will not."

Neurobiological and relational perspectives on trauma

Consistent exposure to racism at the systemic, cultural, and personal levels results in ongoing traumatization for racialized and poor women. Those who wind up in prostitution also frequently have histories of physical and sexual trauma (Farley et al., 1998; Kramer & Berg, 2003; Medrano, Hatch, Zule, & Desmond, 2003; Silbert & Pines, 1982). The trauma literature of recent decades emphasizes that a symptomatic hallmark of traumatic stress is dissociation (van der Kolk, 1996b; Steele & van der Hart, 2009). As early as the late 1800s, Pierre Janet theorized that terrifying experiences which could not be reconciled with existing cognitive schemas were not integrated into conscious awareness (as cited in Schore, 2010). Instead, they were split off from consciousness and voluntary control yet continued to intrude into the present through somatic symptoms, frightening perceptions, and obsessional preoccupations. Trauma and neurobiology research over the past several decades supports this theory, providing evidence for dissociation as "a basic part of the psychobiology of the human trauma response: a protective activation of altered states of consciousness in reaction to overwhelming psychological trauma" (Loewenstein, 1996). The theory of structural dissociation describes how these altered states comprise distinct parts of the trauma survivor's personality, each with its own psychobiological underpinnings (Steele & van der Hart, 2009). Steele and van der Hart (2009) observe that, while this may take the form of clearly alternating "identities" as in dissociative identity disorder, dissociation often manifests more subtly, in the form of ego-alien emotions, body sensations, or persistent and painful relational patterns. Each dissociated aspect of self is accompanied by its own particular physiological states, emotions, belief systems, and sense of self (Steele & van der Hart, 2009). For this reason, I use the term *self-state* throughout this chapter to refer to the constellation of experiences that makes up a dissociated part of the self-system.

Contemporary relational psychoanalysis offers a useful addition to the theory of structural dissociation, by integrating relational concepts of self-other representation. Davies and Frawley (1994) propose that trauma leads to "the organization of mutually exclusive systems of self and object representations" formed in relation to the trauma (p. 45). In the case of childhood sexual abuse, for example, the child finds herself in a double bind, expected to "become two contradictory people simultaneously" (Spiegel, 1986, p. 69): to be both the seductive sexual partner and the "good girl," with the added prohibition that she is not to notice or point out this contradiction. Bromberg suggests that such irreconcilable experiences become "unhooked" from cognitive processing and remain "raw data," unsymbolized except as survival reactions (1998, p. 243). Davies and Frawley (1994) observe that these unsymbolized experiences "lie encrusted in a primitive core of unspeakable terror and phenomenologically meaningless panic, intrusive ideation, and somatic sensation" (p. 45). To manage these terrifying experiences, a split occurs between the self-state that goes on managing the tasks of daily life and those that contain trauma memories and survival reactions that either occurred or were truncated at the time of the trauma (e.g., an impulse to push away that was cut short to avoid escalating the abuse). This split allows the survivor to maintain the original self-object representations characterized by obedience, love, or respect, and simultaneously preserve the capacity to survive by repeating endlessly the responses that proved effective in coping with the original trauma or ensuring the prevention of future pain (Bromberg, 1998).

As a result of this cordoning-off of parts of the self, the adult survivor's relational world comprises complex and shifting relationships between the abuser and the abused, the omnipotent rescuer and the needy child, the uninvolved parent and the unseen child, the seducer and the seduced, each of which arises over and over in the survivor's personal life and the analytic relationship (Davies & Frawley, 1994). With relational matrices in constant flux, trauma survivors often struggle to interpret cues in the present. Instead of overcoming the original trauma through new relational experiences that lead to integration of self-states, the survivor finds herself responding to situations in ways that relentlessly recapitulate the traumatic past. The barriers between dissociated self-states remain obdurate, and those parts responsible for preventing pain become all the more reflexive and unsymbolized. The neurobiology of trauma supports this theory. van der Kolk (1996a) finds that survivors of childhood trauma are often driven to repeat elements of their early traumatic experiences through conditioned responses to stimuli and neuroendocrinologic reactions to stress. The marks of childhood trauma are so indelible that researchers and clinicians have concluded that it increases the propensity to develop strong attachments to abusive partners and decreases the likelihood of leaving dangerous and exploitative relationships (van der Kolk, 1996b).

It is no wonder that childhood trauma, and sexual trauma in particular, is understood to be a common antecedent to entry into street-level and pimp-controlled prostitution (Farley et al., 1998; Kramer & Berg, 2003; Medrano et al., 2003; Silbert & Pines, 1982). Prostitution, in which men demand access to women's bodies, is a clear repetition of early trauma. Even in the absence of childhood trauma, women in prostitution (and, in particular, in street-level and pimp-controlled prostitution) experience higher rates of violence than their counterparts outside the commercial sex trade, and demonstrate high rates of psychological distress, including posttraumatic sequelae and dissociation (Choi, Klein, Shin, & Lee, 2009; Farley et al., 1998, 2004; Hossain, Zimmerman, Abas, Light, & Watts, 2010; Ling, Wong, Holroyd, & Gray, 2007; Mayfield-Schwarz, 2007; Perdue et al., 2012; Rössler et al., 2010; Seib, Fischer, & Najman, 2009; Sloss, 2003; Suresh et al., 2009; Wang et al., 2007). Women in prostitution frequently report physical or mental numbness, going somewhere else in their minds, or using alcohol or drugs to endure sex with johns (Farley et al., 1998; Giobbe, 1990; Mayfield-Schwarz, 2007). Within the framework of structural dissociation, we can understand these strategies as self-states that deploy survival strategies useful for enduring recurrent trauma. Barriers between self-states keep intolerable experiences of violence, powerlessness, and fear in prostitution encounters out of consciousness, and allow for a conscious experience of self as an empowered subject.

If structural dissociation occurs in the face of overwhelming threat, how might dissociation operate for racialized and poor women in a white supremacist society where threat is a part of daily life? Studies show that black, mixed race, and poor people are more likely than whites and people of higher socioeconomic status to be victims of violent crime (DuMonthier, Childers, & Milli, 2017; Morgan & Truman, 2018; Lauritsen & White, 2001). Perceived race-related threat is also correlated with posttraumatic stress symptoms in people of color (Khaylis, Waelde, & Bruce, 2007). From the large-scale traumas of police and community violence, to the daily traumas of life in a white supremacist society that denies one's right to exist, trauma is a fact of life for people of color and poor people in the United States. Racialized and poor people are under tremendous psychological pressure to make themselves acceptable to the dominant culture; any failure to do so may be punished by violence, imprisonment, or death. While I have come across no studies of the interaction between oppressed identities and dissociation, it is my hypothesis that, for women located at the intersection of race, class, and gender oppression, aspects of the self likely to attract dangerous attention can become dissociated as "not me" states, cordoned off from the rest of the self-system for physical and psychological self-preservation.

For women with both racialized and sexual trauma histories, dissociative self-systems might form to facilitate survival of daily life in a white supremacist society, as well as abuse and exploitation by men. What implications do these intersecting traumas and resulting dissociative structures of mind have for the choice to enter prostitution, or the ease with which one might extricate herself from it? I explore these questions, and others, through a case study in the following section.

Structural oppression and intersubjective trauma: case analysis

The following case study is drawn from my work with Shirelle, a 28-year-old African-American woman who sought services from a non-profit agency where I worked, which served survivors of pimp-controlled prostitution. I met her several weeks after she left her pimp, trying to exit prostitution after twelve years in "the life." She sought assistance with transportation, legal advocacy, access to benefits, and mental health. I saw her for psychotherapy over the course of a few months, before she abruptly moved away. The case material is at times graphic, but it is my hope that the details I have chosen to include will illuminate the complex interplay of structural oppression and interpersonal trauma that permeated Shirelle's life. Details have been altered to protect confidentiality.

Case study

Shirelle's parents separated when she was young, and she was raised by her mother, who told her frequently that she wished Shirelle had never been born. Her mother struggled with addiction to crack cocaine; her use often triggered episodes of rage and physical violence toward Shirelle. Shirelle's father, in and out of jail throughout her childhood, had little involvement in her life. Her mother struggled to make ends meet, and other children often teased Shirelle for her dirty clothes. As one of only a few black children at her school, she was taunted about the texture of her hair, her broad nose, and full lips.

Between the ages of 6 and 12, Shirelle was sexually abused by an older male relative, who warned her that if she told her mother, her mother would throw her out of the house. During this period, Shirelle began to experience migraine headaches and frequent nausea. She describes "going somewhere else in my mind" during the nearly nightly rapes, while her body went numb. During the day, she felt "hyper," unable to contain an anxious energy, but at night she describes a "foggy," low-energy state that made it difficult to concentrate on homework. As a result, she struggled academically and developed a reputation among teachers as an unruly student. She was frequently suspended, leaving her with ample time to get into trouble with other neighborhood kids. Two brushes with the police as a teen left her with a juvenile record for shoplifting and public intoxication. As an adolescent, she became hypersexual and describes feeling at that age as though she "might as well just be a whore," because that was all anyone seemed to think she could be.

When she was 16, Shirelle dropped out of high school, left home, and moved to a city several hours away. She had little money saved and struggled to find work with a criminal record and no high school diploma. She met a man named William, who invited her to move in with him while she got on her feet. Shirelle described him as the first person who was nice to her. He bought her clothes, told her she was beautiful, and took her out to eat. He spoke often of their exciting future together, and for the first time Shirelle could imagine a future that looked different than her past. A few months after they moved in together, William suggested that she could make good money if she would "have a little fun" with some of his friends. If she really loved him, he told her, she would do this one small thing for him to help out with the bills. Anxious to please, Shirelle agreed. What she thought would be only stripping turned out to be more when two of William's friends forced her to perform oral sex. She describes feeling filthy and embarrassed but not wanting to let William down. He assured her that this could be the start of a profitable future: he would find the customers, manage the money she brought in, and set aside some of her earnings to help her work toward her goals. Sure that this was a short-term plan and a path to a more stable future, she agreed to keep meeting with William's "friends." William rewarded her with affection, new clothes, and nice dinners.

Soon, however, he was asking her to reach earning "quotas" and encouraged her to solicit sex on the street to attract more johns. When she failed to meet the quota, William would accuse her of stealing "his" money and sometimes threw her out of the house until she made up the difference. Certain these outbursts were her fault, Shirelle redoubled her efforts to attract johns and prove to William that she was loyal and hardworking. His outbursts, however, became increasingly unpredictable and violent; he would slap, punch, and kick Shirelle, sometimes until she was unconscious, and several times he brandished a loaded gun, threatening to kill her if she left him. Her migraines increased in frequency during this time, and she developed an oxycodone addiction in an attempt to manage her pain and anxiety. Despite numerous attempts to get sober, Shirelle struggled with addiction for the next several years. She described it as the only thing that allowed her to "numb out" from the stress of her encounters with johns and her relationship with William. During her years in prostitution, she was raped several times (once by a police officer), arrested twice for solicitation, and served several months in jail.

When I met Shirelle, she was eight months' pregnant and eight months' sober. She had left William after a particularly violent beating left her unconscious with three broken ribs. She wanted her daughter to grow up in a safe home and decided that meant leaving "the life" for good. William had tattooed his name on her neck, which made her easily recognizable, and she was terrified of being spotted and having her whereabouts reported to him. She suffered from frequent migraines and UTIs, bouts of dizziness, and recurrent pain in her neck, back, vagina, and jaw. She was regularly overwhelmed by waves of nausea and was particularly nauseated by her own bodily fluids. Shirelle was worried about giving birth and breastfeeding when her own body repulsed her, yet she was hopeful about bringing her daughter into the world and giving her a better childhood than the one she had known. She had tentatively begun dating a woman whom she described as kind and loving, but Shirelle frequently erupted in anger if she felt her girlfriend had "crossed a line" or was "trying to control" her. Hopeful that this relationship could help her learn to trust again, and terrified of destroying it with her explosive rage, she entered therapy with me for help with her "rollercoaster" moods. While she was doubtful that she could be helped, she believed that her girlfriend deserved better, and that she would need to heal herself in order to offer her daughter the life she deserved.

Relational trauma and intrapsychic adaptations

As a child, Shirelle learned early on that standing up for herself only enraged her mother, unleashing a barrage of insults and sometimes physical blows. It became clear that her needs and their expression threatened her connection with her mother, and so Shirelle's very existence. In time, the part of her that knew and longed to express her own needs was split off, disavowed in favor of the self-state that employed compliance in an effort to maximize what little maternal connection was available to her. So began her tendency toward dissociation. With the onset of sexual abuse, the divide between these self-states was strengthened, as she received near-nightly proof that her needs mattered little to others, whose desires took precedence over even her right to bodily autonomy. When her compliant self-state was foremost, Shirelle felt as if she had no self, no will or desire of her own, aware only of the imperative to submit to the will of others to avoid annihilation. In therapy sessions, she agreed enthusiastically with everything I said and was unnerved when I suggested there might be a part of her, however small, that disagreed with me sometimes, and in time we would want to invite that part to be heard too.

Other dissociated self-states held Shirelle's many survival reactions. She had long heard a voice in her head repeating "nothing ever happened to you," leading her to question her memories of the abuse. Early in our work together she recognized that the quality of this voice was her mother's. We began to wonder whether her mother's refusal to know about the sexual abuse had become incorporated into Shirelle's dissociative system as a self-state to whom the abuse was unreal, and who was, as a result, protected from the painful reality of her traumatic past. Early in childhood, another self-state was heralded by the onset of migraines and dizziness, accompanied by mental fogginess, muscular weakness, and physical and emotional numbness. As a child, this state enabled her to endure the frequent rapes by her male relative. As an adult, it intensified to help her endure encounters with johns. She came to understand this state as a feigned death response that dulled her senses and protected her from the full brunt of the psychological and physical pain of her abuse. The hypersexuality that arose in her adolescence was another self-state's effort at mastering the sexual trauma of her early years. What initially offered the possibility of a sense of control of her body and sexuality led instead to greater torment when a shame-filled state took the reins after each sexual encounter and sent her into a depressive slump. Her "hyper" state, which had frequently earned her suspension during her school years, came with a need in adulthood to talk rapidly and at great length about her traumatic past, which I came to see as a self-state that desperately needed others to understand the depth of her pain and come to her aid. Even as this self-state reached out, another feared the closeness being sought and frequently erupted in anger, staving off the feared intrusion with accusations of manipulation or control. Self-states wired to flee from threat and emotional pain had fueled her addiction, as well as her impulse to uproot and relocate – an impulse that ended our work together only a few months after it began, when she abruptly moved to another state.

These multiple opposing states, originally designed to ensure survival in her childhood environs and prevent future traumatization, ultimately laid the foundation for her exploitation by William. States geared toward proximity-seeking for safety trusted William's good intentions even in the face of mounting evidence of his violence and untrustworthiness, for in these states' relational world, to turn away from William was to be dangerously alone, unloved, vulnerable, and perhaps nonexistent. Those self-states wired to submit in the face of threat ensured that Shirelle could not refuse his requests or the demands of johns. A flight state kept her numb through opiate use that further hindered her ability to set or enforce her own boundaries. When self-states emerged to fight off threat, albeit rarely, by erecting boundaries (with William, with johns, or with police), they were met with violence that further bolstered the other states' impulses to prevent such rash action in the future, and strengthened the hold of freeze and feigned death states that could at least minimize violence and psychic harm. When, against all odds, she escaped this cycle, these self-states continued to intrude forcefully into the present, threatening efforts by some parts of the self-system to forge new relationships for fear that they would mirror the old.

Shirelle's fragmented self-states reflected splintered self and object representations. At times, she spoke with longing of William the ex-boyfriend, and wondered what she had done to cause their relationship to fail. At other times, she spoke with loathing of the pimp who had exploited her trust. One state, eternally desperate to earn the love of a mother who rued Shirelle's very existence, sought endlessly to find fault with herself in order to become perfectly loveable, while the other state railed against the loved object's cruelty and domination. Each self-state, ensconced in its own internal object world, proposed a different script for relationships, trapping her in a cycle of frantic proximity-seeking and angry withdrawal playing out on the stage of dysregulated and dissociated survival defenses. This ongoing dance between dissociated states lays plain the (dis)organizing influence of Shirelle's early experiences on her relational world, such that violence and violation were the price for connection, and awareness of her own needs or desires – let alone their expression – was a prospect fraught with danger.

Structural and cultural trauma

Although an analysis of dissociation lends subtlety to the psychological understanding of Shirelle's situation, it offers only a partial view when applied in the absence of a broader systemic analysis. Shirelle's life was shaped from the outset by forces of structural, cultural, and interpersonal racism. Structural racism can be seen in the way the school system labeled Shirelle "unruly" and issued her frequent suspensions. Likewise, law enforcement was quick to penalize her with a juvenile police record. Cultural racism devalued her physical features that did not conform to dominant group norms, while interpersonal racism confronted her daily in school, where white students taunted her for these traits. The conjunction of these forces led her to drop out of school and, like many poor young people of color with a juvenile record and no high school diploma, she found the informal economy welcomed her much more readily than the world of typed resumés, job interviews, and background checks.

Interlocking systemic oppression and personal trauma influenced Shirelle's experiences in prostitution as well. As a poor, black woman, Shirelle was statistically more likely to face violence in prostitution than her white counterparts (Vanwesenbeeck, 1994), and, when she reported these attacks to police, she was less likely to be believed (Cooper, 1990; Herndon, 1990; LaFree, 1989; Richie, 2012). As a black woman, she was more likely to be arrested and jailed for prostitution than a white woman (Lucas, 1995). Violence and betrayal by pimps, johns, and police reinforced relational models based on early experiences of abuse and neglect, deepening Shirelle's sense of herself as powerless and further constricting her sense that other ways of relating were possible. Shirelle's experiences demonstrate that oppression experienced along multiple axes of identity reinforces both internalized and actual positions of subordination in external power hierarchies.

The Gordian knot of intersectional oppression and trauma

To understand the impact of marginalization on the psyche, it is useful to draw on psychological theories of racism and oppression. Shirelle's hypersexual self-state, for example, can be understood as a response to the sexual trauma she endured as a child, but it can also be explained through the lens of racialized projection and introjection. Because white society projects its sexual desire into black and brown bodies, Shirelle was doubly sexualized: by a society that assumes women and girls of color to be lascivious – that both demands this of them and shames them for it – and by a family system that reinforced this message through sexualized abuse. How might the introjection of her abuser's messages and white societal projections have interacted to deepen her sexualized self-state's convictions about her worth, about what was expected of her, and about what kind of intimacy was available to her? Shirelle's contention that she "might as well just be a whore" is not uncommon for childhood sexual abuse survivors. Might it not also reflect a taking-in of a white supremacist culture's beliefs about black women that, given the chink in her armor left by personal trauma, could take hold to shape Shirelle's sense of self?

We might also wonder how Shirelle's compliant and rageful self-states were shaped by the violence of white supremacy. When whites project their aggression into black and brown people, black women are portrayed as unreasonably and inappropriately angry, and white society attempts to control this feared rage through rules and expectations normed on dominant group ideals of propriety, respectability, and comportment. These expectations were communicated to Shirelle by classmates who reminded her how far outside the (white) norm she was, by a school system that required adherence to behavioral norms, and by police who targeted her for existing outside the moral social order. How might these experiences have entwined with her relational traumas to support the emergence of a compliant and non-threatening self-state organized to protect her from interpersonal and structural violence? Meanwhile, Shirelle's justified rage toward a dehumanizing system of dominance had to be dissociated to protect her from the violent backlash that often meets resistance by black and brown people. Yet, this rageful and defiant state appeared repeatedly in the context of her relationship with her girlfriend, intent on reclaiming a sense of agency and empowered selfhood that often felt out of reach.

An agentic self-state was evident in the way she spoke of the lure of "the life" as a world that seemed to offer the opportunity to live outside the norms of "square" society, resist its oppressive power, and forge her own identity. This conscious state of resistance expressed a liberatory vision of strength in the face of contempt and derision. Yet unconsciously, it expressed internalized white supremacist values, for it is precisely white supremacist, capitalist patriarchy that bars racialized and poor women from the formal economy and funnels them into an informal marketplace where they are expected to sell their bodies as commodities. Shirelle's strivings for agency through engagement in this exploitative system could be seen as a self-state reflecting internalized commodification. Patricia Hill Collins (1986) argues that self-valuation is a vital way for members of dominated groups to embrace and value those aspects of themselves that allow them to survive denigration by dominant society – yet she notes this can only be a useful resistance strategy as long as it does not replace one set of controlling images with another. Although the term "sex worker," for example, seems to hold promise for black women to reject the stereotype of sexual degeneracy and embrace their sexual agency, it simply replaces that stereotype with white, middle-class, capitalist values of respectability and productivity. The fetishization of individualism, the commodification of women's bodies, and the false narrative of unfettered agency obscure the roles of racism, capitalism, and patriarchy in creating and sustaining prostitution, masking the way that racialized and poor women are marked for sexual exploitation. By failing to critically analyze how the system of prostitution relies on the existence of certain classes of women who can be exploited, the "sex work" method of self-valuation ignores the race and class oppression inherent in the commercial sex industry.

When we interrogate the intersections of race, gender, class, and personal trauma, it is plain that for Shirelle prostitution could never be a truly liberatory tactic. Forced as a child into sexual submission, raped and beaten into compliance later in life, cast by the dominant culture as a vehicle for men's gratification long before she made the "choice" to prostitute – Shirelle was conscripted into prostitution, bound by a Gordian knot of structural and personal trauma and their intrapsychic sequelae. Far from liberatory, prostitution in fact further entrenched her in a cycle of exploitation. When intersectional oppression and psychological trauma are given their due, it becomes inescapably clear that the question of agency is far more complex than traditional feminist debates on prostitution allow.

Psychotherapy at the intersection of oppression and trauma: implications for psychoanalytically oriented treatment with women with prostitution histories[2]

The racialized and sexualized trauma faced by many women in prostitution is trauma enacted on the body. A psychoanalytic approach to treatment with these women, and with other chronically traumatized patients, must be grounded in a model of mind that incorporates the contributions of psychobiological trauma research. As noted earlier, the research points to the chronic nervous system dysregulation resulting from persistent exposure to trauma; however, attention to physiological dysregulation is rarely prioritized in psychoanalytic treatment approaches, with their emphasis on verbalization rather than a more sensate focus. In their pioneering work on the inclusion of the body in psychotherapy for traumatized patients, Ogden, Minton, and Pain (2006) convincingly argue that insight and words, while valuable elements of therapeutic intervention, are limited in their ability to treat the dysregulated neurophysiological states caused by trauma. Free association and discussion of traumatic events are too activating for most trauma survivors and risk causing hyper- or hypoarousal of the autonomic nervous system – states in which cognitive processing and integration cannot take place (Siegel, 1999). Pat Ogden, Peter Levine, and others have been instrumental in illuminating these challenges to traditional psychotherapy with trauma survivors, and have proposed integrated body-mind approaches that support regulation from the "bottom up" as well as the "top down" (Levine & Frederick, 1997; Ogden et al., 2006).

The current two-person paradigm in psychoanalysis is highly compatible with a more embodied approach. The relational framework has given increasing attention to the "unthought known" of both therapist and patient – those internal states that have yet to be articulated (Bollas, 1987). Trauma survivors live perpetually in the realm of the unthought known, as unsymbolized trauma responses surface over and over, rendering higher-level cognitive processing unavailable. Instead, it is the language of internal sensation, movement, and sensory perception that is available in the consulting room. As Schore (2005) notes, "the intersubjective field co-constructed by two individuals includes not just two minds but two bodies" (p. 2). Trauma survivors need the analytic process to begin at the somatic level before trying to process trauma and achieve integration at the affective and cognitive levels (Ogden et al., 2006).

An embodied approach likewise allows for greater capacity to work with the dissociated states that so often accompany trauma. Eldredge and Cole (2008) have noted that traditional, interpretation-focused techniques, based in a repression model of the mind, can be highly disorganizing for patients who rely predominantly on dissociation rather than a more flexible array of psychological defenses. Verbalization-based approaches can trigger unsymbolized trauma experiences, leading to hyperarousal and emotional flooding, or hypoaroused depressive withdrawal in an effort to protect against the overstimulating traumatic material (Eldredge & Cole, 2008; Ogden et al., 2006). This may even exacerbate dissociation as the therapy recreates the overwhelming experience that required the dissociative response in the first place (Eldredge & Cole, 2008). To counteract psychic disorganization and work more effectively with physiological hyper- and hypoarousal, Eldredge and Cole suggest an embodied psychoanalytic approach that emphasizes psychoeducation, resourcing, attention to physiological sensation, and use of language that "gives the locus of control to the patient" (2008).

Eldredge and Cole (2008) suggest a greater focus on psychoeducation than would normally be employed in psychoanalytic psychotherapy, with emphasis on offering information about the nervous system. This normalizes the patient's experiences and counteracts the patient's shame and sense of inherent "badness" (Eldredge & Cole, 2008). To this I would add a second psychoeducational component regarding dissociation, especially as it relates to dissociated trauma survival responses and how and why those reactions intrude into the present. This has been profoundly organizing for my patients, illuminating what were previously mysterious and unfathomable psychophysiological experiences. Dysregulated self-states are often calmed when patients learn about dissociated survival defenses, as this model implicitly communicates the therapist's respect for each state's ongoing efforts to protect the self-system. Others have noted that communicating a welcoming and respectful stance toward all self-states greatly facilitates the working alliance not only with whichever state may be emergent, but also with the whole constellation of self-states that will inevitably appear in the consulting room (Schwartz, 1995). For women with prostitution histories, this model is particularly valuable, as the interlocking effects of structural racism, classism, misogyny, and personal trauma create dissociated states that are loathed and feared by other parts of the self-system, which have internalized perspectives and projections of the dominant culture and their respective abusers.

Dissociated states and nervous system activation can be effectively regulated through moment-to-moment tracking of the patient's affective and physiological arousal and by use of regulatory techniques (Levine & Frederick, 1997; Ogden et al., 2006). A directive approach that invites patients to attend to the effects of their narrative on their internal experience can prevent retraumatization by helping patients stay regulated. Active attention to present-moment experience helps the patient "encounter the therapist in the present, rather than in the context of the traumatic situation" (Eldredge & Cole, 2008, p. 91). Women with histories of prostitution often have a strong aversion to noticing their bodily sensations, and some may object to the word "body" altogether, so attention should be given to the pace and means by which the therapist invites this new awareness. The therapist may encourage increasing attention to "what happens inside" as she senses incipient dysregulation, and may even explore with the patient what sensory perceptions and movements counteract dysregulation. The patient is thus assisted to return to a more regulated state from which therapeutic traction can be restored (Eldredge & Cole, 2008).

An embodied approach also facilitates constructive engagement with the continually shifting transference-countertransference positions inevitable in psychoanalytic work with trauma survivors. Davies and Frawley (1994) have noted that, because these recurring relational positions encompass the patient's dissociated self and object representations, they are usually perceptible only through the therapist's careful attention to her own countertransferential reactions. The therapist's capacity to notice her moment-to-moment body experiences is an invaluable asset in this process. For example, the therapist may notice she has entered an activated state in the face of a patient's helpless tears, evident by her clenched jaw, shallow breath, and elevated heart rate. She may begin to hypothesize that she has been pulled into the role of perpetrator in an abuser-victim complementarity. If the therapist can self-regulate and return to a more centered state, she regains the flexibility and balance needed to make use of the countertransference to explicate the relational constellation being enacted. Further, research on dyadic regulation demonstrates that the therapist who can regulate her own internal states can also effect change in the patient's state, facilitating regulation for the patient who cannot yet auto-regulate (Schore, 2005). For women with prostitution histories, many of them survivors of early childhood abuse, the capacity for self-regulation of internal states may never have developed (Schore, 2010), but a somatically informed therapist can support the gradual development of such skills through mindful attention to the nonverbal components of the co-created intersubjective field.

These suggestions for an embodied approach to psychoanalytic psychotherapy represent only the tip of the iceberg. Attention to the sensate in psychoanalytic work holds great potential to alter the way traumatic experiences are held and organized, consciously and unconsciously, by the survivor. Those who wish to incorporate "bottom-up" interventions into their work will find many invaluable resources in the body-oriented trauma treatment literature (see Eldredge & Cole, 2008; Levine & Frederick, 1997; Ogden, Pain, Minton, & Fisher, 2005; Ogden et al., 2006; van der Kolk, 2014). Embodied psychoanalytic approaches hold particular promise for women with prostitution histories, who have so often undergone especially embodied forms of trauma. Attention to present-moment internal experience offers a way for prostitution survivors to reclaim a sense of power over, and power within, their own bodies, and expands the scope of healing to encompass the fullness of body and mind.

Conclusion

Throughout this chapter I have argued for linking prostitution with the perpetuation of white supremacist patriarchy. The intersection of race, class, and gender oppression with psychological trauma scripts racialized and poor women for prostitution and reinforces race and class hierarchies among women, yet the power of these forces is obscured by the enduring focus on individual agency in prostitution debates. An intersectional analysis exposes these forces and is enriched when we examine how interlocking structural and psychological trauma create and perpetuate external power structures and internalized subordination. This integrative perspective has much to offer to prostitution discourse, whether for activists, policy-makers, or clinicians. Through this lens, we might begin to imagine social justice movements that do not simply aim to "improve the lot" of women in prostitution but rather pursue strategies to destabilize the complex oppressive structures that create a system within which racialized and poor women's exploitation is normalized. For policy-makers, this perspective provides a more complex and nuanced analysis that could inform legislative efforts at anti-subordination, such as the decriminalization of women in prostitution. In the consulting room, this lens reminds us that women's striving for agency, authorship, and subjectivity must be understood alongside the realities of intersectional marginalization and psychological trauma. To undo internalized subordination and the fragmentation of self that result from trauma and oppression, we must be willing to engage with them as they arise in the intersubjective space. The embodied psychoanalytic approach offered in this chapter is a powerful and effective strategy for this liberatory work. Only when we acknowledge the full impact of interlocking structural oppression and psychological trauma can we truly pursue anti-subordination for all women, within the consulting room and without.

Notes

1 Although an analysis of the role of heterosexism, cissexism, ethnocentrism, and other systems of oppression would add much to the prostitution literature, such a broad-reaching analysis is beyond the scope of this chapter. I hope others will pick up these threads to enrich our understanding of the complex tapestry of oppressive systems at play in prostitution.

2 An intersectional-psychological analysis of prostitution also has implications for social service provision, legislative reform, and other arenas, thorough discussion of which is beyond the scope of this chapter.

References

Alexander, M. J. (1994, Autumn). Not just (any) body can be a citizen: The politics of law, sexuality and postcoloniality in Trinidad and Tobago and the Bahamas. *Feminist Review*, *48*, 5–23.

Akhtar, S. (2014). The mental pain of minorities. *British Journal of Psychotherapy*, *30*(2), 136–153.

Altman, N. (2010). *The analyst in the inner city: Race, class, and culture through a psychoanalytic lens* (2nd ed.). New York, NY: Routledge.

Benjamin, J. (1988). *The bonds of love: Psychoanalysis, feminism, and the problem of domination.* New York, NY: Pantheon.

Bollas, C. (1987). *The shadow of the object: Psychoanalysis of the unthought known.* New York, NY: Columbia University Press.

Boren, Z. D. (2014, September 14). Daniele Watts: Django unchained actress detained by Los Angeles police after being mistaken for a prostitute. *The Independent*. Retrieved from www.independent.co.uk/news/people/daniele-watts-arrested-django-unchained-actress-detained-in-los-angeles-after-being-mistaken-for-a-prostitute-9731871.html

Bromberg, P. M. (1998). *Standing in the spaces: Essays on clinical process, trauma & dissociation*. Hillsdale, NJ: The Analytic Press.

Choi, H., Klein, C., Shin, M-S., & Lee, H-J. (2009). Posttraumatic stress disorder (PTSD) and disorders of extreme stress (DESNOS) symptoms following prostitution and childhood abuse. *Violence against Women*, *15*(8), 933–951.

Chuang, J. A. (2010). Rescuing trafficking from ideological capture: Prostitution reform and anti-trafficking law and policy. *University of Pennsylvania Law Review*, *158*(1655), 1655–1728.

Clarke, R. J., Clarke, E. A., Roe-Sepowitz, D., & Fey, R. (2012). Age at entry into prostitution: Relationship to drug use, race, suicide, education level, childhood abuse, and family experiences. *Journal of Human Behavior in the Social Environment*, *22*(3), 270–289. https://doi.org/10.1080/10911359.2012.655583

Collins, P. H. (1986). Learning from the outsider within: The sociological significance of Black feminist thought. *Social Problems*, *33*(6), S14–S32.

Collins, R. (1971). A conflict theory of sexual stratification. *Social Problems*, *19*(1), 3–21.

Cooper, C. J. (1990, September 16). Nowhere to turn for rape victims: High proportion of cases tossed aside by Oakland police. *San Francisco Examiner*, p. 1A.

Crenshaw, K. (1989). Demarginalizing the intersection of race and sex: A Black feminist critique of antidiscrimination doctrine, feminist theory and antiracist politics. *University of Chicago Legal Forum*, 139–167.

Crenshaw, K. (1991). Mapping the margins: Intersectionality, identity politics, and violence against women of color. *Stanford Law Review*, *43*(6), 1241–1299.

Davidoff, L. (1995). *Worlds between: Historical perspectives on gender and class*. New York, NY: Routledge.

Davies, J. M., & Frawley, M. G. (1994). *Treating the adult survivor of childhood sexual abuse: A psychoanalytic perspective*. New York, NY: Basic Books.

Doezema, J. (2000). Loose women or lost women? The re-emergence of the myth of white slavery in contemporary discourses of trafficking in women. *Gender Issues*, *18*(1), 23–50.

DuMonthier, A., Childers, C., & Milli, J. (2017). *The status of Black women in the United States* (Report No. R478). Retrieved from https://iwpr.org/wp-content/uploads/2017/06/The-Status-of-Black-Women-6.26.17.pdf

Duncan, N. (1996). Renegotiating gender and sexuality in public and private spaces. In N. Duncan (Ed.), *BodySpace: Destabilizing geographies of gender and sexuality* (pp. 127–145). New York, NY: Routledge.

Dworkin, A. (1997). Prostitution and male supremacy. In *Life and death*. New York, NY: Free Press.

Eldredge, C. B., & Cole, G. W. (2008). Learning from work with individuals with a history of trauma: Some thoughts on integrating body-oriented techniques and relational psychoanalysis. In F. S. Anderson (Ed.), *Bodies in treatment: The unspoken dimension* (pp. 79–102). New York, NY: The Analytic Press.

Erbe, N. (1984). Prostitutes: Victims of men's exploitation and abuse. *Law & Inequality: A Journal of Theory and Practice*, *2*(2), 609–628.

Farley, M., Baral, I., Kiremire, M., & Sezgin, U. (1998). Prostitution in five countries: Violence and post-traumatic stress disorder. *Feminism & Psychology*, *8*(4), 405–426.

Farley, M., Cotton, A., Lynne, J., Zumbeck, S., Spiwak, F., Reyes, M. E., . . . Sezgin, U. (2004). Prostitution and trafficking in nine countries: An update on violence and posttraumatic stress disorder. *Journal of Trauma Practice*, *2*(3–4), 33–74.

Fellows, M. L., & Razack, S. (1998). The race to innocence: Confronting hierarchical relations among women. *The Journal of Gender, Race & Justice*, *1*, 335–352.

Foucault, M. (1978). *The history of sexuality* (R. Hurley, trans.). New York, NY: Random House.

Gilman, S. L. (1985). Black bodies, White bodies: Toward an iconography of female sexuality in late nineteenth-century art, medicine, and literature. *Critical Inquiry*, *12*(1), 204–242.

Giobbe, E. (1990). Confronting the liberal lies about prostitution. In D. Leidholdt & J. G. Raymond (Eds.), *The sexual liberals and the attack on feminism* (pp. 67–81). New York, NY: The Teacher's College Press.

Giobbe, E. (1996). An analysis of individual, institutional and cultural pimping. *Michigan Journal of Gender & Law*, *1*, 33.

Goldberg, D. (1993). *Racist culture*. Oxford: Blackwell.

Herndon, R. F. (1990, August 19). Race tilts the scales of justice. Study: Dallas punishes attacks on whites more harshly. *Dallas Times Herald*, p. 1A.

Hidalgo, D. A. (2006). Sex workers' rights movements. In S. Seidman, N. Fischer, & C. Meeks (Eds.), *Handbook of the new sexuality studies* (pp. 499–503). New York, NY: Routledge.

Holmes, D. (2006). The wrecking effects of race and social class on self and success. *The Psychoanalytic Quarterly*, *75*(1), 215–235.

Hong, Y., Zhang, C., Li, X., Liu, W., & Zhou, Y. (2013). Partner violence and psychosocial distress among female sex workers in China. *PLoS ONE*, *8*(4), e62290. https://doi.org/10.1371/journal.pone.0062290

Hossain, M., Zimmerman, C., Abas, M., Light, M., & Watts, C. (2010). The relationship of trauma to mental disorders among trafficked and sexually exploited girls and women. *American Journal of Public Health*, *100*(12), 2442–2449.

Jordan, W. D. (2012). *White over Black: American attitudes toward the Negro, 1550–1812* (2nd ed.). Chapel Hill, NC: University of North Carolina Press.

Khaylis, A., Waelde, L. C., & Bruce, E. J. (2007). The role of ethnic identity in the relationship of race-related stress to PTSD symptoms among young adults. *Journal of Trauma & Dissociation, 8*(4), 91–105.

Kissil, K., & Davey, M. (2010). The prostitution debate in feminism: Current trends, policy and clinical issues facing an invisible population. *Journal of Feminist Family Therapy, 22*(1), 1–21.

Kramer, L. A., & Berg, E. C. (2003). A survival analysis of timing of entry into prostitution: The differential impact of race, educational level, and childhood/adolescent risk factors. *Sociological Inquiry, 73*(4), 511–528.

LaFree, G. (1989). *Rape and criminal justice: The social construction of sexual assault*. Belmont, CA: Wadsworth Publishing Company.

Lauritsen, J. L., & White, N. A. (2001). Putting violence in its place: The influence of race, ethnicity, gender, and place on the risk for violence. *Criminology & Public Policy, 1*(1), 37–60.

Leidholdt, D. A. (2003). Prostitution and trafficking in women: An intimate relationship. *Journal of Trauma Practice, 2*(3–4), 167–183.

Levine, P. A., & Frederick, A. (1997). *Waking the tiger: Healing trauma*. Berkeley, CA: North Atlantic Books.

Ling, D. C., Wong, W. C. W., Holroyd, E. A., & Gray, S. A. (2007). Silent killers of the night: An exploration of psychological health and suicidality among female street sex workers. *Journal of Sex & Marital Therapy, 33*(4), 281–299.

Loewenstein, R. J. (1996). Dissociative amnesia and dissociative fugue. In L. K. Michaelson & W. J. Ray (Eds.), *Handbook of dissociation: Theoretical, clinical, and empirical perspectives* (pp. 307–336). New York, NY: Plenum.

Lucas, A. M. (1995). Race, class, gender, and deviancy: The criminalization of prostitution. *Berkeley Women's Law Journal, 10*(1), 47–60.

MacKinnon, C. A. (1993). Prostitution and civil rights. *Michigan Journal of Gender and Law, 1*, 13–31.

Mayfield-Schwarz, L. (2007). *Severity of trauma exposure and complex post-traumatic stress disorder symptomatology in women who prostitute* (Doctoral dissertation). ProQuest Digital Dissertations.

Medrano, M. A., Hatch, J. P., Zule, W. A., & Desmond, D. P. (2003). Childhood trauma and adult prostitution behavior in a multiethnic heterosexual drug-using population. *The American Journal of Drug and Alcohol Abuse, 29*(2), 463–486.

Mohanty, C. T. (2013). Transnational feminist crossings: On neoliberalism and radical critique. *Signs, 38*(4), 967–991.

Morgan, R. E., & Truman, J. L. (2018). *Criminal victimization, 2017* (NCJ 252472). Retrieved from www.bjs.gov/index.cfm?ty=pbdetail&iid=6466

Ogden, P., Minton, K., & Pain, C. (2006). *Trauma and the body: A sensorimotor approach to psychotherapy*. New York, NY: W. W. Norton & Co.

Ogden, P., Pain, C., Minton, K., & Fisher, J. (2005). Including the body in mainstream psychotherapy for traumatized individuals. *Psychologist – Psychoanalyst, 25*(4), 18–19.

Perdue, T. R., Williamson, C., Ventura, L. A., Hairston, T. R., Osborne, L. T. C., Laux, J. M., . . . Nathan, V. M. (2012). Offenders who are mothers with and without experience in prostitution: Differences in historical trauma, current stressors, and physical and mental health differences. *Women's Health Issues, 22*(2), e195–e200.

Pinderhughes, E. B. (1989). *Understanding race, ethnicity, and power: The key to efficacy in clinical practice.* New York, NY: The Free Press.

Pokorak, J. J. (2006). Rape as a badge of slavery: The legal history of, and remedies for, prosecutorial race-of-victim charging disparities. *Nevada Law Journal, 7*(1), 1–54.

Portlock, K. S. (2007). Status on trial: The racial ramifications of admitting prostitution evidence under state rape shield legislation. *Columbia Law Review, 107*(6), 1404–1436.

Razack, S. (1998). Race, space, and prostitution: The making of the bourgeois subject. *Canadian Journal of Women & the Law, 10*(2), 338–379.

Richie, B. E. (2012). *Arrested justice: Black women, violence, and America's prison nation.* New York, NY: New York University Press.

Roberts, D. (1994). *The myth of Aunt Jemima: Representations of race and region.* New York, NY: Routledge.

Rössler, W., Koch, U., Lauber, C., Hass, A-K., Altwegg, M., Ajdacic-Gross, V., & Landolt, K. (2010). The mental health of female sex workers. *Acta Psychiatrica Scandinavica, 122*(2), 143–152.

Schore, A. N. (2005, Fall). Notes from Allan Schore's groups in developmental affective neuroscience and clinical practice. *Psychologist – Psychoanalyst, 25*(4), 18–19.

Schore, A. N. (2010). Attachment trauma and the developing right brain: Origins of pathological dissociation. In P. F. Dell & J. A. O'Neill (Eds.), *Dissociation and the dissociative disorders: DSM-V and beyond* (pp. 107–141). London: Routledge.

Schwartz, R. C. (1995). *Internal family systems therapy.* New York, NY: Guilford Press.

Schweitzer, D. (2000). Striptease: The art of spectacle and transgression. *The Journal of Popular Culture, 34*(1), 65–75.

Seib, C., Fischer, J., & Najman, J. M. (2009). The health of female sex workers from three industry sectors in Queensland, Australia. *Social Science & Medicine, 68*(3), 473–478.

Shaver, F. M. (1994). The regulation of prostitution: Avoiding the morality traps. *Canadian Journal of Law & Society, 9*, 123.

Siegel, D. J. (1999). *The developing mind: How relationships and the brain interact to shape who we are.* New York, NY: Guilford Press.

Silbert, M. H., & Pines, A. M. (1982). Victimization of street prostitutes. *Victimology, 7*(1–4), 122–133.

Sloss, C. M. F. (2003). *The mental health needs and service utilization of women who trade sex* (Doctoral dissertation). ProQuest Digital Dissertations.

Smith, C. A. (2014). Putting prostitutes in their place: Black women, social violence, and the Brazilian case of Sirlei Carvalho. *Latin American Perspectives, 41*(1), 107–123.
Smith, V. (1990). Split affinities: The case of interracial rape. In V. Smith, M. Hirsch, & E. F. Keller (Eds.), *Conflicts in feminism* (pp. 271–287). New York, NY: Routledge.
Spiegel, D. (1986). Dissociation, double binds, and posttraumatic stress in multiple personality disorder. In B. G. Braun (Ed.), *Treatment of multiple personality disorder* (pp. 61–78). Washington, DC: American Psychiatric Press.
Steele, K., & van der Hart, O. (2009). Treating dissociation. In C. A. Courtois & J. D. Ford (Eds.), *Treating complex traumatic stress disorders: Scientific foundations and therapeutic models* (pp. 145–165). New York, NY: Guilford Press.
Suresh, G., Furr, L. A., & Srikrishnan, A. K. (2009). An assessment of the mental health of street-based sex workers in Chennai, India. *Journal of Contemporary Criminal Justice, 25*(2), 186–201.
van der Kolk, B. A. (1996a). The body keeps the score: Approaches to the psychobiology of posttraumatic stress disorder. In B. A. van der Kolk, A. C. McFarlane, & L. Weisaeth (Eds.), *Traumatic stress: The effects of overwhelming experience on mind, body, and society*. New York, NY: Guilford Press.
van der Kolk, B. A. (1996b). The complexity of adaptation to trauma: Self-regulation, stimulus discrimination, and characterological development. In B. A van der Kolk, A. C. McFarlane, & L. Weisaeth (Eds.), *Traumatic stress: The effects of overwhelming experience on mind, body and society* (pp. 182–213). New York, NY: Guilford Press.
van der Kolk, B. A. (2014). *The body keeps the score: Brain, mind, and body in the healing of trauma*. New York, NY: Viking Penguin.
Vanwesenbeeck, I. (1994). *Prostitutes' well-being and risk*. Amsterdam: VU University Press.
Volkan, V. D., & Sinclair, C. (1997). *Bloodlines: From ethnic pride to ethnic terrorism*. New York, NY: Farrar, Straus & Giroux.
Wang, B., Li, X., Stanton, B., Fang, X., Yang, H., Zhao, R., & Hong, Y. (2007). Sexual coercion, HIV-related risk, and mental health among female sex workers in China. *Health Care for Women International, 28*(8), 745–762.
Weitzer, R. (2011). Sex trafficking and the sex industry: The need for evidence-based theory and legislation. *Journal of Criminal Law and Criminology, 101*(4), 1337–1370.

Chapter 4

Skin memories

On race, love, and loss

Sue Grand

In every psychoanalysis, there is a prevailing motif and a transference dynamism in which that motif comes alive. In my first analysis, that theme was aborted grief. For me, that grief had collective meanings, which would be illuminated by a racialized transference. But like all analyses, this process would begin in my personal past. When I was 7, I lost my Russian Jewish grandmother, who cared for me while my parents labored seven days a week. Grandma died and I was lost: lost to my parents' attention, small at her funeral, invisible to the adult mourners, all of them larger, more vocal, more clamoring than myself. I was without tears, without comfort, without her enveloping body. She was 5 foot 1, and sometimes she weighed 250 pounds. She had pendulous arms and a vast bosom. To me, her body was bountiful. It held me and nourished me, and now it was gone.

My parents were first-generation Americans. Grandma came through Ellis Island with her parents, in flight from conscriptions and pogroms. Then, there was World War I, the Great Depression, unemployment and starvation, and then, World War II. My father witnessed atrocities in battle, and after the liberation he was stationed at Dachau. Life was full of catastrophic reversals and moral imperatives. What we had was humor, our wits, and our labor. Children's lives were rough and tumble; they worked, if they could get it, and when they weren't working, they ran in the streets. After Grandma was gone, I knew I would raise myself, on city streets. Childhood had already passed on. Of course, there was still laughter. There were riotous family stories, but none were told about Grandma. Where Grandma had been, there were vague memories of Russia and the disappearance of others. There were absolute goodbyes, and impossible distances. There were always holes in our mourning, and, now, after my grandmother's death, there was another hole in our stories.

If we were silent about her absence, that absence would be felt in Brooklyn. In life, Grandma was a presence. There was nothing inert about her heft. No: her bulk seemed to make her a formidable force. In Brooklyn, she knew who ran things; they owed her favors, and she could make things happen. By day, she bustled about, and kibitzed, and cooked and cleaned. In the evenings, she took off her apron and stepped out. She had always lived from hand to mouth. But on Saturday nights, her flesh poured out of her strapless gowns. She put on lipstick and powder, long white gloves, costume jewelry. Glorious in her plentitude, the Queen of Canarsie, she sallied forth to some political event. She schmoozed, and deals were struck. For family and neighbors, there were rent reductions, free doctoring; immigration officials melted away. Grandma had a kind of nurturing insistence, and she wouldn't back down. She saw need, and she took care of it. *With* me, she was tender, but she was also fierce *for* me.

But what inspired her to take care of Brooklyn? Even in the absence of stories, I sensed that there were other bodies nesting inside of her body. I often played with those Russian puzzle dolls, painted, rotund, wooden figures that contained ever-smaller replicas of themselves. Grandma was Russian, and she had the same shape. I thought those dolls must be alive inside of her. This would explain her devotion, and her bulk. But exactly *who* were these bodies sequestered inside Grandma? This mystery found commentary in my grandmother's hands. Broad and calloused, they were full of competence, grace, and intention. They never stopped moving. And yet, each hand had several mutilated fingers; there were just rough stumps ending at the knuckles. Gradually, I absorbed the discrepancy between her hands and my own. One day, I asked, "Grandma, what happened to your fingers?" "I was working in a factory. They were severed in an accident. We were poor. We didn't have enough to eat. I was lucky to be working. I had to feed your father."

She goes on kneading dough, and I am riveted by those fingers. I slip into the folds of time, assembly lines, harrowing sounds, and sharp, implacable machines. The Great Depression, and my grandmother, bleeding. No money for a hospital or a doctor. No one else to feed the family. I see her being saved by other, hungry, working hands. Those times layered into present time: there are mountains of food emerging from her deft movements. Now, she is feeding Brooklyn, defying poverty's implacable machine. She is corpulent; she eats in memory of hunger, and for those who had nothing to eat.

Years after my analysis, I find myself visualizing her hands. They were a miracle of post-traumatic resilience and provision; they were proud, and they moved without shame, or fear. But all of this is reawakened memory, a luxurious, unfolding vision, loosened by my psychoanalysis. When I came to see my analyst, I was depressed. I knew Grandma mattered, and I knew that she had died. What followed was a remarkable analytic excavation, between an African-American analyst and a Russian-Jewish patient. Between us, there were complex trans-generational legacies, interleaved with racial/ethnic identities, inscribed on our woman bodies.

In an analysis between a white patient and an African-American therapist, issues about racism will surface. But in *this* treatment, race trouble became a direct conduit to the plantation. It was as if racism moved swiftly backwards in time: the assassination of MLK, Jr; Medgar Evers; Emmett Till; the bridge at Selma; lynchings; Jim Crow; Reconstruction; the Civil War; and then, we arrived at the cotton fields, and the slave block. I have always been vulnerable to dual vision: life, here, now; and the long, tangled history of violence. And this is what I knew at the beginning of my analysis. In my first consultation, I met an analyst who appeared to be white. After the first few sessions, I had random encounters with two white people who knew her. Each of them told me that my analyst identified herself as African-American. One of them had known my analyst in college and described her as an African-American student who was a political activist in the sixties. And I knew this: her name didn't sound like Brooklyn. It sounded like the Deep South.

So what, then, did I know? I knew we lived in racial categories and that I had shame, and guilt, for perpetuating those categories. I wanted to be color-blind (see K. Leary, 2002). But I also knew, as Cornel West (2001) would put it, that 'race matters' – that an African-American identity references an objective history of oppression (also K. Leary, 2002). And I knew that there was a gap, a tension, between her *apparent* whiteness and her identification as black. I knew too that she could 'pass' as white, but that she had refused to pass. This is what I understood: that she had important familial and community attachments. She had a political position and solidarity with those who *could not pass*. What to do with this in my analysis? I knew that she thought I thought she was white. I thought she thought that I was 'passing' her. As Kim Leary (1997) puts it, "Passing always occurs in the context of a relationship: it requires, on the one side, a subject who does not tell, and on the other, an audience who fails to ask" (p. 85). But what my analyst didn't know is that I knew without asking. Discovering her racial identification from external sources, it was as if I had plundered Pandora's box. I had forbidden, extra-analytic knowledge. I had the puzzle of white skin, black identity. I had questions that had no place in classical psychoanalysis.

It was the 1970s. My analyst and I were ten years apart; we were both products of a radical era: anti-war protests, feminism, the civil rights movement. But we were also embedded in a white psychoanalysis, which did not inquire into trauma, or the intersection of psyche and culture. She was a politically active African-American who was also successful in the white world of psychoanalysis. But insofar as Faimberg, Laub, and Bergmann and others had begun to recognize trans-generational transmission, this new lens was trained on the Holocaust and excluded slavery (for exceptions, see: Bass, 2003; Gump, 2010; J. Leary, 2005; Smith, 2011). Eventually, we would trust each other enough to talk race trouble. But in the trans-generational area of what Akbar (1996) calls 'plantation syndrome' or J. Leary (2005) calls 'post-traumatic slave syndrome' there were no words yet for the phantasms that would appear in my transference. From the first, my analysis was haunted by the ghosts who were, as Reis (2007) puts it, carrying "their mute messages and their enigmatic demands, seeking witness to hidden catastrophe" (p. 622). As Davoine (2012) might suggest, history emerged through unexpected events, through symptoms, and the interpenetration of our psyches.

My transference would be personal, plastic, healing, and imaginary. But it would also be defined by a real, and terrible, history. My racial conundrum referred to what Laub and Podell (1995) call 'trauma's empty circle': a residuum of mass atrocity that exceeds speech and narration, in which "we are implicated in each other's traumas" (Caruth, 1995, p. 24). I knew, or sensed, that my therapist's 'white' skin was *not* due to generations of mutual, and loving, intercourse. In the United States, interracial love was as rare as it was forbidden and dangerous. For much of our history, it was illegal 'miscegenation'. But the rape of black women by white men was ubiquitous. White skin, African-American identity: this insinuated the predicament of slave women, whose descendants would emerge with light skin. Lying on the couch, I glimpsed these slave women in the shadows. They cried out at the edge of my consciousness, and they are crying out still. Of all the things I shared with my analyst, of this, I never spoke.

Missing stories: testimonies of the skin

White skin, African-American identity. I was silent, in a country that has kept its own brutal secrets for almost 500 years: women and girls, kidnapped in Africa, sold into slavery. The violence of white incursions was written, and rewritten, on their bodies, and on the skin of succeeding generations. There are the euphemisms for rape that persist in histories of slavery, even those written in 2012 (Swarns, 2012): that white masters 'fathered' children with their female slaves. That more enlightened white masters, like Thomas Jefferson, had slave 'mistresses' or 'wives'. One could say that these terms capture the varieties of love and desire that *could* exist between slave and master (see Berlin, 2003; Deramus, 2005; Fox-Genovese, 1988; Scharfstein, 2011; Swarns, 2012). They may acknowledge the rare, courageous love relationships that did occur (Berlin, 2003; Deramus, 2005). For example, R. M. Johnson, vice president to Van Buren, took his black wife and children with him to Washington, D.C., in 1836, before slavery ended (see Berlin, 2003, p. 182). We cannot presume her consent. But, at times, there were complex erotic/romantic switchbacks in the relationship of master and slave, and relative degrees of agency available to some slave women (Gorden-Reed, 2008). But as Hartman (1997) elaborates in her excellent critique of 'seduction' during slavery, 'fathering' and 'mistress' presume a woman's freedom to say *yes*, when it is impossible to say *no*. As a slave, she cannot refuse her master. Nonetheless, in the 'erotics of terror' (Hartman, p. 81) the rape of slave women is

> Embraced, denied, inverted and displaced in the law of slavery . . . the enslaved is legally unable to give consent or offer resistance, (but) she is presumed to be always willing (Hartman, p. 81.). . . . The legal transposition of rape as sexual intercourse shrouds this condition of violent domination with the suggestion of complicity.
>
> (p. 85)

Thus, even the most brilliant and compassionate histories of slavery (e.g., see Berlin, 2003) embrace these euphemisms and fail to adequately narrate this sexual trespass. I am white, but I am a woman, and I have a vagina, and I know what rape is. I know about power and submission. I know that permanent wariness and predatory menace. I am a 'free' white woman. I can try to escape. I always had some laws to protect me. Slave women were bred like cattle, assaulted by their masters, coerced into sex with threats and promises. With a husband, or parents, who would be brutalized, or killed, for trying to protect her. Then: she is pregnant with another slave, with lightening skin, a child scarred by this heritage, and yet perversely privileged by that scar.

In a universe of such racial madness, this incursion of whiteness into black vaginas yielded a trans-generational legacy of shame, rage, terror, and a tendency to blame the victim (see hooks, 2001). But it also yielded children *who had the potential for race change*. As Kim Leary (1997) notes, "the very ability to pass from black to white – unlike other cultural or ethnic masquerades – is dependent on antecedent traumas like the sexual exploitation of African women and girls during slavery (p. 89)" (see also hooks, 2001). These children bore the complex stigmata of slavery. A girl's lightened skin spoke of her forebears' abjection. That skin still speaks of this abjection in contemporary America, but this historical violence is obscured by our collective 'malignant dissociative contagion' (Grand, 2000).

But such was the perversity of this atrocity: that sexual violation also conferred degrees of whiteness on succeeding generations of slaves. This yielded a complex 'color caste' system (see hooks, 2001) in which light-skinned blacks were considered superior to dark-skinned blacks. The master's offspring might receive easier work, better care, even some affection or education. During slavery, these children were denied and were often persecuted by their master's shame and fear, and by the mistress's jealousy and vengeance (see Fleischner, 1996; Fox-Genovese, 1988). But these children could also be humanized by proximity; becoming the locus of white ambivalence. When the Spanish dominated the Louisiana territory,

> Manumission began inside the slave owners' household. Among the first to be freed were the *lovers* and children of the slave owners themselves. During the first decade of Spanish rule, numerous masters freed their *slave wives* and the children they bore, for reasons of 'love and affection'.
>
> (Berlin, 2003, p. 93, italics mine)

In Berlin's text, 'lover' and 'wife' insinuate consent in a system of total subjugation. What a strange legacy of oppression. Through sexual exploitation, a woman is degraded. Her child becomes the ambiguous sign of a new category between black and white, perhaps the first beneficiary of freedom. Indeed, as Berlin (2003) notes, it was not mysterious that "the free colored population grew physically lighter as the slave population – much of it just arrived from Africa – grew darker" (p. 152).

Thus, for slave girls, to be 'mulatto' was to become something between the human and the sub-human. This child could become semi-human to her mother's rapist, by whom she is owned, and by whom she can be freed. But like all slave girls, she is also prey for her master/father. Whether she succumbed to threats and promises, or was the object of a more violent assault, a girl understood her fate. This fate continued to mingle familial links and DNA. The whiter these children became, the more they exposed the sexual predation of their white masters. They complicated the ideology of slave masters and threatened the racial categories that sustained white dominance. But if light-skinned blacks kept awakening white ambivalence and moving towards emancipation, it would pose an economic loss, requiring the master class to keep purchasing new slaves. And so, the 'one drop rule' was established to define blackness (Sharfstein, 2011). New laws insured that these children would follow the condition of their mother. Now, the offspring of rape *increased* slave holdings and multiplied wealth. Even as the color line blurred, official racial categories often became *more* rigid and *less* permeable. Destabilized by racial ambiguities, the brutality of whites often escalated (Berlin, 2003; Sharfstein, 2011).

Nonetheless, sexual predation kept threatening the power hierarchies that it was consolidating. Thus, historian Charles Beard could comment, rather poetically, on the way resistance eventually triumphs over regimes of violence, because the "bee fertilizes the flower that it robs". Indeed, rape fertilized women's bodies with the racial ambiguities that could destabilize white dominance. These contradictions kept infecting succeeding generations. Race change became increasingly possible (Sharfstein, 2011), even as racism was perpetuated and internalized. Re-enacting the 'color caste system' imposed on them by sexual violence (and by the relative privileges 'lightness' had conferred) blacks would also become divided against themselves. 'Lighter' skin became a marker of possibility and worth; dark skin potentiated shame, hopelessness, and self-hatred (J. Leary, 2005; hooks, 2001; Powell, 2012; Thompson, 2012). The 'erotics of terror' (Hartman, 1997) continued to be bedrock to white privilege, as Baldwin (1972), Fanon (1952), Hernton (1965), Hine (1993), and others have noted. Whites continued to be paranoid and persecutory about black men raping white women (thereby polluting their imaginary, untainted, 'virginal', whiteness), while white men continued raping black women. Beginning with slavery, this "white culpability was displaced as black criminality" (Hartman, 1997, p. 83.). As Young-Bruehl (1996) notes, throughout the generations, this perversity has been worked out on black bodies: through sexual projections and sexual transgressions; through "the rapacious 'whitening' of the darker race" (p. 491); and through centuries of white secrecy. The subterranean intercourse between 'races' contradicted our mythologies of racial hierarchies and separation. The result was a passing mechanism which "depended upon its operating in silence. Passing was a conspiracy of silence not only for the individual but for a biracial society, which had drawn a rigid color line based on visibility. Unless a white man was a white man, the gates were open to endless slander and confusion" (Jordan, 1968, p. 174).

This history takes a splintered pathway in post-traumatic slave syndrome. In their bodily experience, African-American women describe difficulty feeling beautiful, sensuous, *and* safe (McCoy-Wilson, 2007; hooks, 2001). There are also descendants of rape who could 'pass' to live in a white world. Later, *their* descendants might discover slaves in the family (see Ball, 1998; Swarns, 2012). They might find themselves asking: am I really 'white'? What do these categories really mean? And: are my ancestors both the rapist and the raped (Swarns, 2012)? All of this is attended by mystification and loss, the awareness of missing kin, and by familial pockets of what Patterson (1982) calls, 'social death'. For, as Kim Leary (1997) puts it, passing becomes "a traumatic accommodation that produces traumatic losses of its own" (p. 88). Having lost so many forebears to death, sale, and separation, African-Americans felt forced to reproduce those broken attachments, in order to pass. Afraid to be 'outed' by contact with their own relatives, people severed all ties to their past. African-Americans often kept the secret even within a loving interracial marriage (Gates, 1996; K. Leary, 1997; Sharfstein, 2011; Swarns, 2012).

When I arrived on the couch, I was just beginning to know that the Atlantic and Domestic slave trade lasted more than 300 years. Millions lived and died in chains (see Berlin, 2003; Hochschild, 2005). African-American slavery was one of the most sustained forms of mass violence perpetrated by humanity. And in every epoch of mass violence, women are violated, and these wounds are embodied in their descendants. But in the 1970s, this traumatic legacy had not registered in psychoanalysis. As Gump (2000, 2010), and Alan Bass (2003) note, slavery is still not adequately recognized in trauma studies. Although we now have an expanding literature on the influence of race within psychoanalysis (Altman, 2000; Bonovitz, 2012; Holmes, 2012; Leary, 1997; Suchet, 2007, etc.), with the notable exceptions of Apprey (2003), Alan Bass (2003), Janice Gump (2010), slavery has not found a place in the trans-generational turn in psychoanalysis. This very absence may be a trans-generational legacy, an inherited trace of the belief that slaves were incapable of deep feeling. As haunted as he was by slavery, Thomas Jefferson promoted this view:

> Their griefs are transient. Those numberless afflictions . . . are *less felt and sooner forgotten with them.* In general their existence appears to participate more of sensation than reflection.
>
> (Jefferson, as quoted in Williams, 2012, p. 90; italics mine)

This conviction neutralized the master's guilt. For post-traumatic slave syndrome to gain recognition in the trans-generational turn in psychoanalysis, another voice must be heard:

> I was compelled to stand and see my wife shamefully scourged and abused by her master: and the manner in which this was done, was so violently and inhumanely committed upon the person of a female, that I despair. . . . My happiness or pleasure was then all blasted; for it was sometimes a pleasure to be with my family even in slavery. I loved them as my wife and child. . . . But oh! When I remember that my daughter, my only child, is still there, destined to share the fate of all these calamities, it is too much to bear. . . . If ever there was any one act of my life while a slave, that I have to lament over, it is that of being a father and a husband of slaves.
>
> (Henry Bibb, 1849 [ex-slave] as quoted in Williams, 2012, p. 114)

Slave women on the couch: ghosts in the transference

In the 1970s, I had not heard this voice. But somehow, its claims had penetrated my existence. I felt guilt about my whiteness, and I wanted to make repair. In the wake of the civil rights movement, I wanted to be color-blind. So I tried to have a colorless analysis, in a psychic world divorced from politics and culture. But in the United States, color blindness is wishful phantasm; this phantasm can actually negate the others' historical subjectivity (see K. Leary, 2002). As a young, progressive white woman, I had no exit from this loop. But I was also a Jew whose father had witnessed Dachau. And so, my analysis would proceed in two registers. There was a 'black analysis' in which history was trying to break in. There was a 'black' analyst, with whom I was white and bad. There was a 'white analysis', configured as a 'pure' and 'untainted' psychic excavation. In this register, I had a 'white analyst' with whom I was also white and with whom I could be good. Sometimes, these registers were split off and dissociated, but mostly they were inter-penetrating in my transference. My analyst became two grandmothers. Sometimes, these grandmothers were both in *ambiguous* racial categories. The Jewish one was not really white (see Altman, 2000; Suchet, 2007), and the African-American one was not really black. Sometimes, they were *both* messengers of history. One fled from Russian pogroms and left her relatives behind. In claiming her African-American identity, and refusing to 'pass', the other would *not* leave her people behind. These figures were in flux; they moved in and out of shadows, and they morphed through time.

From the beginning of my analysis, I needed a reparative bond of identification. I needed my analyst to be an intact Bubbie from Brooklyn. I was suffering from attachment trauma. I wanted a sense of sameness with my analyst, a sameness that was both familiar and safe. *Not* our shared female vulnerability in a sexist culture. *Not* our legacies of persecution. In the United States, race has been the foundational marker for difference, conflict, and alienation. Skin color has been a firewall between 'us' and 'them'; it has subverted bonding and identification. If my analyst was going to be 'like me', she would have to be white. It wasn't difficult to erase racial difference, because she appeared to be white. Still, I have wondered. How did I create this Jewish grandmother trans-position, in a treatment infused with the 'un-thought known' (Bollas, 1986) of slavery? My analyst was young and slender and graceful, almond-eyed, olive-skinned, with long brown hair that flowed to her waist. Her posture was relaxed and erect, and she moved like a dancer. In both body and in spirit, one would have said these women were opposites: my analyst didn't have Grandma's noise or heft or her moxie. She was quiet and gentle and receptive, and her words were chosen with care. Her empathic attunement seemed meditative and transcendent. Grandma wouldn't know from this kind of quiescence. Clearly, my analyst maintained herself on exercise and salad, not on blintzes and chicken fat. When she spoke, it was educated and articulate, without a trace of a Yiddish accent. There was no reason to think she was a Brooklyn Jew. There was every reason to think that she wasn't. Her first name was resonant with the Deep South. And yet, my 7-year-old self recognized my Bubbie. I sobbed unexpectedly the first time she went away. Every session, I watched for the changes that would presage her disappearance.

Over time, my love for my analyst became, in many ways, reciprocal, faithful, and tender. But my 'normative unconscious' (Layton, 2006) was also infused with cultural prejudice; it repeated hegemonic practices (Hollander, 2011), which disqualified her African-American identity. To have an *intact* maternal bond, I had to have a *white mother*. I was a white child; how could I have a black mother? Wasn't race the ultimate sign of the 'not me' and the 'not mine'? On the one hand, I kept re-constructing racist categories, and *excluding a black woman as a legitimate love object for a white child*. But I was also living in the switchbacks of my analyst's trans-generational past. In my analyst's name, there were echoes of the plantation: mothers in the cotton fields and on the slave blocks. They were howling, chained, beaten, reaching helplessly, for their children. There were mothers searching for their children, and children searching for their mothers (Williams, 2012). There were privileged white sons and daughters of the slave-masters. Cared for by these slave mothers who were bereft about their own children. Then these white children grew up to enslave their nanny and her children, recycling cruelty and loss into the very heart of her attachments.

For more than 300 years, the protective maternal shield had been violated. If my analyst was black, I became white and bad. As a white child, how dare I ask her for enduring love? If I ask her to love me, am I turning her into my 'black mammy'? If I acknowledge racial difference, will I discover that her love for me is tainted with resentment and hatred? To claim her love must I become her black child? But if I am her black daughter,

I will share her fate. And I can be sold to another master, howling, again, as I am separated from Mother. To Fleischner (1996), the loss of Mother is the originating moment of psychic enslavement for girls born into slavery.

So it is dangerous to be my analyst's black child, and it's impossible to be her white child. Our histories are thick with transgression and loss. So, I passed my analyst, *but I never forgot* that she was African-American and that she would not pass herself. In the folds of this paradox, I re-enacted persecutory history, but I was also trying to resist, and repair, this history. By *knowing* my analyst as an African-American woman who I could *imagine* as my white Bubbie, I trespassed on my analyst's subjectivity. But in the mad thicket of race, I was also creative and insistent: I wanted an intact, and inviolable, maternal shield. In my 'black' analysis, this search kept testifying to the memories of slave children:

> My mammy (recalled Fannie Moore of South Carolina) she work in de field all day and piece and quilt all night. . . . I never see how my mammy stand such hard work. She stand up for her chillen though. De old overseer he hate my mammy, 'cause she fought him for beatin' her chillen. Why she get more whippin' for dat dan anything else.
>
> (as quoted in Genovese, 1972, p. 499)

These memories bore witness to the ferocity of Mother, even as she was forcibly separated from her own children:

> John Randolph of Roanoke, a slaveholder himself, who had known Patrick Henry, Henry Clay, and all of the great orators of the day, and who himself ranked at the top, was asked whom he thought to have pride of place. "The greatest orator I ever heard," he replied, "was a woman. She was a slave and a mother and her rostrum was an auction block."
>
> (quoted in Genovese, 1976, p. 456)

This mother is not a 'dead mother' (Green, 1986) of massive trauma. This was the 'Alive Mother', described by Silberg (2012) and Main (2000). Her maternal capacity was fierce and unbroken. My analyst signified those slave women, who risked torture to find, and protect, their children (Williams, 2012), despite 300 years of severed attachments. And my analyst signified those who sustained strong familial and communal bonds, as they crossed into freedom (see Cross, 1998). In my treatment, this maternal figure is a condensation of history. She is Sojourner Truth and Harriet Tubman and Septima Clark and Rosa Parks. But this mother is also a primal imago, a wish fulfillment, a fantasy of an indefatigable super-Mother, larger than persecution, abjection, sickness, separation, and death. She is a slave mother, who cannot be vanquished by the chains or by the whip. She is an obese, Russian Jewish grand-Mother from Brooklyn, who can live forever on chicken fat, without dying of a heart attack. For African-American women, this imago can repeat stereotypes. As Hine notes, it is problematic to "create myths of the super-heroic black woman who stoically met every obstacle, endured total debasement, only to rise above her tormentors and captors" (Hine, 1993, p. 340). Still, I would suggest that this phantasm lurks in the unconscious of children who have been separated from Mother, by death or violence. This imago contains longing and hope; it is an exemplar of justice and human dignity. It is an archetype of what hooks and West (1991) call the 'love ethic' in the civil rights movement, and in African-American faith and resistance.

In my analyst's steadfast empathic attunement, in her refusal to pass, I felt her keeping faith with this mother. And so, my analyst became a 'transformational object' (Bollas, 1986); she was gentle, but she had all of Grandma's strength, devotion, and moxie. If lost Russian relatives were fed inside my Grandma's body, persecuted generations were sheltered in my analyst's racial solidarity. Even as I imagined her ethnic *sameness* with Grandma, it was actually her racial *difference* that restored the maternal bond. The 'un-thought known' (Bollas, 1986) of slavery was actually *resurrecting* Grandma and repairing the wounds of history, even as part of me negated race. It was here, between knowing and not knowing massive psychic trauma (see Laub & Auerhahn, 1993) that I had the sense that

> When the world within us is destroyed, when it is dead and loveless, when our loved ones are in fragments, and we ourselves in helpless despair – it is then that we must re-create our world anew, re-assemble the pieces, infuse life into dead fragments, re-create life.
>
> (Segal, 1952, p. 199)

My African-American analyst, my Russian Jewish grandmother: they were so different in size and temperament and history. But they *did* have an essential sameness: they had *maternal dignity and clarity and force*. They possessed a queenly grace and womanly assurance; they bore their wounds with resilience and their pain with compassion. They were fierce; I knew that *they would fight for their children.*

All of this was distilled in my transference. My analyst's gentle strength was ameliorating my depression and restoring the 'love ethic' to human connection. But for me, this love ethic was also infused with doubt. I, me, and mine: *white people* had befouled the very Mother that I longed for. This truth mirrored a more personal moment, before my grandmother's death. *Grandma is in congestive heart failure. She is seated, ashen, and still, in her apartment. Grandma is never still; I can sense that she isn't well. My heart breaks for her suffering. Carefully, I approach her, my hand outstretched in tenderness. An adult voice stops me: "Don't touch. Grandma isn't well. You will hurt her." I freeze. I never touch her again, and, in fact, I never see her again. My love is forever conflated with Grandma's destruction. I am it: the boss man, the machine that severed her fingers; the Cossacks who murdered her relatives in Russia. I can make no reparation: Grandma is dead. I am caught in paranoid-schizoid splitting and in severe depressive anxiety.*

Analytic love: answering shame and the memory of evil

In the second year of analysis, I am revisiting this memory. Once, I tried to touch Grandma's suffering. Now, I am approaching the wound of race. I know that I am experiencing transference, but I also know that, as Holmes (2012) put it, "there is always an external reality of race. The lived reality of race in Western culture is that it always asserts itself" (p. 268). My *personal* melancholia seems to refract Cheng's (2001) notion of 'white racial melancholy'. Here, I was

> teetering between the known and the unknown, the seen and the deliberately unseen, (where) the racial other constitutes an oversight that is consciously made unconscious – naturalized over time as absence, as complementary negative space.
>
> (p. 16)

To Cheng, this co-constructs the 'legislated grief' (p. 8) and 'ambulatory despair' (p. 23) that is the melancholic predicament of the racially oppressed. From her perspective, the past is not dead, it is not past, and it cannot be 'gotten over'. Instead, 'social, political and subjective beings' must grieve (p. 7). Will this be possible in my analysis? Or will I be repudiated, struck down, again, for my destructiveness? For the 'micro-aggressions', and the 'micro-traumas' I may have inflicted? There was no psychoanalytic discourse in which to speak this. How could I talk about passing, and not passing, and the historic significance of her white skin? How could I talk without becoming the evil other of history?

Then, too, my treatment was already overflowing with *one* abandoned 7-year-old child in relation to *one*, lost mother. In my family, we had emigration memories: grown women, howling, as they were parted, forever, from their Russian mothers. We had Dachau memories, millions of mothers and children, separated, forever, by the gas. If race were to actually arrive on my analytic couch, Jewish cries would be amplified by the cries of African mothers, reverberating back to the Middle Passage. Such trauma is always too much to bear and too terrible to speak (see Grand, 2000; Howell, 2005; Laub & Auerhahn, 1993, etc.). I was in a paralytic predicament, when life intervened.

My analyst was in a high-rise building; I had to take the elevator to the twenty-sixth floor. Today, in the lobby, the elevator door opens. And there, inside is a black man, looking very 'street'. My heart starts to pound with terror, anticipating rape, before I can arrive at my analyst's floor. At the elevator, we stare at each other. I hesitate, and I know what he's seeing: another racist white woman, projecting violence onto an innocent black man. To reverse discrimination, I must override my panic, get in the elevator, risk what feels like certain assault. If I don't get in, what am I? He is my analyst's people. I mumble an excuse. As I turn away, I see the bitterness in his eyes. I want to cry out that I am sorry, but I just can't. I want to tell him: I was a girl, an adolescent, a young woman, on city streets. I grew up hard and fast in some rough neighborhoods; I didn't feel privileged. By 17, I was living, alone. I worked in a factory, and I took college courses at night. I returned home through violent landscapes. Men of every color have exposed themselves, chased me, threatened me, stolen my purse, called out obscenities, grabbed my breasts, put their hands up my skirt on crowded subways. Once, a man came to the door of my apartment, claiming to be a repairman. I knew I hadn't called a repairman. I wouldn't let him in. He went away and raped a more trusting woman on the next floor. I am wary, and I have eyes on the back of my head. I don't trust strange men in enclosed spaces. As the elevator closes, I want to cry out, really, it's not just because of your skin and your 'hoodie'.

But if he had been white and dressed in a suit, I would have taken the risk. I take the next elevator, and I arrive, shaken with anxiety and shame and guilt. How can I tell my analyst this? At this moment, our racial legacies seem salient. I am not expecting any solidarity about women's rape-dread, from a sister who also moves through city streets (see Grand, 2009). I am anticipating black rage. The man on the elevator is her brother, son, father. He represents generations of black men, falsely accused, brutalized, strung up: he is one of Billy Holiday's 'strange fruit'. I am trying to tell my analyst what just happened, and I tell her I am having trouble telling it. She asks me about my discomfort. I squirm and cringe, and reveal what I have always known: that she is African-American. That she looks white and that she doesn't pass. That she was a political activist in college. I am sure she will be offended by my behavior at the elevator. She is quiet, and the moment lasts forever. Is this the end of our bond? Have I turned her into another dead mother? Then, she says that I seem very frightened, and she asked me about my fear. I said I knew it was wrong to be so terrified of his violence, just because he is black. But I just couldn't get on that elevator. She asks me about memories of sexual trespass and about my fears of black men. I tell her. I can't believe what I am telling her: about poverty and urban violence and racial projections, and all of the molestations. Later, much later, I will wonder: why are regimes of power infused with the 'erotics of terror' (Hartman, 1997)? How have we constructed these trans-generational 'elevator moments', so that my white vagina now appears as the sacrificial site for racial repair and restitution?

But in that moment in the analysis, a miracle was occurring: I was making a racist confession, and I still felt her with me. Perhaps, she isn't gone. I was weeping, and I said as much as I could ever say at that time. I never spoke about the slave women crouching in the shadows of her office. I never spoke about black vaginas, held hostage to their masters. I never spoke about vaginas held hostage to white shame. I didn't link slave children's lightening skin to my analyst's ability to pass, centuries later. And I didn't talk about white children on plantations, mothered by slave mammies. I didn't talk about 'miscegenation', the criminalization of interracial love, and the ubiquitous sexual predation by generations of white power. I could only talk about the racism that we had words for, at that time.

It took everything I had to confess that I didn't think I could have a 'black mother'. I didn't think that a black mother could want me, as a white child. I confessed that I was looped into these racial categories and contradictions, when I should be 'color-blind'.

Now, it seems to me that this conversation could have unfolded over years. Inside me, this story has continued to unfold for the past thirty years. It has informed my reading, my writing, and my political consciousness. In the analysis, we could have deepened our awareness of our trans-generational ghosts: her legacy from slavery, my Russian ancestors, and the memory of Dachau. We could have talked about the condition of women that prevails, during mass violence. We could have shared what it was like to be a girl, on city streets – the menace, and the appropriation, of our bodies. But I only gave this a few, very painful, sessions. Nonetheless, I did find my courage. To love, we must be willing to know the other. I reached into my own 'love ethic', as I had, long ago, as a child: *Grandma, what happened to your fingers?* I asked about her racial experience and her racial heritage. What was it like to be taken for white among whites, as they expressed racist attitudes towards blacks? What was it like to be taken as white among blacks who could not pass as white? Had I hurt her by treating her like she was white?

In those days, we didn't ask personal questions in analysis, and we didn't expect our analysts to answer. But the African-American activist broke through her more classical constraints. Her response was sensitive and reflective and cautious. She didn't reveal much, but for those times, she said a lot. I was frightened to hear the truth and awed by her trust. I kept bursting into tears. She was tender, as always, towards my fear of loss. She said, "You are afraid you can't belong to me." And, "you are afraid I see you as bad." My sobbing got deeper. And, then, I asked her about her anger at white people like me. How could she love me? Finally, she said that her life had allowed her to love lots of different kinds of people. I could hear the experience, the sadness, and the compassion, in her voice. She was human. Her people had been wounded, and still, she was an unbroken mother. I was flawed; I was human, but I was not the agent of her destruction. She was someone real, with whom I could grieve and with whom I could make amends.

In this moment, I recovered the truth that I had witnessed in my grandma's hands: that abjection's memory is inscribed on women's bodies; that massive trauma forecloses mourning and keeps breaking up our bonds; that resilience can transform that history into compassion; that history's wound is not really eradicated by time; but that the maternal capacity does survive the lost generations, even though that original love has been lost. In speaking of race, this truth opened up other questions. Can healing *one* interracial bond help to heal 300 years of history? Will love ever soften my white shame and turn my guilt into a generative force? So much was spoken between us, and yet, there was still so much that would remain unspoken: the ancestral howls that haunted our relationship. African, Jewish, Russian. The recurrent breaks in the imago of Mother. The recurrent breaches of attachment, which had spanned 300 years. For that era, we had courage. But together, we returned to an intra-psychic psychoanalysis; we moved away from the ghosts of history. But like all ghosts, ours continued to speak through us.

One day, my analyst announced that she was relocating to another state with her family. After everything she knew about Grandma, and everything we had tried to repair, I found myself betrayed. Like Grandma, she seemed to love me, and like Grandma, she was leaving me forever. She was taking her *real children and leaving me behind.* I had six months to grieve, and for six months I raged and wept and howled, while she kept her empathic center and weathered the storm. Once again, I am standing at my grandmother's funeral. This time, I wasn't invisible. I kicked and fought. Raging, I regained cinematic memories: Grandma's hands, baking; the texture of her house dresses; the faded wallpaper in her kitchen; her old-lady shoes and dentures; the hard candy with the soft fruity center that she always carried in her purse; her long white gloves and costume jewelry; and her graceful, zaftig arms. There was her immaculate, threadbare parlor; her bedroom simple, but cascading with light. Outside that window, clothes were fluttering from clotheslines, reeled in by pulleys. Then: the tiny bungalow at Rockaway, its ancient linoleum and its paper-thin walls; the joy of sand beneath my feet, and Grandma, fanning herself on the beach. I could hear the Yiddish inflections in her speech, and I could taste her food in my mouth.

In the cinema of those memories, I retrieved another ghost: Elzora, Grandma's black maid/sister/soul mate. They were standing at the kitchen sink, moving in their fluid rhythms, cleaning dishes, one washing, and the other drying, They were bustling, rotund replicas of each other. Their heads tilted towards each other in their woman secrets; they crowed in private laughter. They were twins: bossy and nurturing, quarrelsome, formidable, generous, and kind. In the back of my mind, I am wondering: What was Grandma doing with a black maid? She was working class. She lived from hand to mouth. She cooked and cleaned her own apartment;

she didn't have servants. If Grandma was the boss, you wouldn't know it. If Elzora got a paycheck, I don't know where it would come from. Knowing Grandma, their financial arrangement was one interdependence, and which of them had which urgent bill to pay when. Their intimacy was a peculiar artifact of racism and poverty, and love, and infirmity, and the strange solidarity of their widowhood and persecution. I last saw Elzora at the funeral, weeping, in a sea of white faces. Then, Grandma's white sisters took up their official mourning posts, and Elzora vanished. I am twice abandoned. No one can really tell me where they've gone.

Now Elzora reappears: Grandma's truest sister, my black grandmother, whose vanishing is renewed in my analyst's departure. I am finding, and losing, both of my grandmothers. Their racial markers are becoming blurred and their racial markers are illuminated by our collective, historical truth. Before age 7, I think I was color-blind. But Elzora was a 'black maid'; she couldn't be Grandma's 'real' sister, and she didn't belong to our family. She resides in the deepest core of my silence, her existence occluded by Cheng's 'legislated grief' and by what Patterson (1982) calls 'social death'. Six months later, I say goodbye to my analyst. I wailed to the very end. My termination echoed with the grief of generations, and with the 'sorrow songs' of slavery (W. E. B. DuBois as cited in Cheng, 2001, p. 20). Are we all fated to re-live the dislocations and disconnections of the past? Will we ever repair our legacies of violence and create a sacred register for children and their mothers?

In the end, my analyst answered my despair with hope: we could find ways to stay attached. Our attachment has morphed, and deepened, for more than 30 years. The analysis has held, my depression lifted. My grandmother speaks to me, every day. Now, her body is nested inside my own. Over the years, I have heard my analyst's stories about her own formidable grandmother. My analyst has continued to live by the 'love ethic' of Martin Luther King, Jr. With her, I have learned that "[l]ove takes off the masks that we fear we cannot live without and know we cannot live within." (Baldwin, as quoted in hooks, 2001, p. xxv.) She has never forgotten me, and she has never let go of my hand.

References

Akbar, N. (1996). *Breaking the chains of psychological slavery*. Tallahassee, FL: Mind Productions and Associates.

Altman, N. (2000). Black and white thinking: A psychoanalyst reconsiders race. *Psychoanalytic Dialogues*, *10*, 589–603.
Apprey, M. (2003). Repairing history: Reworking transgenerational trauma. In D. Moss (Ed.), *Hating in the first person plural* (pp. 3–29). New York, NY: Other Press.
Baldwin, J. (1972). *No name in the street*. New York: Random House.
Ball, E. (1998). *Slaves in the family*. New York, NY: Ballantine Books.
Bass, A. (2003). Historical and unconscious trauma: Racism and psychoanalysis. In D. Moss (Ed.), *Hating in the first person plural* (pp. 29–45). New York, NY: Other Press.
Berlin, I. (2003). *Generations of captivity: A history of African-American slaves*. Cambridge, MA: Belknap Press.
Bollas, C. (1986). *The transformational object in the British school of psychoanalysis: The independent tradition*. New York, NY: Hogarth Press.
Bonovitz, J. (2012). White analysts seeing Black patients. In S. Akhtar (Ed.), *The African American experience* (pp. 377–403). New York, NY: Jason Aronson.
Caruth, C. 1995. *Trauma: Explorations in memory*. Baltimore: Johns Hopkins University Press.
Cheng, A. A. (2001). *The melancholy of race: Psychoanalysis, assimilation, and hidden grief*. London: Oxford University Press.
Cross, W. E. (1998). Black psychological functioning and the legacy of slavery. In Y. Danieli (Ed.), *International handbook of multigenerational legacies of trauma* (pp. 387–403). New York, NY: Plenum Press.
Davoine, F. (2012). The psychotherapy of psychosis and trauma: A relentless battle against objectification. *Psychoanalysis, Culture and Society*, *17*(4), 339–348.
Deramus, B. (2005). *Forbidden fruit: Love stories from the underground railroad*. New York, NY: Atria Books.
DuBois, W. E. B. (1989). *The souls of Black folks*. New York, NY: Bantam Press.
Fanon, F. (1952). *Black skin, White masks*. New York, NY: Grove Press.
Fleischner, J. (1996). *Mastering slavery: Memory, family, and identity in women's slave narratives*. New York, NY: New York University Press.
Fox-Genovese, E. (1988). *Within the plantation household: Black and White women of the old South*. Chapel Hill, NC: The University of North Carolina Press.
Gates, H. L. (1996). White like me. *The New Yorker*, p. 17.
Genovese, E. D. (1976). *Roll, Jordan, roll: The world the slaves made*. New York, NY: Vintage Books.
Gorden-Reed, A. (2008). *The Hemingses of Monticello*. New York, NY: W. W. Norton & Co.
Grand, S. (2000). *The reproduction of evil: A clinical and cultural perspective*. Hillsdale, NJ: The Analytic Press.
Grand, S. (2009). Strange vaginas. *Psychoanalysis, Culture and Society*, *14*(1), 58–64.
Green, A. (1986). *On private madness*. London: Hogarth Press.

Gump, J. (2000). A white therapist, an African-American patient – shame in the therapeutic dyad. *Psychoanalytic Dialogues*, *10*, 619–632.

Gump, J. (2010). Reality matters: The shadow of trauma on African American subjectivity. *Psychoanalytic Psychology*, *27*(1), 42–54.

Hartman, S. V. (1997). *Scenes of subjection: Terror, slavery, and self-making in nineteenth century America*. Oxford: Oxford University Press.

Hernton, C. C. (1965). *Sex and racism in America*. New York, NY: Grove Press.

Hine, D. C. (1993). In the kingdom of culture: Black women and the intersection of race, gender and class. In G. Early (Ed.), *Lure and loathing: Essays on race, identity, and the ambivalence of assimilation*. New York, NY: Penguin Press.

Hochschild, A. (2005). *Bury the chains: Prophets and rebels in the fight to free an empire's slaves*. New York, NY: Houghton Mifflin Company.

Hollander, N. (2011). *Uprooted minds: Surviving the politics of terror in the Americas*. New York, NY: Routledge Press.

Holmes, D. E. (2012). Racial transference reactions in psychoanalytic treatment: An update. In S. Akhtar (Ed.), *The African American experience: Psychoanalytic perspectives* (pp. 363–377). New York, NY: Jason Aronson.

hooks, b. (2001). *Salvation: Black people and love*. New York, NY: Perennial Press.

hooks, b., & West, C. (1991). *Breaking bread: Insurgent Black intellectual life*. Boston: South End Press.

Howell, E. F. (2005). *The dissociative mind*. Hillsdale, NJ: The Analytic Press.

Jordan, W. D. (1968). *White over Black: American attitudes toward the Negro 1550–1812*. Chapel Hill, NC: University of North Carolina Press.

Laub, D., & Auerhahn, N. C. (1993). Knowing and not knowing massive psychic trauma: Forms of memory. *International Journal of Psychoanalysis*, *74*, 287–301.

Laub, D., & Podell, D. (1995). Art and trauma. *International Journal of Psychoanalysis*, *76*, 991–1005.

Layton, L. (2006). Racial identities, racial enactments, and normative unconscious processes. *Psychoanalytic Quarterly*, *75*, 237–269.

Leary, J. D. (2005). *Post traumatic slave syndrome: America's legacy of enduring injury and healing*. Milwaukee, OR: Uptone Press.

Leary, K. (1997). Passing, posing and "keeping it real". *Constellations*, *6*(1), 85–96.

Leary, K. (2002). Race in psychoanalytic space. In M. Dimen & V. Goldner (Eds.), *Gender in psychoanalytic space: Between clinic and culture* (pp. 313–331). New York, NY: Other Press.

Main, M. (2000). The organized categories of infant, child and adult attachment: Flexible vs. inflexible attention under attachment-related stress. *Journal of the American Psychoanalytic Association*, *48*(4), 1055–1095.

McCoy-Wilson, S. (2007). *In "rememory": Beloved and transgenerational ghosting in Black female bodies*. Graduate English Association New Voices Conference.

Patterson, O. (1982). *Slavery and social death: A comparative study*. Cambridge, MA: Harvard University Press.
Powell, D. R. (2012). Psychoanalysis and African Americans: Past and present. In S. Akhtar (Ed.), *The African American experience: Psychoanalytic perspectives* (pp. 59–85). New York, NY: Jason Aronson.
Reis, B. E. (2007). Witness to history: Introduction to symposium on transhistorical catastrophe. *Psychoanalytic Dialogues*, *17*(5), 621–626.
Segal, H. (1952). A psycho-analytical approach to aesthetics. *International Journal of Psychoanalysis*, *33*, 196–207.
Scharfstein, D. J. (2011). *The invisible line: Three American families and the secret journey from Black to White*. New York, NY: Penguin Press.
Silberg, L. M. (2012). Ghostbusting transgenerational processes. *Psychoanalytic Dialogues*, *22*, 106–122.
Smith, B. F. (2011). *Transcending the legacies of slavery: A psychoanalytic view*. London: Karnac Books.
Swarns, R. L. (2012). *American Tapestry: The story of the Black, White, and multiracial ancestors of Michelle Obama*. New York, NY: Amistad.
Suchet, M. (2007). Unraveling whiteness. *Psychoanalytic Dialogues*, *17*, 867–886.
Thompson, C. L. (2012). The African American patient in psychodynamic treatment. In S. Akhtar (Ed.), *The African American experience: Psychoanalytic perspectives* (pp. 337–363). New York, NY: Jason Aronson.
West, C. (2001). *Race matters*. New York, NY: Vintage Books.
Williams, H. A. (2012). *Help me to find my people: The African American search for family lost in slavery*. Chapel Hill, NC: The University of North Carolina Press.
Young-Bruehl, E. (1996). *The anatomy of prejudices*. Cambridge, MA: Harvard University Press.

Part III

Immigrant experiences

Chapter 5

Intersectionality in the immigrant context

Pratyusha Tummala-Narra

Although psychoanalytic perspectives on immigration have contributed significantly to understandings of psychological processes involved in the migration and post-migration context, less attention has been directed toward intersectionality as it relates to the intrapsychic and interpersonal experiences of immigrants and the children of immigrants. In fact, prior literature has primarily reflected a compartmentalized approach to identity, as though multiple identities develop independently from one another (Greene, 2012). Yet, identity development is dynamic, driven by various sociocultural contexts and intrapsychic and interpersonal experiences within these contexts (Ruth, 2012; Suchet, 2011). Further, identity reflects fluid and shifting experiences of social locations shaped by power dynamics (Cho, Crenshaw, & McCall, 2013). In the case of immigration, individuals face both challenges and opportunities in developing and making visible a sense of self that reflects their authentic experiences of the premigration context and post-migration context. The acculturation process and the negotiation of loss inherent to the immigrant's journey are closely connected with the intersections of multiple social locations and identities, and marginalization and privilege, in pre-migration and post-migration contexts.

This chapter addresses some ways in which first-generation racial minority immigrants (those who arrived to the U.S. as adults) and the second generation (those born and raised in the U.S.) experience these intersections, and the implications of these experiences for relational life, conflict, and identity. Specifically, I explore the role of discrimination and stereotyping, the experience of multiple identities, and marginalization and privilege among racial minority immigrant-origin individuals. The chapter underscores the importance of recognizing unconscious processes underlying complex identifications concerning gender, race, and sexuality, and the sociopolitical context that shape these identifications. Clinical case material is provided to illustrate theoretical points related to psychoanalytic psychotherapy with racial minority immigrants, focusing on issues such as experiences of invisibility and marginalization.

Discrimination and stereotyping in the U.S.: race, gender, and sexuality

Immigrants' experiences of multiple identities such as those connected with race, culture, gender, sexuality, social class, dis/ability, and immigration status are often invisible within mainstream American society because of racism and stereotyping. The increasing presence of racial minority immigrants in the U.S. is met with collective anxiety which triggers dissociative defenses in which majority individuals create psychological distance and dehumanize immigrants (Ainslie, 2009). The ongoing debate concerning immigration policy and border security (e.g., U.S./Mexico "border wall"), and the perceptions of immigrants as terrorists, rapists, and criminals, reflect this collective anxiety. The destructive responses to such anxiety are evident in the travel ban of individuals from numerous majority Muslim countries, and the "zero tolerance" policies of the Trump administration which has directed systematic abuse of undocumented children and adolescents, through policies of forced family separations, detentions, and deportation.

The term, "Trump Effect" has been coined to describe the rise in explicit forms of racism, xenophobia, sexism, homophobia, and transphobia faced by children and adults immediately following the 2016 presidential election (Zimbardo & Sword, 2017). Specifically, immigrant children have been threatened by classmates and teachers and told that they or their family members would be deported or placed into camps (Southern Poverty Law Center, 2016). The "Trump Effect" is also evident in the rise of violence against black and brown people and LGBTQ+ people since early 2017 (National Center for Transgender Equality, 2019). The rise in explicit hate and discrimination coupled with macro-level policies (e.g., ban of transgender people in the military) based in racist, anti-immigrant, and anti-LGBTQ+ people have important implications for how racial minority immigrants and subsequent generations are perceived and treated in the U.S. context, and for how they experience and negotiate identity.

The stereotypes underlying and reinforcing racist ideology not only carry inaccurate information about individual experience, but also serve to consolidate pre-existing conscious and unconscious feelings of rage, envy, and desire. Stereotypes remove the subjectivity of a person by reducing reality to suit the needs of dominant groups (Bhabha, 1994; Young-Bruehl, 2007). Additionally, they become internalized by both dominant groups and targeted groups. For example, the prevalent notion of the "model minority" applied to Asian-Americans, assuming that they are academically and professionally successful because of innate or cultural traits, is typically viewed as a positive stereotype. However, studies have indicated that internalizing this stereotype can contribute to psychological distress, particularly when Asian-Americans cannot meet these expectations of academic and/or professional success (Thompson, Kiang, & Witkow, 2016; Yoo, Miller, & Yip, 2015). The stereotype also perpetuates the notion that Asian-Americans face fewer challenges than other racial groups in the U.S., and that they are somehow immune to racist ideology and racial hierarchies in educational and workplace settings. The model minority stereotype is internalized by Asian-Americans such that it reifies silence and stigma concerning psychological distress and traumatic experience, and the belief that these problems rarely occur or carry less importance within Asian-American communities (Kanukollu & Mahalingam, 2011). It is important to note that the model minority stereotype co-exists with other, more negative stereotypes. In particular, there are persistent mainstream gendered stereotypes of Asian-American men as asexual and physically unattractive, and of Asian-American women as exotic and submissive (Mukkamala & Suyemoto, 2018). Subgroups of Asian-Americans, such as South Asians, particularly Muslims and Sikhs, are stereotyped as terrorists. Importantly, stereotypes can also be fluid in that they are reformulated to meet the needs of the dominant group. For example, stereotypes of South Asian women as exotic have shifted in the post-9/11 era to a stereotype of asexuality. As such, the content of stereotypes becomes redefined, even while the suppression of subjectivity of the targeted individual or group persists (Bhabha, 1994).

The contradictory aspects of stereotypes and the shifting nature of stereotypes serve to bury the complexity of subjective experience and inhibit the expression of this complexity in various contexts. Intersectional stereotyping, such as that directed against South Asian men or women, aims to dehumanize not only one's racial or cultural background, but also to desexualize and disempower individuals and communities. My client, Lekha, a 30-year-old second-generation Indian-American straight-identified, cisgender woman, coping with depression, commented, "Boys in school never looked at me. I was not the white, blonde girl who got all of the attention. I mean literally no one looked at me." As we explored her self-image, she told me that she always compared her body to that of white female models and stated, "I just exercised all the time, paid attention to what I wore constantly. I still do this same thing. It didn't matter how thin I was, and even when guys began to ask me out, I felt like this strange object, like interesting but never anyone you could really be with in the long run."

Lekha proceeded in this session to describe her experiences of racism and stereotyping, such as when a classmate told her that her clothes smelled and when another classmate assumed that she would have an arranged marriage forced by her parents. Experiences of racism contributed to her belief that no one would find her attractive because of her dark skin and Indian heritage. Within her family, Lekha experienced herself as unattractive because of negative messages about her darker skin tone. The impact of negative messages at home, and racial and ethnic stereotypes to which Lekha was exposed throughout her life was profound in that she was unable to reconcile the repeated messages about her body and appearance, even when friends and co-workers complimented her on her physical beauty. Her sense of undesirability permeated her mental life to the extent that she became hopeless about someone loving her, and the feeling of undesirability was repeatedly reinforced through ongoing interactions in which she was either ignored or exoticized. Importantly, stereotypes not only suppressed others' recognition of her subjective experience, but also suppressed Lekha's access to the complexity of her own desires. Lekha had become unable to recognize what she had enjoyed and desired from a partner, and instead, her experiences of racism and colorism constrained how she experienced herself and her romantic and sexual relationships.

Lekha's experiences of racism, colorism, and stereotyping are steeped in racial and gender-based ideologies within and outside of her Indian-American community. The lack of sense of belonging and acceptance that developed early in her life is a core aspect of her identity as an Indian-American woman, and the tenacity of her psychic sense of undesirability is rooted in her family and a broader society which devalues and/or "others" her physical body. The invisibility of her experience is shared by many racial minority immigrants who operate across cultural contexts where colorism, racism, and sexism are normalized (McGuire, Casanova, & Davis, 2016; Mukkamala & Suyemoto, 2018). Fakhry Davids (2009) described internal racism as a "normal pathological organization," referring to the ways in which marginalized racial minority members serve to protect the dominant group's anxieties about the marginalized group, and how defensive structures develop such that fantasies about the marginalized group are perceived to be facts. These fantasies, which are mistaken as facts, are internalized by members of majority and minority groups. The rigidity of these fantasies, as manifested in stereotypes, can intensify under particular sociopolitical conditions, as is evident in the post-Trump era in the United States. Even when individuals consciously resist and/or deny certain stereotypes, all people internalize these stereotypes unconsciously and enact them in interpersonal relationships. In fact, racism, sexism, and other forms of prejudice and discrimination are most often experienced within intersubjective spaces. For example, my client, Francisco, a 37-year-old Mexican-American cisgender man who emigrated from Mexico in his early twenties, described an interaction with his boss: "I thought that he respected me. We worked together for two years. Then, one day, we were talking about where we went to college, and he said, 'Oh, those kinds of schools are always looking to get more minorities.' I was taken aback, couldn't believe it. What do I say?" When I asked Francisco about how he responded, he said, "Nothing. I did nothing. I was too shocked." He proceeded to wonder when he will feel "completely free" of these stereotypes and posed the question, "When will this guy actually see me as a person?" The microaggression (Sue, Capodilupo, Nadal, & Torino, 2008) left him feeling invisible, as his boss's racial stereotypes drove his perceptions of Francisco's abilities, despite the years that they had spent working together.

The impact of racism, stereotypes, and microaggressions on intrapsychic and interpersonal life cannot be overstated. There is clear evidence of the negative impact of racism, stereotypes, even "positive stereotypes," and microaggressions based on race, gender, sexual orientation, and religion on mental health symptomology and well-being (Nadal et al., 2015). It is also important to note that stereotypes of race, gender, and sexuality impact racial minorities from an early developmental age throughout the course of their lives, albeit in varying forms and contexts (Garcia Coll &

Marks, 2012). The negative social mirroring (Suárez-Orozco, 2000) which racial minority children and adolescents face, particularly at school and broader society (e.g., social media, Internet) has lasting impact on their developing sense of self in relation to others and to broader systems. Further, experiences of stereotyping and discrimination do not have an endpoint, and rather, they persist over time and contexts. The vignettes of Lekha and Francisco highlight the ways in which the recognition of individual subjectivity continues to be constrained in the context of ongoing experiences of prejudice well in adulthood.

Immigrant experiences of multiple identities: race, gender, and sexuality

Immigrants' experiences of race, gender, and sexuality can vary significantly between their pre-migration and post-migration contexts. The process of migration, even in circumstances in which an individual is not fleeing traumatic circumstances, is inherently stressful and often encompasses traumatic intrapsychic shifts. Salman Akhtar (2011) has described the traumatic shifts that occur because of separation from loved ones, familiar surroundings, and objects, and the culture shock associated with adapting to the new cultural environment. For many racial minority immigrants, moving to the U.S. involves stark differences in environmental surroundings and cultural norms. Akhtar has delineated the ways in which these shifts mark both anxiety and the pain of mourning. He also highlighted the experience of "figure-ground incoherence" (Akhtar, p. 10), in which there is heightened awareness of one's actions, such as that occurring when speaking in a new language. Acculturative stress, rooted in language and communication barriers and experiences of racism and xenophobia, further impinge on immigrants' transitional experience, as metaphor is less accessible in a new linguistic and cultural context (Akhtar, 2011). As such, adaptation to new and divergent cultural contexts can necessitate the compartmentalization of subjectivity and dissociated self-states (White, 2015).

The lack of sense of continuity in the immigrant's experience typically remains unconscious as efforts to meet the demands of survival in the new cultural context dominate everyday life (Boulanger, 2004). In fact, for many immigrants, securing economic stability and family structure, attaining access to education, and successfully navigating language are key aspects of survival. Immigrants also seek to secure a better future for their children in relation to the opportunities available in the country of origin. As such, the psychological losses inherent to cultural change are perceived as necessary sacrifices for fulfilling these goals. Additionally, the conflicts associated with cultural shifts lie largely in unconscious experience, as immigrants forge on toward adaptation while at the same time retain their heritage culture and minimize the pain of loss and separation (Akhtar, 2011). Importantly, the second and later generations have different experiences as compared with earlier generations of immigrants. The second generation typically seeks to both retain aspects of their heritage culture and immerse in mainstream society, moving beyond the goal of survival (Tummala-Narra, 2016). Growing up in the U.S. poses fundamental differences in second-generation racial minority immigrants as they develop a sense of identity within a context of race, gender, and sexuality that contrasts with that of their parents. Empirical studies, in fact, indicate that stress related to racism, while experienced by racial minority immigrants of all generations, has a greater negative impact on second-generation racial minority immigrants (Tummala-Narra, Inman, & Ettigi, 2011). These findings parallel the "immigrant paradox," a phenomenon in which second-generation racial minority immigrant-origin individuals have been found to have worse mental health and educational outcomes when compared with the first generation (Alegria et al., 2008; Garcia Coll & Marks, 2012).

These studies call attention to divergent developmental experiences of first and second generations and of the specific contexts in which development occurs. The dilemmas arising from "acculturation gaps" is one illustration of developmental challenges unique to each immigrant generation. The term "acculturation gap" has been used to describe cultural worldview differences between immigrant children and their parents (Prathikanti, 1997). However, it is important to note that acculturation gaps reflect mirroring occurring outside of the home context, where children are exposed to new ideologies concerning race, gender, and sexuality, which contrast with the ideologies of the parents' pre-migration context. Further, the acculturative stress experienced in contexts outside the parent-child dyad is typically not discussed in immigrant homes (Tummala-Narra, 2016). In particular, children tend not to share their experiences of isolation, alienation, discrimination, or bullying with their parents and caregivers whom they perceive as stressed by the demands of acculturation. Parents and caregivers are most often not aware of the acculturative stress faced by their children and tend to assume that if their children are fluent in English and have more exposure to mainstream American context, that they are better able to adapt. Children, in parallel, do not have access to a sensory experience of their immigrant parents' experience of growing up in their countries of origin. The ability to imagine and experience each other's developmental context is significantly challenged as an increasing sense of alienation and isolation can develop between older and younger members of a family.

Parents may respond to a growing sense of distance from their children by fostering a connection to the heritage culture and/or religion, which provides a sense of pride in belonging to the heritage culture or group. Children in turn may or may not respond with interest in the heritage culture, depending on a range of factors, such as their experiences with school, peers, and friends. The disconnection that immigrants and their children can develop in the face of acculturative stress contributes to what Alan Roland (2006) has coined as the "dual sense of self." Individuals can develop separate, compartmentalized self-states such that only partial experiences are shared among family members and friends. Therefore, the subjective experiences of the first and second generations are not only invisible to broader U.S. context but also within families and ethnic and religious communities. The experience of compartmentalization is illustrated in the experience of my client, Jasmine, who is a 21-year-old second-generation lesbian cisgender woman, coping with anxiety related to coming out to her mother. Jasmine's mother is a Filipino, Catholic immigrant to the U.S, who condemns LGBTQ+ identities, and believes that being gay is a sin. Jasmine's father died of an illness when she was 3 years old, and she is the only child. Jasmine sought help to cope with her anxiety of possibly coming out to her mother, and particularly how her mother would bear learning about her sexual identity. She stated, "I don't agree with my mom's views, but she worked so hard all her life. She was a single mother and never complained about it. She just worked all the time for me. I get so exhausted just thinking about telling her. I know I eventually have to, but I don't want to break her heart. It's just hard." Jasmine spoke of how her mother was her most important role model, especially with respect to how she engendered a view of women as powerful and independent. Throughout much of her childhood, Jasmine had worked hard to fulfill her mother's wishes of succeeding academically at school and "avoiding trouble." In doing so, Jasmine never disclosed to her when she was called racial slurs in elementary school and middle school. She worried about "adding more stress" to her mother's life. Jasmine had spent much of her adolescence "hiding" aspects of her life, as she became aware of her sexual identity. She identified as a Catholic and attended church regularly with her mother. Going to church was an important source of connection with her mother and with her Filipino community. Being a part of the church was also significant to the mourning of her father's death, and she often found comfort in reading the Bible. However, as she grew into adolescence, Jasmine felt disillusioned by her Church's beliefs concerning sexual orientation and felt as though she was living a "double life," one which offered opportunities for exploring her sexual identity, particularly in college, and the other which offered a sense of connection with her mother and heritage culture and religion. Jasmine's experience of these split-off aspects of her identity marks critical dilemmas concerning her authentic sense of self. She often felt as though her worlds could never meet. The prospect of coming out to her mother left her feeling as though she had to decide between sacrificing her mother and sacrificing herself, which posed an impossible bind.

From a psychoanalytic perspective, it is critical to closely examine how contradictory self-states develop as a function of the migration and acculturation process, as different aspects of identity are shaped by new cultural experiences and demands (Bromberg, 2010; White, 2015). For Jasmine's mother, retaining and passing on her heritage culture and religion was necessary to raise her daughter in the U.S. and maintain her husband's memory and presence in the family. For Jasmine, it was vital to be able to express her sexual identity freely and to secure spaces of acceptance across all of her life contexts, including her family, school, and friendships. She stated, "I just want to be me and not be hated for it." Yet, Jasmine's recognition of her mother's anxiety concerning sexuality and experiences of racism outside of her home posed significant challenges to fulfilling this wish.

It is important to note that Jasmine's identifications with race, gender, and sexuality are intertwined with other aspects of identity and social location, such as social class and immigration status. Specifically, she grew up in a lower-middle class family, where her mother struggled financially to meet all of the family's living expenses, holding multiple jobs. She and her mother carry ongoing fears of changing immigration policy as they have relatives who are undocumented. Recent policies of deportation and separation of families have triggered alarming levels of anxiety in the family

(Yoshikawa, Suárez-Orozco, & Gonzales, 2016), and for Jasmine, these policies exacerbate her fear of losing her mother both physically and psychologically. The interaction of these multiple identities poses ongoing and new challenges in multiple contexts. The silence on immigration status is invisible in her college campus context, where she is careful about revealing her concerns about immigration policy, and in her home context, her sexual identity is invisible to her family. Yet, both sets of concerns lie at the core of her anxiety.

For many racial minority immigrants, sexual orientation is a stigmatized topic in families and ethnic and religious communities. Max Belkin (2018, p. 3) noted that the separation and isolation of LGBTQ+ individuals is "a powerful weapon of discrimination and persecution." The pathologizing of sexual minorities in communities worldwide dismisses the internal experiences and basic human rights of sexual minorities. For many immigrants, with origins in countries where sexual minority status is linked to alienation, physical abuse, and even death, open dialogues concerning sexuality are experienced as threatening. Further, LGBTQ+ immigrants are especially vulnerable to harassment and danger during returns to the country of origin and racially based violence in the U.S., and under threats of deportation (APA, 2012). These ongoing threats to safety contribute to depression, anxiety, substance abuse, and suicidal ideation, and pose serious challenges to developing an authentic sense of self. These external threats further impose intrapsychic and interpersonal constraints on the expression of subjectivity.

Additionally, immigration poses new dilemmas concerning gender roles and gender identity. Racial minority immigrants often contend with contradictory social norms concerning gender roles. For example, women immigrants may experience a sense of independence and self-reliance in different ways within the new cultural context, where they secure new educational, professional, and financial success. At the same time, many women and men experience shifts in gender roles as incongruent with their cultures of origin. Changes in gender roles can signal movement away from heritage culture, where there may be a sense of urgency in managing this particular threat to ethnic identity. For example, a young woman may be complimented by her family for her success in her academic work, and at the same time be told that she should be modest about her success in the presence of men who may feel threatened by her success. This message is situated within a cultural value of modesty, a value which is internalized by the woman in this example. While the young woman may feel more connected with her family and ethnic community through this shared cultural value of modesty, she may also experience it as conflicting with mainstream American values of self-assertion and pride in one's personal accomplishments. In this case, "goodness" is associated with a heritage cultural value of modesty and "badness" with the American value of expression of pride in one's accomplishments.

Gender identity is another area of potential contention in the formation of identity within the context of immigration. Similar to sexual orientation, gender identity is a topic that is seldom discussed openly in many immigrant communities. While parents from all racial and cultural backgrounds have fantasies of their children's gender identities (Spivey & Greene, 2014), many immigrant parents have an additional set of expectations concerning their children's gender in relation to their extended families and communities in the U.S. and country of origin. Gender non-conforming people in most countries are demeaned and punished, and the reality of these dangers and prejudiced attitudes lie at the core of why many immigrants tend not to engage in dialogue regarding gender identity (Singh, 2016). Such circumstances constrain the possible ways in which gender non-conforming immigrants and children of immigrants explore gender identity.

It is important to consider some other aspects of identity that intersect with race, gender, and sexuality, which have important intrapsychic and interpersonal implications for identity development among racial minority immigrants. Specifically, the lightness and darkness of skin color can be associated with goodness and badness, respectively, and with a sense of being an authentic member of an ethnic group (Tummala-Narra, 2007). For example, multiracial people who are "white passing" may be seen as outsiders to a particular ethnic group, even if their cultural and/or religious identifications reflect insider status. The splitting of good and bad immigrants by racial minority immigrants is shaped by pre-migration beliefs regarding race, class, caste, gender, and sexuality. This is evident when a first- or second-generation immigrant carries pre-migration beliefs regarding the superiority and inferiority of certain social class or caste groups into the new cultural context. These pre-migration beliefs interact with beliefs about social class, race, gender, and skin color within the U.S. in such a way that can reinforce discriminatory ideologies. Further, within the broader context of living in the U.S., many immigrants engage in efforts to secure a positive image of their heritage culture and communities to those outside of the ethnic group as a way to mitigate racism and other forms of discrimination and prejudice (Mahalingam, Balan, & Haritatos, 2008). Yet, this impression management can undermine, minimize, or dismiss the stress experienced by immigrants and their children.

The complexity of developing cultural identifications in the face of pressures and demands within and outside of racial minority immigrant communities implicates the process of mourning. The anxiety and sadness that accompanies separation from loved ones and culture of origin poses dilemmas concerning the extent to which immigrants feel connected to heritage culture, community, and family, and to other new cultural contexts (Akhtar, 2011). The cultural norms and sociopolitical structures specific to the U.S. contribute to a sense of disillusionment in the American Dream. For example, in the case of Asian-Americans, the notion of model minority sharply contrasts with the stereotype of the perpetual foreigner where an individual is perceived to be a foreigner, even when they are born and raised in the U.S. The experience of loss and disillusionment resulting from the recognition that Asian immigrants and their children may never truly belong or be accepted as Americans marks racial melancholia (Eng & Han, 2000). Coming to terms with the realities of race in the U.S. can complicate mourning related to other aspects of identity, such as gender. For instance, my client, June, a 26-year old Chinese-American cisgender woman, shared, “I want to stay connected with my family. They mean everything to me, but I can’t deal with how they want me to be a woman.” June was born and raised in the U.S., and her parents are immigrants from a large city in China. June’s parents’ expectations of women as caregivers to others overwhelmed her, as she identified increasingly with a Western, feminist perspective of women and men as equally responsible for caregiving responsibilities in the family. June often felt as though she had to meet the expectations of multiple contexts and felt as though she was betraying her family if she did not meet these expectations. On several occasions in psychotherapy, she posed the question, “I feel like I can’t be a good Chinese woman if I don’t listen to my family. I know that this isn’t true in a sense, but it’s how I feel. The thing is, I’m not really sure what it means to be good and Chinese outside of what my parents think. Life is not as easy for people who are not white.” In this session, June referred not only to the constriction she feels in defining her identity and roles as a woman, but also the constriction she feels with regard to being a

Chinese-American. Her dilemma underscores the ways in which cultural identifications are often experienced as contradictory, indicating goodness and badness, and how she feels that she must make a choice within the parameters of constraint (Tummala-Narra, 2016). June's conflicts challenge the ability to consider other possibilities where she could experience herself as "in between" her Chinese and American spaces (Bromberg, 2010; White, 2015; Yi, 2014).

Marginalization and privilege

From a contemporary psychoanalytic perspective, identity develops through an interaction of intrapsychic, relational, and societal factors, and individuals experience identity along unique and distinct developmental lines (Ruth, 2012). In the immigrant context, each person has a distinct pre-migration history and context, early developmental history, family dynamics, migration journey, post-migration context, acculturation process, losses, separations, and traumatic experiences. As such, each immigrant's experience is inherently intersectional, and each individual within a particular group (based on race, ethnicity, gender, language, immigration status, sexual orientation, social class, and dis/ability) has unique experiences of their families and groups of affiliation and identification (Greene, 2012). Further, the ways in which individual members of a family experience colorism, racism, sexism, and heterosexism can vary considerably as a result of relationships with parents, caregivers, siblings, and other family members, and to interactions within mainstream U.S. context. An important underlying force that contributes to these differences relates to the issue of privilege versus marginalization within families, communities, and broader society.

Intersectionality refers not only to subjective experiences of multiple identities, but also encompasses the role of structural inequalities that underlie the relationships among marginalized and privileged identities and social locations (Crenshaw, 1989; Shin et al., 2017). Crenshaw (1989) introduced the term "intersectionality" to describe how race and gender in interaction with each other influence black women's employment, noting that black women's experiences could not be understood by examining the dimensions of gender and race separately from each other. This intersectionality framework has called attention to the unique experiences of women of color as distinct from white women and from men of color, and to the unique experiences of people within any given racial or ethnic community based on differences in structural power. Crenshaw's work on intersectionality in the 1980s concerning the marginalization of women of color continues to be a contemporary problem, where ciswomen of color and transwomen of color are harassed, abused, and murdered at alarmingly high rates (National Center for Transgender Equality, 2019). Relatedly, harassment and assaults of Muslim women wearing hijab have been on the rise in the post 9/11 and Trump era.

The realities of structural inequality and marginalization have important implications for how multiple, intersectional identities develop, and for how they are experienced. For example, racial minority Muslim women experience gendered forms of Islamophobia in the U.S. (McGuire et al., 2016), where prejudice is thought to be justified by dominant groups. Women wearing hijab can be perceived by non-Muslims as though they are being oppressed and repressed by men, a collective anxiety that is projected to a group of people with less social and political power in the U.S. The hijab can also represent to non-Muslims a symbol of 9/11 and carry associations of terrorism. The internal experience of a woman wearing hijab can reflect a sense of pride in her faith and tradition, and at the same time anxiety about being watched, monitored, and targeted (McGuire et al., 2016). The surveillance of people of color in the U.S. can be viewed as justifiable by some white people who claim that such surveillance is necessary for national security or for maintaining the white race. In a sense, the "good aggression" of this white subgroup is thought to contain the "bad aggression" of people of color (Holmes, 2012). The distorted messages such as those regarding aggression, foreignness, attractiveness, and intelligence are internalized and become intertwined with how multiple identities, such as race, gender, and religion, are formed and negotiated throughout one's life.

Racist messages further create conflicts for how racial minority immigrants cope with racial trauma. For example, a second-generation Vietnamese-American, single, straight-identified client, Binh, shared with me that he had hoped to marry someone white so that his children could potentially pass as white or "at least lighter Asian." He had come to equate lightness and white physical features with social and economic status and power, and had hoped that his children would be able to secure privilege that was inaccessible to him. As he shared this wish with me, he also expressed feeling ashamed for wanting to move away from his

Vietnamese heritage. Yet, the economic struggles and racism that he and his family faced in the U.S. lay at the root of his identity conflicts. Experiences of marginalization contributed to a feeling of being less American, even though he was born and raised in the U.S. One way to reconcile the pain of discrimination was to pre-empt racism and secure a sense of acceptance for his children.

Intersectionality further implicates the role of privilege as co-existing with marginalization. Intersectional marginalization and privilege are most often context specific, and therefore, identity work involves consciously and unconsciously assessing which contexts promote or impede a sense of power and authenticity (Belkin, 2018; Cho et al., 2013; Gray, Mendelsohn, & Omoto, 2015; Greene, 2012; Tummala-Narra, 2016). For example, a racial minority bisexual cisgender woman may experience marginalization based on sexual orientation and gender within her ethnic community and mainstream society, and yet, experience privilege as a light-skinned person in both of these contexts. A survivor of childhood sexual abuse may be silenced by members of his family and religious community, and in these same contexts, he enjoys more freedom with respect to his career and dating choices as compared with women in his family and community. It is important to consider the structural power held by people who are privileged within racial minority immigrant communities, as these individuals define the group's cultural norms. Beverly Greene (2012, p. 85) noted the disparity between those with privilege and those with disadvantage within ethnic and racial groups: "What is presented as the requirements of authenticity in the culture as well as what defines the culture and the group's boundaries are articulated by the most powerful members of the group, not the most vulnerable or marginalized." This disparity is evident in many racial minority immigrant communities in which cisgender male and heterosexual members of the group carry authority over how heritage culture and religion are interpreted and transmitted to subsequent generations (Greene, 2012, 2013).

People with multiple minority positions develop resilience and the ability to hold multiple perspectives in navigating across these various contexts, and at the same time, this process of navigating can come at the cost of developing a true self, one that carries a sense of continuity across time and context (Winnicott, 1971). In the case of a survivor of trauma mentioned earlier, the lack of access to openly discussing the trauma and its effects with trusted members of his family and community may then create psychological distance that cannot be bridged when he feels that they must avoid talking about the trauma in order to remain connected with his family and community. Kris Yi's (2014) conception of cultural dissociation speaks to the experience of a survivor distancing the self from engaging with an ethnic community, such as practicing cultural traditions or speaking a heritage language as a way of coping with being traumatized within one's family or community. Yi (2014) formulated cultural dissociation as an untenable position when the individual faces discrimination in mainstream context and has disconnected from the heritage culture or community, marking challenges to standing in the spaces among dissociated self-states (Bromberg, 2010).

Intersectionality from a psychoanalytic perspective further considers the experience of identities across different developmental contexts and transitions. Specifically, particular aspects of identity may be experienced as more significant during particular developmental periods (Greene, 2012). For example, my client, Abraham, a 21-year-old cisgender gay man, who emigrated from the Dominican Republic to the U.S. when he was 10 years old, described his experience of race becoming more prominent in his life as a college student and after the presidential election of Donald Trump. In high school, he came out to close friends but had not talked about his sexual orientation to his parents. In college, he began dating his partner whom he finds to be supportive and loving. In psychotherapy, he felt as though it was not possible to talk with his parents about his sexual orientation, as the problem of racism on his college campus pre-dominated his everyday experiences. He stated, "Right now, it just feels like I'm dealing with so much hate toward people of color. Being with Mark (partner) just gives me some respite from all the craziness of Trump." While Trump's rhetoric has been damaging to people of color and LGBTQ+ people, Abraham's relationship with his partner has helped to buffer against some of the toxic effects of homophobia. However, because of growing incidents of racism on campus, he continued to feel targeted primarily as a person of color. At the same time, it is worth considering that he continues to feel unsafe in coming out to his family. The shifting nature of the salience of identities underscores the reality that identities are not fixed, but rather fluid, dynamic, and interactive. In psychoanalytic psychotherapy, it is critical then to explore why certain identities become salient in any one particular context and developmental juncture (Greene, 2012).

Holding the complexity of identity in the therapeutic relationship

Exploring and holding the complexity of intersectionality in psychotherapy requires a recognition of the hybridity and multiplicity of identity and context (Tummala-Narra, 2016). It is important that therapists simultaneously recognize that intrapsychic experience of identity has no boundaries and is not defined by socially constructed categories, and that social constructions of race, gender, and sexuality have important implications for social inequities faced by racial minority immigrants, and therefore shape intrapsychic and interpersonal life (Greene, 2013). Intersectionality has been conceptualized as an "analytic disposition" or a "way of thinking about the problem of sameness and difference and its relation to power" (Cho et al., 2013, p. 795). In this view, identity is in a continual process of being created and re-created through the dynamics of power, privilege, and marginalization (Cho et al., 2013). Within the context of psychoanalytic psychotherapy, this analytic sensibility toward intersectionality manifests in the therapeutic relationship. The experience of sameness and difference in psychotherapy is rooted in early object relations and adulthood attachments, and comes to life in the transference. In psychoanalytic psychotherapy, the therapist and client embark on a collaboration in which the interplay of self-states is shaped by earlier interpersonal experiences of the therapist and client and through enactments within the therapeutic relationship (Bromberg, 2010). Belkin (2018, p. 10) suggested that "dissociation and curiosity are inexorably linked: whenever one of them moves to the foreground, the other one recedes to the background." As such, the experience of knowing and not knowing is shared by the therapist and client, and aspects of identity are more visible and palpable at varying moments in the therapeutic process.

The client's and therapist's defenses play an important role in guarding against anxiety and discomfort that are associated with race, gender, sexuality, and other aspects of identity and social location. Racial minority clients may manage the discomfort of white therapists by denying or minimizing the role of marginalized status on their lives (Greene, 2012;

Tummala-Narra, 2016). Yet, it is critical for the therapist, when relevant, to validate that the client's distress stems from systemic injustice, and that distress derived from racism, xenophobia, sexism, transphobia, heterosexism, classism, and ableism is an appropriate response to injustice (Greene, 2012; Adames, Chavez-Duenas, Sharma, & La Roche, 2018). In fact, such validation is a part of witnessing where the therapist recognizes the client's experiences of privilege and marginalization and their accompanying dissociative emotional experiences (Belkin, 2018). Without the therapist's initiative in exploring sameness and difference, and the multiplicity of identity, both that of the client and the therapist, impasses ensue, leaving the client potentially further isolated and marginalized.

Exploring sameness and difference with racial minority immigrants can bring to conscious awareness a range of suppressed and repressed feelings, such as fear, anger, sadness, curiosity, and shame. These affective experiences are uniquely produced through an interaction of the histories, identities, and social locations of the therapist and client. At varying points in psychotherapy, the therapist and the client may avoid or become excessively curious about each other's sociocultural identities, at times reifying pre-existing stereotypes and fantasies about each other's groups of affiliation (Comas-Díaz, 2012; Tummala-Narra, 2016). Interestingly, because of shared socialization experiences of compartmentalizing identity, the therapist and the client may selectively focus on only certain aspects of the other's identity. For instance, a client's associations to the therapist's gender may be a core component of the transference, or a therapist's attention to the client's racial background may dominate the exploration of conflicts related to social class. The attention to singular aspects of identity impedes a deeper understanding of the full range of experiences among racial minority immigrants, including migration history; acculturation; immigration status; language; experiences of race, gender, sexuality, social class, and dis/ability; and differences across immigrant generations. It can also serve to defensively protect against painful experiences of shame and guilt concerning privilege and marginalization, consequently perpetuating a fragmented sense of self (Ferguson & Miville, 2017; Greene, 2012).

Nevertheless, the therapeutic relationship offers a space in which multiple aspects of identity can be explored, but only insofar as therapists are willing to examine the multiplicity of their own identities and their experiences with privilege and marginalization (Greene, 2012; Belkin, 2018). The therapist's awareness of intersectionality and willingness to bear the unknown and work through mistakes and impasses are necessary for this type of work (Steinfeld, 2018; Tummala-Narra, 2016). The therapeutic relationship has the potential to offer a transitional space in which the client can explore dissociated, contradictory self-states associated with different sociocultural contexts and begin to bridge disconnected intrapsychic spaces (White, 2015). Through this relationship, the therapist too is transformed as his/her/their own identity work is re-engaged. A contemporary psychoanalytic lens is not only concerned about the immigrant's intrapsychic transition to a new cultural context, but also to the intrapsychic and interpersonal transformations of each part of identity and the interplay among these aspects of identity within shifting social, cultural, and political contexts across the lifespan. The following case vignette illustrates some aspects of intersectionality in my psychotherapeutic work with a first-generation immigrant client.

Case vignette: Talia

Talia is a 40-year-old Sudanese-American, Muslim, cisgender woman from a middle-class background. She was referred to me by her primary care physician after suffering from depression for more than a year. Talia emigrated from Sudan to join her maternal aunt's family in the United States when she was in her early twenties. Her maternal aunt left Sudan after being targeted by growing political conflict. Talia's mother persuaded Talia to move to the U.S. as the conflict in Sudan persisted. Her mother and father remained in Sudan and cared for their younger children. Talia lived with her aunt's family, which consisted of her aunt, aunt's husband (uncle), and their three children, in a suburban area within the East Coast of the U.S. Talia's initial adjustment to living in the U.S. was difficult, as she deeply missed her mother, father, and siblings with whom she had a close relationship. Her visits to Sudan were infrequent, and over time she felt emotionally distanced from her family there. While she felt comfortable with her aunt's family, she felt alienated outside of the home and found it challenging to make friends. She attended a community college where she struggled academically for the first several months. With the assistance of her aunt, she was able to adjust to the new academic environment and gradually came to excel in her coursework. Her experience of fitting in with other students was complicated by feeling as though others gazed at her and made insulting comments about her clothing and her accent.

Talia often felt anxious when she witnessed other black immigrants and African-Americans being targeted with racial slurs and physical attacks, reminiscent of violence in Sudan. At the same time, the racism of the U.S. felt foreign to her, and she felt as though she could not connect to American racist ideology that devalued black people.

In her last year of college, she met a man who emigrated from Morocco, and they eventually married. She felt close to her husband who was supportive to her and encouraged her to pursue her interest in science. She worked as a lab technician, and several years later, after the birth of her daughter, she stayed home to take care of her. Talia became increasingly anxious and depressed as her daughter became an adolescent and sought the help of a physician who referred her to work with me. In our initial sessions, Talia shared with me that she was unsure about what to talk about with me in psychotherapy. She stated, "I don't know where to start and what all to talk about. I've just been sad and tired, worried about my daughter." She proceeded to tell me that she has felt increasingly detached from her husband and has few people in her life with whom she can talk to honestly about her concerns. Talia worried about her daughter's growing sense of independence, which she associated with becoming American.

Talia's ambivalence about being in the U.S. and far away from her family in Sudan heightened as her fantasy of someday returning to Sudan diminished. She worked hard to pass on Sudanese cultural traditions and faith in Islam to her daughter, and at the same time felt guilty about having opportunities that were not available to her siblings. She stated, "I think sometimes my daughter doesn't know what she has here. She takes it for granted." At other moments, she expressed her concern for her daughter's future in the U.S. She mentioned in one session, "I wish I could leave and go back to Sudan. It's too racist here. If you are black, then they think you are dangerous or not pretty. If you are black and Muslim, then there is no end to this here. Why do I want my daughter to stay here?" When I asked her about what she imagines for herself and her daughter if they lived in Sudan, she responded, "The problem is there that it is hard for women. We don't have the same chance at studying and working, being on our own." In a subsequent session, she stated, "You are working, independent. I want that for my daughter. Then again, I think you must have given up your culture to be here doing this work." I responded to Talia by asking her to tell me more of what she imagined that I have given up. She stated, "Maybe you don't follow your traditions anymore, or don't have a family. Then again, you seem comfortable with yourself, not sad or worried like me. I know you too must go through racism in this country." I experienced Talia's fantasies of me as someone who reflected what she may have both wished and feared. At times, she experienced me as too American, an immigrant from India who had to give up parts of herself to become American, and other times, a woman who secured her own independence, something she valued for herself and her daughter. My own experience as a child immigrant to the U.S. was challenging, and I could relate to Talia's sense of alienation in her initial years in the U.S. Yet, my experiences as an Indian-American woman transformed over time, and my anxieties about living in the U.S. were both similar and distinct from those experienced by Talia. At times, my identity as a woman was more salient to her, and at other times my identity as an immigrant became more significant. She imagined that I shared her anxiety about losing a sense of connection and authenticity within our heritage cultures, and a part of me felt anxious as well. Working with Talia brought to conscious awareness my anxiety of separating from my Indian heritage, and from earlier ideals of "good" Indian women inculcated in my upbringing.

In subtle ways, Talia shared her concerns about my lack of understanding of Islam. She periodically made comments such as, "You wouldn't know this but in the mosque, we can't wear sleeveless tops. My daughter wants to wear them, but I don't allow it in the mosque." Interestingly, in this particular session, I had worn a sleeveless blouse, which I noted to her. She stated, "Yes, but maybe it is OK in your culture, for Hindus." I responded, "Some Hindus are OK with sleeveless tops and others may not be." Through these conversations on sameness and difference, Talia was increasingly open to considering new possibilities for herself and her daughter. For example, she stated in one session:

> My daughter asked if she can be a black Muslim girl who likes to dress up and wear lipstick. I told her, 'Why not?' Then, I felt a bit scared that I told her that. I thought of all the racism against black girls and Muslim girls. I still said it though.

Talia's anxiety about raising her daughter as a black, Muslim, immigrant-origin girl persisted but took new forms in ways that no longer felt debilitating. Rather, she engaged with her anxiety as a way to expand the range of possibilities for her identity. I continued to sit with her anxiety, sadness, and the unknown, and the realities of racism and sexism that would continue to affect her life and mine.

Conclusion

Racial minority immigrants experience stress, marginalization, and resilience in the process of acculturation. The contemporary sociopolitical climate in the U.S. poses new challenges and dangers for many racial minority immigrants facing explicit forms of hate and anti-immigrant sentiment. Within immigrant groups, marginalization of women and LGBTQ+ individuals among others produces increased vulnerability which constricts access to a full range of possibilities with regard to hybrid identities. A contemporary psychoanalytic perspective values the examination of intersectionality with a recognition of the fluid and dynamic nature of identity, which is mirrored in the therapeutic relationship. Psychoanalytic psychotherapy with racial minority immigrants involves the transformation and re-working of sociocultural identities for both the client and the therapist.

References

Adames, H. Y., Chavez-Duenas, N. Y., Sharma, S., & La Roche, M. J. (2018). Intersectionality in psychotherapy: The experiences of an AfroLatinx queer immigrant. *Psychotherapy*, *55*(1), 73–79.

Ainslie, R. C. (2009). Regression in the construction of the immigrant other. *Psychoanalysis, Culture, & Society*, *14*(1), 49–57.

Akhtar, S. (2011). *Immigration and acculturation: Mourning, adaptation, and the next generation*. New York, NY: Jason Aronson.

Alegria, M., Chatterji, P., Wells, K., Cao, Z., Chen, C., Takeuchi, D., . . . Meng, X. (2008). Disparity in depression treatment among racial and ethnic minority populations in the United States. *Psychiatric Services*, *59*(11), 1264–1272.

American Psychological Association. (2012). *Crossroads: The psychology of immigration in the new century*. Report of the APA Presidential Task Force on Immigration. Washington, DC: American Psychological Association.

Belkin, M. (2018). Who is queer around here? Overcoming rigid thinking and relating in patient and analyst. *Contemporary Psychoanalysis*, *54*(3), 484–510.

Bhabha, H. K. (1994). *The location of culture*. London: Routledge.

Boulanger, G. (2004). Lot's wife, Cary Grant, and the American dream: Psychoanalysis with immigrants. *Contemporary Psychoanalysis*, *40*, 353–372.

Bromberg, P. M. (2010). Minding the dissociative gap. *Contemporary Psychoanalysis*, *46*(1), 19–31.

Cho, S., Crenshaw, K. W., & McCall, L. (2013). Toward a field of intersectionality studies: Theory, applications, and praxis. *Signs: Journal of Women in Culture and Society*, *38*(4), 785–810.

Comas-Díaz, L. (2012). *Multicultural care: A clinician's guide to cultural competence*. Washington, DC: American Psychological Association.

Crenshaw, K. W. (1989). Demarginalizing the intersection of race and sex: A Black feminist critique of antidiscrimination doctrine, feminist theory and antiracist politics. *University of Chicago Legal Forum*, *1989*, 139–167.

Davids, M. F. (2009). The impact of Islamophobia. *Psychoanalysis and History*, *11*(2), 175–191.

Eng, D. L., & Han, S. (2000). A dialogue on racial melancholia. *Psychoanalytic Dialogues*, *10*(4), 667–700.

Ferguson, A. D., & Miville, M. L. (2017). It's complicated: Navigating multiple identities in small town America. *Journal of Clinical Psychology: In Session*, *73*(8), 975–984.

Garcia Coll, C., & Marks, A. K. (2012). *The immigrant paradox in children and adolescents: Is becoming American a developmental risk?* Washington, DC: American Psychological Association.

Gray, N. N., Mendelsohn, D. M., & Omoto, A. M. (2015). Community connectedness, challenges, and resilience among gay Latino immigrants. *American Journal of Community Psychology*, *55*, 202–214.

Greene, B. (2012). Intersections of multiple identities and multiple marginalizations: Clinical and paradigmatic considerations. In R. Nettles & R. Balter (Eds.), *Multiple minority identities: Applications for practice, research, and training* (pp. 81–91). New York, NY: Springer.

Greene, B. (2013). The use and abuse of religious beliefs in dividing and conquering between socially marginalized groups: The same-sex marriage debate. *Psychology of Sexual Orientation and Gender Diversity*, *1*(S), 35–44.

Holmes, D. E. (2012). "Why can't we simply treat people's problems, not their race (or physical disability, or sexual orientation)?!" A psychodynamic approach to the therapeutic relevance of multiple minority identities. In R. Nettles & R. Balter (Eds.), *Multiple minority identities: Applications for practice, research, and training* (pp. 187–205). New York, NY: Springer.

Kanukollu, S. N., & Mahalingam, R. (2011). The idealized cultural identities model on help-seeking and child sexual abuse: A conceptual model for contextualizing perceptions and experiences of South Asian Americans. *Journal of Child Sexual Abuse*, *20*(2), 218–243.

Mahalingam, R., Balan, S., & Haritatos, J. (2008). Engendering immigrant psychology: An intersectionality perspective. *Sex Roles*, *59*, 326–336.

McGuire, K. M., Casanova, S., & Davis, C. H. F. (2016). "I'm a Black female who happens to be Muslim": Multiple marginalities of an immigrant Black Muslim woman on a predominantly White campus. *The Journal of Negro Education, 85*(3), 316–329.

Mukkamala, S., & Suyemoto, K. L. (2018). Racialized sexism/sexualized racism: A multimethod study of intersectional experiences of discrimination for Asian American women. *Asian American Journal of Psychology, 9*(1), 32–46.

Nadal, K. L., Davidoff, K. C., Davis, L. S., Wong, Y., Marshall, D., & McKenzie, V. (2015). Intersectional identities and microaggressions: Influences of race, ethnicity, gender, sexuality, and religion. *Qualitative Psychology, 2*, 147–163.

National Center for Transgender Equality. (2019). *These are the 2017 victims of anti-transgender homicides*. Retrieved from https://transequality.org/blog/these-are-the-2017-victims-of-anti-transgender-homicides

Prathikanti, S. (1997). East Indian American families. In E. Lee (Ed.), *Working with Asian Americans: A guide for clinicians* (pp. 79–100). New York, NY: Guilford Press.

Roland, A. (2006). Across civilizations: Psychoanalytic therapy with Asians and Asian Americans. *Psychotherapy: Theory, Research, Practice, Training, 43*(4), 454–456.

Ruth, R. (2012). Contemporary psychodynamic perspectives on multiple minority identities. In R. Nettles & R. Balter (Eds.), *Multiple minority identities: Applications for practice, research, and training* (pp. 163–184). New York, NY: Springer.

Shin, R. Q., Welch, J. C., Kaya, A. E., Yeung, J. G., Obana, C., Sharma, R., . . . Yee, S. (2017). The intersectionality framework and identity intersections in the *Journal of Counseling Psychology* and *The Counseling Psychologist*: A content analysis. *Journal of Counseling Psychology, 64*(5), 458–474.

Singh, A. A. (2016). Moving from affirmation to liberation in psychological practice with transgender and gender nonconforming clients. *American Psychologist, 71*(8), 755–762.

Southern Poverty Law Center. (2016). *The Trump effect: The impact of the 2016 presidential election on our nation's schools*. Retrieved from www.splcenter.org/20161128/trump-effect-impact-2016-presidential-election-our-nations-schools

Spivey, P., & Greene, B. (2014). Gender-nonconforming, Black, male children: Endangered, misunderstood, and mistreated. In K. C. Vaughans & W. Spielberg (Eds.), *The psychology of Black boys and adolescents* (vol. 1–2, pp. 99–105). Santa Barbara, CA: Praeger.

Steinfeld, M. (2018). Learning in safety: Intersectional awareness and the expiration of ignorance through its embrace. *Psychoanalysis, Culture, & Society, 23*(2), 211–216.

Suárez-Orozco, C. (2000). Identities under siege: Immigration stress and social mirroring among the children of immigrants. In A. Robben & M. Suárez-Orozco (Eds.), *Cultures under siege: Social violence & trauma* (pp. 194–226). Cambridge: Cambridge University Press.

Suchet, M. (2011). Crossing over. *Psychoanalytic Dialogues, 21*(2), 172–191.

Sue, D. W., Capodilupo, C. M., Nadal, K. L., & Torino, G. C. (2008). Racial microaggressions and the power to define reality. *American Psychologist, 63*(4), 277–279.

Thompson, T. L., Kiang, L., & Witkow, M. R. (2016). "You're Asian; You're supposed to be smart": Adolescents' experiences with the model minority stereotype and longitudinal links with identity. *Asian American Journal of Psychology, 7*(2), 108–119.

Tummala-Narra, P. (2007). Skin color and the therapeutic relationship. *Psychoanalytic Psychology, 24*(2), 255–270.

Tummala-Narra, P. (2016). *Psychoanalytic theory and cultural competence in psychotherapy*. Washington, DC: American Psychological Association.

Tummala-Narra, P., Inman, A. G., & Ettigi, S. (2011). Asian Indians' responses to discrimination: A mixed-method examination of identity, coping, and self-esteem. *Asian American Journal of Psychology, 2*(3), 205–218.

White, C. J. (2015). Strangers in paradise: Trevor, Marley, and me: Reggae music and the foreigner other. *Psychoanalytic Dialogues, 25*, 176–193.

Winnicott, D. W. (1971). *Playing and reality*. New York, NY: Routledge.

Yi, K. (2014). From no name to birth of integrated identity: Trauma-based cultural dissociation in immigrant women and creative integration. *Psychoanalytic Dialogues, 24*(1), 37–45.

Yoo, H. C., Miller, M. J., & Yip, P. (2015). Validation of the internalization of the model minority myth measure (IM-4) and its link to academic performance and psychological adjustment among Asian American adolescents. *Cultural Diversity and Ethnic Minority Psychology, 21*(2), 237–246.

Yoshikawa, H., Suárez-Orozco, C., & Gonzales, R. G. (2016). Unauthorized status and youth development in the United States: Consensus statement of the society for research on adolescence. *Journal of Research on Adolescence, 27*(1), 4–19.

Young-Bruehl, E. (2007). A brief history of prejudice studies. In H. Parens, A. Mahfouz, S. W. Twemlow, & D. E. Scharff (Eds.), *The future of prejudice: Psychoanalysis and the prevention of prejudice* (pp. 219–235). Lanham, MD: Aronson.

Zimbardo, P., & Sword, R. (2017). Unbridled and extreme present hedonism. In B. X. Lee (Ed.), *The dangerous case of Donald Trump* (pp. 25–50). New York, NY: St. Martin's Press.

Chapter 6

Strangers in paradise

Trevor, Marley, and me: Reggae music and the foreigner other

Cleonie White

Shaping identities

Music has a way of transporting you to that intersecting corner where selfhood and otherness bump up against each other; where, though unscripted, you come to know what only moments before arrival there you did not know: that the tremors of uncertainty and sadness that rocked you before you got there are not to be feared – there, where you come to grasp the unifying power inherent in being interpersonally alive. The philosopher, Ian McGilchrist (2009), has something to say about the power of music:

> It has been said that music, like poetry, is intrinsically sad . . . not, of course, that there is no joyful music, but that even such music appears to be joy torn from the teeth of sadness, a sort of holiday of the minor key. It is what we would expect in view of the emotional timbre of the right hemisphere; and there is strong affinity between the right hemisphere and the minor key.
>
> (p. 73)

I am Jamaican – and other things as well, of course, but we'll get to that. As a tiny girl, I frequently stood on my auntie's feet and, together, we danced gleefully to the tunes of classical music (White, 2012). My grandfather, on the other hand, much to the consternation and expressed contempt of my very proper, English-identified Jamaican granny, perfected the rhumba box and performed music endemic to those among us Granny summarily dismissed as "mere commoners." Ouch! "How could he [Grandfather] consort with *those people* and play *that* 'music'?" Granny lamented, "How could he so shame the family?"

"Sigh!" *Shame* is my experienced affect in this public recall of my cultural beginnings.

The disquietude that framed my grandmother's "me" – "not-me" sensibilities was rooted in the broader culture's unease with its racial and socioeconomic complexity. This anxiety is, of course, derived from rigidly ingrained patterns of cultural attachment and identity formation, transmitted intergenerationally through the lens of colonialism. Alan Schore's commentary in his foreword to Bromberg's *The Shadow of the Tsunami* (2011) bears relevance here. Schore writes that "[d]uring episodes of the intergenerational transmission of attachment trauma the infant is matching the rhythmic structure of the mother's dysregulated arousal states" (p. xviii). Dysregulated patterns of attachment are transmitted in the broader culture as well, for "mind," "self," and "cultural contexts" cannot be understood as independent entities (Aron, 1996). The argument could be made, therefore, that, for the colonized, mental representations of self and other swirl robustly in the rhythms and attachment patterns of inter-generational transmissions of colonial tyranny.

For me, rhythms of attachment were powerfully informed by my grandmother's stiff upper lip – her classic, elitist appetite for all things European. But beneath it all, a less associated sensibility "drank" symbolically, surreptitiously, of the spirited euphoria that "freed" my grandfather of England and propelled him, in these rhumba-box, mento-jamming sessions, toward closer communion with "those people" in whom his dissociated, more Afrocentric self-states appeared seamlessly embodied. Of course, neither grandparent could symbolize the paradoxical nature of J. Wray and Nephew's overproof (63% ABV) white rum – as reliever of pain and as living "proof" of continued insertion of sugarcane plantation culture into the Jamaican psyche. Slavery, if its name had to be spoken, was regarded simply as an unfortunate chapter in our history that was now long past and needed not to be reconstituted with every turn of memory. So, my grandfather simply drank the rum, and my grandmother disapproved. Both needed it for sustenance of flawed, illusory identities. Was either of them truly free? Leonard Cohen (2001) captures their dilemma beautifully in song, as he articulates his recognition of the implicit human dilemma inherent in attempting to rid oneself of that part of self that is the carrier of current, and historical trauma: Quite paradoxically, Cohen suggests, even in the fight against the ravishes of alcohol, the actor does so while simultaneously awash in the spirits she/he wishes to avoid.

The melodies of Europe and the rhythms of Africa resided restlessly – dissociatively – within me. Yet, always, in the presence of music, a life-enhancing, transformational space opens up in me, and I happily inhabit the "*in-between*" (McGilchrist, 2009). Music evokes in me complex, organic yearnings for spiritual awakening in *time before Time*. But in my Jamaican home, the starting line of my history was set in 1655, when the British conquered (. . . er. . . "civilized"?) the island. This misguided account of my identity could not be sustained, of course – not in a place where my curiosity was daily awakened by the mysteries of unseen Maroons who, unyielding in their rebellion against enslavement, secured their freedom long before the Emancipation Proclamation, and created dwellings and communities in the Cockpit mountains that curtained the home of my childhood.

My growing-up consciousness of obvious differences in Jamaican society, my secret identification with my mento-playing grandfather, and my yearning to know and to narrate the complex spaces that yawned between self-states, pointed my path to the U.S. where, paradoxically, were it not for the promise of Jamaica's "white gold" (sugarcane), *my* ancestors might have disembarked into American slavery. Why migrate? Well, "[g]ood ideology presents itself as if it is the natural order of things. It is only when you depart can you see the water you swam in" (Guralnik, 2011, p. 125). Migration goes hand in hand with a wondering mind, which itself attests to a certain *habit of being* – a certain state of readiness for full immersion into the realm of the unknown.

America held, for me, unending possibilities to be heralded into the unknown; and my natural capacity for complete absorption into what was, for a newly arrived resident, the cacophony of minds that is American culture, was later to be of service in the course of my work with my Jamaican patient, Trevor. In our intersubjective stretches across colonial fault lines, Trevor and I negotiated, and over time transcended, binaries of race and class that tormented our Jamaican minds with shame. We dwelled together in the universality of Jamaica's music – *Reggae* – and held our cultural looking glass up to ourselves and up to each other as we struggled to locate our place as foreigners in a foreign land.

Playing with variance

The analytic relationship comprises multiple variances – constantly shifting, multiply determined, experientially contradictory, self-states within and between the analytic dyad. What I conclude, then, is that *the art, the music of psychoanalysis, resides in its function* – as *the analysis of variance*. Intersubjectivity, as I see it, encompasses musical relationships – between melody and rhythm, between self and other – while holding constant individual differences en route to locating commonalities. *The "we-ness" of "us" is predicated upon recognition and validation of the "you-ness" of you and of the "I-ness" of me* (White, 2004).

"Can we talk?" That was an underlying question that repeatedly confronted Trevor and me. Given our history, we knew that individually, and together, we had "Many Rivers to Cross," as Jimmy Cliff (1972) poignantly lamented. But, while we understood that the water ran darker, or clearer, depending on which side of the river banks we stood, we sought, in our analytic overtures toward each other, to compose symphonies of subjective and intersubjective transformations beyond the limits of guilt and shame.

Where am I? roots and foundations

The music on the radio in my waiting room functioned as part of my "noise machine system" to secure privacy: Self-organizing binaries we construct between "inner" and "outer," between what constitutes "dissonance" and what "harmony," lay down their weight at our analytic feet in our daily efforts to engage the complexity of our patients' and our own interiority. Hopefully, we remain mindful of social, external contexts that exert influence. My radio's signal always transmitted the soothing waves of classical music.

"You play this music all the time," Trevor complained. "You nuh (not) Jamaican, man? How come you stray so far from your roots?"

"I beg your pardon?!" This was my startled response, "not knowing," even as I *knew* exactly what he meant.

"In the three years since I've been coming here," Trevor e-x-p-l-a-i-n-e-d, "not once me hear you play anything that reflects yuh Jamaican roots. What about some *Roots Reggae*, man?"

Grasping the complexity of this question, including meanings embedded in Trevor's mixture of Jamaican patois and English, necessitates a brief "detour" from the analytic room into exploration of cultural and historical influences, not only upon the development of reggae music, but upon the trajectory of our lives that brought Trevor and me into this moment of relational reflection and negotiation – into what, in the clouds of ganja-induced, "spiritual" language of Jamaica's Rastafarian culture, is romanticized as "Reasoning." To be clear, while "reasoning" between Trevor and me involved implicit, subject to subject, mind to mind communications and connections, we dwelled in unconscious spaces (alas!?) *sans* "ganja!"

Jamaica: "Four Hundred Years of History . . ." (The Wailers 1970)

Not to worry. Jamaica's history is anything but dull; but you, the reader, will be spared the full journey. Anyway, I am neither a historian nor a musicologist. I write, instead, from my position as a Jamaican, who arrived in America and into psychoanalysis, riding the waves of African culture and British colonial ideology across the Caribbean Sea.

Jamaica's recorded history covers some 400 years of occupation, first by Spain (1494–1655), and then by Great Britain which, in 1655, lay claim to the real estate and to the minds and bodies of Jamaicans, only to perpetuate the crime of slavery first initiated by the Spanish. For the next three hundred years, until our independence in 1962, Jamaica remained a colony of the British Empire. How does an enslaved mind robbed of history preserve memory and create subversive identities in the midst of imposed truths and externally constructed realities? Jamaican scholar and social critic, Professor R. M. Nettleford (2006), captures the struggle for a self-constructed cultural/historical narrative in his challenge of unreflected "truths" of history. He challenges received historical "facts" in his position that indigenous Indians discovered Columbus – Jamaica's first European tourist – on their shores, and not the other way around. Surprising? Perhaps. But then again, "[e]ven Columbus and the cowboys are not heroes forever" (Stern, 1997, p. 65).

Nothing more drives a spirit into creative acts of survival than the stifling experience of coercion and control that subvert complexity of being. When current contexts render freedom apparently unattainable, then new, creative, morally charged sensibilities that question imposed truths and entrenched realities emerge. In their stories, art, poetry, jokes, music, and language, for example, Jamaicans have constructed a vibrant, complex, most inspiring cultural narrative that demonstrates the struggles and conflicts inherent in any process of emergence from unsymbolized experience to mentalization and knowing. How might we grasp this exquisite human capacity to rise from the ashes, so to speak, and to create ourselves anew?

Creativity might be understood to be an abstract human potential – "a creative impulse . . . that can be looked at as a thing in itself" (Winnicott, 1971, p. 92).

Can we understand that, not unlike the process entailed in the creation of an oyster's pearl, transition from "creative impulse" to actualization is triggered by, and cannot be "unlinked" from (Layton, 2006, p. 108) the creator's personal, social, or cultural contexts? And yet, here is the extraordinary thing – what might be considered a paradox: In this stimulated awakening into creative productivity, the actual product, *the symbolization of creative potential, is always new because it is unplanned; it emerges without summons* ("unbidden" in Stern's, 1990 language) so that the artist, herself, perceives her creation with surprise. This, surely, is one critical factor that accounts for differences and for the unique character of each culture's creative productions.

In Jamaica, music remains an always emergent, creative arrangement that informs, and is, itself, influenced by, complex processes of identity formation. One readily discerns in early folk songs the function of music as a critical, cultural schema for transmitting messages and securing witnessing to simple and complex events in the everyday lives of the community. Stories of relationships – marriages, births, steamy love affairs, of pain, sadness, *obeah*, danger, conflict, and resolution – were transmitted in song. They were, furthermore, sung in *patois*, another ingenious "weapon" of survival – the language of rebellion and self-preservation!

Jamaica's music

According to Chang and Chen (1998), *Mento* was the prevailing music of choice in Jamaica from the late nineteenth century into the 1930s. But up until the late 1950s, mento (made popular in the U.S. by another singer of Jamaican descent, Harry Belafonte) was the prevailing music of choice played both on the radio and certainly in tourist regions of Jamaica. By the 1950s, though, Jamaicans were ready for a new rhythm. *Ska* emerged. Still, mento has undergone popular revival as "dancehall mento." In spirited celebrations of Jamaica's musical roots, for example, the performance group, Fab Five (2007) reminds audiences that, all pretensions aside, there is no escape from the powerful impact of mento music. True, man . . . true.

Ska fired the imagination of Jamaica's underclass, who were at this point enamored of the music's fast pace that seemed both to reflect and to herald the country's pre- independence mood of optimism. In London's East End, the music hit the white skinhead underground class like a great "Ball of Fire" (Skattalites, 1967); and, although the musical scene in Jamaica continued its evolution into new genres, this particular aspect of the Jamaican brand has defied extinction across the globe. By the late 1960s, however, in concert with social and political life in Jamaica, yet another musical genre emerged.

Rock Steady reflected the growing disappointment among Jamaica's ghetto poor who, more than one hundred years since Emancipation, found no star in Jamaica's diamond-studded heavens upon which to affix a subjective gaze. A "rude boy" culture, memorialized in the music of Desmond Dekker ("007 [Shanty Town]," 1967), became an increasing source of concern for authorities, as the artist openly described the rude boy shooting and bombing in one of Jamaica's poorest, shattered communities. The situation was no less troubling to the authorities a year later, when Dekker dropped his next hit, "Poor Me, Israelite" (1968), in which he paid homage to the horrific plight of disenfranchised Jamaicans, struggling against their limited odds for survival of self and family. Dekker's "Poor Me, Israelite" might be imagined as anticipatory to Bob Marley's call to social consciousness ("War," 1976). And, ominously, Dekker predicted the consequences of silence and neglect on the part of the power elite: Rebellion. And, as rock steady emerged from ska as a slower, more relaxed genre, so, too, did rock steady give way, in the grip of seemingly unending social and political schisms, to yet another musical turn. From the embers of rock steady's fifteen months of glory during the late 1960s into the early 1970s, another beat, *Reggae*, emerged. Rastafarian spirituality and socio-political commentary were taken up as the cause célèbre of this new sound. Reggae music is transformative. It penetrates the mind. It challenges stereotypes, shifts perceptions, and dismantles rigidly constructed barriers. Still slower, and more pensive, but without loss of the all-important "riddim" (rhythm)-and-dance element, the music reaches the listener at an affective level. It robs the body of its will toward stillness and incites it into movement: Intellect and affect, mind and body, become one. Allow yourself full immersion in the lyrics and rhythm, and you will agree that reggae music elevates us into complex fellowship with our humanity!

Roots reggae

Reggae is Jamaica's music. Giuseppe Verdi (1813–1901) wrote the operas of Europe. Samuel Coleridge Taylor (1875–1912), "the African Mahler," was Britain's biracial composer of classical music. Now, since my ancestry dates back to African slaves and European slave holders, how fortunate it is that these musical forms cannot but be embedded in the core of who I am? *They are my rapture*. They transport me through the roundabouts of life and take me to the brink of the universe. Nevertheless, as I have indicated, some aspects of "my rapture" lived only surreptitiously within me. And this fact became the laced centerpiece of my work with Trevor. Our analytic relationship unfolded through the lenses of culture, politics, race, class, and dissociation.

As it was Trevor's main point of focus, I discuss "Roots reggae" (late 1960s to the early 1980s) as the radical voice of Jamaica's repudiated class – those who were "remembered," it often seemed, only when the sound of downtown ghetto "rude boy" gunfire penetrated the silence of the uptown class and shattered denial! In retrospect, I understand Jamaica's post-colonial "rude boys" in context of Fanon's (1963) theorizing of Algeria's colonized "fella" for whom

> living does not mean embodying moral values or taking his place in the coherent and fruitful development of the world. To live means to keep on existing. Every date is a victory: not the result of work, but a victory felt as a triumph for life.
>
> (p. 308)

Roots reggae, so named to distinguish it from later reggae styles (e.g., Dub, Dancehall), more powerfully than had its musical antecedents communicated the social, political, and economic conditions that blotted the lives of Jamaica's "fellas." In unapologetic rebellion against the colonizing *lingua franca* (British English) and all its social and political implications, reggae was written and sung in Jamaican patois, the language of public dissidence and subversion. Reggae identified the pain and frustration of the common man. Bob Marley and the Wailers (1974a) named them – the suffering, hungry, and angry citizens among us – and challenged the uptown class to take account of its own role in creating the conditions to which it now responded with repulsion, anxiety, and alarm. In his soulful, acoustic rendition of

"Redemption Song" (1980), Bob Marley understood very well that, like my grandparents, no Jamaican could escape the anxiety of the colonized.

Marley broadcast the voices of demoralized Jamaicans into the staid drawing rooms uptown. He held up to all Jamaicans a cultural looking glass of subjectivity and the imperative was clear: psychological revolution – on all sides. Marley, in his "Redemption Song" (1980), channeled the writings and passions of Marcus Garvey (1937), another Jamaican social/political activist, who challenged the downtrodden to rise up and take charge of their own destiny. And, in the stubborn absence of structural and political change, Marley's loyalties nestled squarely in the corner of the voiceless majority, as did those of other reggae artists.

Reggae music became a clarion call to socially disadvantaged Jamaicans to claim their subjectivity – their agency – and to transform these into political action. Marley and the Wailers (1973) incited their politically and economically oppressed listeners to protest against their elite oppressors on their own behalf. In the footsteps of ska and rock steady, reggae carries a pulsating, syncopated bass line in 4/4 time, with deliberate emphasis on the second and fourth beats in each bar. With drums and bass guitar carrying the beat; with keyboard, acoustic, and electric guitar; with soprano and tenor saxophones evoking spirituality; and with the mesmerizing call-and-response passion of the lyrics and vocal message, *reggae* transports the listener/dancer/activist/psychoanalyst into ancient, affective realms from which she emerges renewed – with peace and hope in the unifying force of "One Love" (Bob Marley and the Wailers, 1977a). The Holy Bible figures largely as a vehicle of transport for, and validation of, the messages of rebellion, redemption, and possibility in reggae's lyrics. How did the Bible come to figure so prominently in reggae music?

Reggae and Rasta: music of Jah (God's) people

Jamaica is the idyllic, "fun-in-the-sun, rum-punch-drinking paradise" it is purported to be (remember "Take me to Jamaica/Where the rum comes from"?). But Jamaica is, as well, a deeply reflective, generally conservative (primarily Christian), society. Slaves embraced the Bible (King James Version – KJV). It was their mooring "in the Valley of the Shadow of Death. . . . [for] In the prophets, patriarchs, psalmists, [they] found comfort and hope. The Jewish story had for [them] an almost unbearable, piercing relevance" (Sherlock & Bennett, 1998, p. 39). And for Jamaicans in rural and underserved communities, the crux of religion resided in moral fellowship – "the common pot of the tenement yard" (Sherlock & Bennett, 1998, p. 358).

Rastafarians relied heavily on Old Testament teachings of The Holy Bible (KJV) for construction of their religious ideology. Disparaged by the elite class as Jamaica's "social outcasts," Rastafarians were particularly intrigued with Marcus Garvey's ideas. Garvey established his Back to Africa Movement under the auspices of the Universal Negro Improvement Association, which he founded in 1914. In America and the Caribbean, he advocated black pride, black hope, and the return of Africans in the diaspora to the African homeland. Garvey proclaimed that "We are going to emancipate ourselves from mental slavery, because whilst others might free the body, none but ourselves can free the mind" (1937). Rastafarian sensibility was aroused by Garvey's message, as they searched for their own spiritual and political foundation. Despite controversy on this point, they credit Garvey with having "predicted" around 1927, that in Africa, a black man would be crowned king. Goldman (2006) notes that Garvey frequently cited biblical references to Ethiopia: "Ethiopia shall soon stretch out her hands unto God" (Psalm 68:31). Indeed, by 1930, one Ras Tafari, a self-proclaimed descendant of the tribe of Solomon, was crowned King of Ethiopia. This seemed the materialization of biblical prophecy (Revelations 5:2–5). With this coronation, Rastafarians hailed Marcus Garvey a prophet, Haile Selassie their King and Savior, and Ethiopia their promised land. They adopted the King's pre-coronation name, Ras Tafari (the "i" pronounced as "eye"). Rastafarians cite many biblical passages critical to their search for divine awakening and guidance in the conduct of their daily lives (food, dress, language) and in their style of worship. Their doctrines include biblical prohibitions against cutting the hair (Leviticus 21:5), hence the lion-like "dreadlocks" for which they are known; and, of course, they locate in biblical passages support for spiritual use of "herbs."

Roots reggae musicians were also driven by their quest for political awakening, and the return of black Jamaicans to their particularly African-centric, Jamaican subjectivity, if not to Africa. The alienated poor were "God's Chosen People," and their lamentations resonate symbolically in the gospel chants of the Melodians' "By the Rivers of Babylon" (1970), with their rendition of the Holy Bible's Psalm 137 (KJV):

By the rivers of Babylon
There we sat down, yea, we wept

When we remembered Zion.
We hung our harps
Upon the willows in the midst of it.
For there those who carried us away captive
asked of us a song, . . .

How shall we sing the Lord's song
In a foreign land?

And they chant – hauntingly, they chant. And the soul is awakened from dissociated somnolence, the mind's eyelids lifted from habitual states of not seeing. Reggae music has that kind of power!

Bob Marley, perhaps the most well-known of the Rasta reggae artists, amplified the spiritual and political aspects of Rastafarian philosophy, and internalized their idiosyncrasies in speech. Jehovah became "Jah" (Psalm 68:4), and Rastafarians adopt the term, "I and I" (first person pronoun, doubled, for "you and I"). They expunge from their repertoire any language form that insists upon constructing artificial dichotomies that promote differences as markers of inequality.

Marley's music proved an effective instrument of change as Trevor and I traveled into our shared history and reflected upon our divergent paths. We encountered strangeness in ourselves, and as "not-me" projections into each other, and realized that we could not fully comprehend the foreignness we experienced as we attempted to negotiate the challenges of our adopted home – America – without painful confrontation of another truth: That, in our Jamaican paradise home, where our motto: "Out of Many, One People," promotes cultural and political hybridity, each of us, independently, struggled against haunting experiences of alienation.

I was of many minds regarding my place in the uptown domain I called home. On one hand, I took full advantage of the privileges it afforded. But in that community, the air I breathed reeked of hegemony. So, on the other hand, a sense of moral unease disturbed the comfort of my middle-class life. I voiced opposition on behalf of disaffected proletariats. With this attitude I was, predictably, thrust toward the lip of uptown. But I survived; I did not fall upon the tracks that led downtown. Nothing in my experience approximated the tributaries of social trauma coursing through the veins of ghetto residents like Trevor. I remained, in the end, a privileged "rebel" peering into the ghetto from the safety of my faraway verandah (yes, I had a verandah!). Despite my ambivalence, I could not have found a place in Trevor's place. Yet, we both understood that in our own ways we were, in fact, "strangers in paradise." Is it not, then, paradoxical that it is in a foreign country, and in the foreignness of psychoanalysis, that two Jamaicans sought meaning to their native experiences of strangeness? Trevor and I were confronted with myriad questions relevant to individual, and shared identities: Does hybridity preclude individuality? Who is the stranger – the foreigner? How does strangeness live within/between us? How do we negotiate difference? What is "an immigrant," and how does this designation inform identity? We had much to learn in our quest to know each other.

"I and I": intersubjectivity

Philip Bromberg (2012) proposes that "[t]he fact that we all need otherness as part of self-wholeness inherently challenges the security of mental stability. Where does "I" end and "we" begin?" (p. 273). As if, themselves, contemplating this critical question, Rastafarian's philosophy asserts: "I and I": Self and other subjectivity is incontrovertible. Rastafarians do not, of course, posit psychoanalytic theories. Yet, one grasps in the wisdom inherent in their "first person-pronoun-doubled" ideology, a relational stance that asserts equality across and within subjectivities. *There can be no end to "I."* It is the threat of volcanic engulfment in hybrid "we" states, to the detriment of "*not-we*" subjectivities, that potentiates the terror of psychological annihilation. The possibility of entering an intersubjective "we" space resides in recognition of this truth – that *it is two subjective "I" sensibilities that stretch across psychic chasms*. Trevor and I learned this only too well.

Trevor is a handsome Jamaican man who, despite his marbled ebony, his beauty and sharp mind, could not feel himself to fit into American culture. Perhaps it was his "stand-out" lion's "dreadlocks," he thought. "People don't understand." He had long expressed envy of the apparent ease with which I negotiated my immigrant, and professional status. I seemed to have slipped seamlessly into this new world of whiteness and power. In what felt to be a carryover of his experiences in Jamaica, Trevor seemed oblivious to the fact that, in America, we could pretend, we could mimic, but never would we truly enjoy those privileges organically assigned to whiteness. But Trevor's earlier question, "What about roots reggae?" was an unarticulated accusation of those Jamaicans to whom history had been kinder, while society's less fortunate members still, symbolically, harvested implanted fear and anxiety in the concrete "plantations" (government housing/political bureaucracy) of post-colonial Jamaica. In his mind, my lighter skin tone alone afforded me privileges he, and others in his neighborhood, could not imagine.

Trevor hailed from a family rich in hope, but poor – very poor by any economic standards. He grew up in Trench Town, one of many "shantytowns" or ghettoes in Kingston, romanticized in the music of Bob Marley (1974b, 1975). It was a town spotted with "government yards" (tenements) and with what gave the appearance of hurriedly constructed tin "shanties" its residents called home. Trevor and other hungry children wandered the streets searching, always searching, it seemed – minds fogged, hearts pounding, stomachs agitated – for things they could not clearly identify. Like the character, Ivanhoe Martin, in Jamaica's culture film, "The Harder They Come" (1972), Trevor (and his family) abandoned the serenity of country life and headed to post-independence Kingston, the crowded city of big dreams and little change for poor, unfortunate, dreamers. Though smart, my patient lacked the academic preparedness required for entry into one of Jamaica's elite secondary schools. Now what? The future stretched long past imagination, and hope became no more than a ghostly mirage.

"T'ings was tough, you know," Trevor recalled, his head shaking negatively against unsolicited memory, his tears flowing free, as if to wash him clean of shame and pain. "Black people really suffa [suffered]!"

"Yes," I told myself, "I know," but in truth I had been spared his reality – what for him was an all too familiar inferno. Could I see him now? Would I permit his gaze to penetrate *my* veil of shame? Would I train my gaze into the depths of our cultural looking glass? Kapuscinski's (2006) keen reflections helped clarify what I "knew": "Others cast a new light on my own history for me" (p. 45).

Trench Town's rivers of rage could not be dammed. Trevor's stomach churned mercilessly with pangs of hunger and despair, and he fully identified with the ghetto desperation described in Bob Marley's (1974a) lyrics, in which he excoriates Jamaica's wealthy elites who secure all the good, at the expense of those who suffer. Yes, so it was for Trevor. Very angry, and feeling increasingly less able to internalize his mother's hope for him, he decided, at the age of 12, to join the gangs of Kingston. Like Sunday morning church bells beckoning his mother to prayer, the sounds of "rude boy" chiming in the recesses of his splintered mind haunted and buoyed this young boy's troubled soul.

I say that, as lives the common man, so is he marked the prophet of the Nation that is the place of his dwelling. And thus began this young prophet's adventures on the negative side of the law. Trevor is riddled with shame for his actions as a gangster:

> I brought drugs into my community, and I can't hide from responsibility. People were murdered!

He denied having killed anyone, though he commanded "respect" with powerful weapons he easily secured as his constant companions. His guilt was, nevertheless, palpable. Now, I had never before been this close to an admitted gangster and, despite my conscious self, and the fact that, by this time, I had been working with Trevor for some years, my initial response to the story was fear . . . followed by shame, for I caught myself in the act of Othering! In front of me sat one of "those people"! But another sensibility caught hold of me – thankfully; and, as Trevor and I, two subjectivities, reached across difference in this moment of witnessing, Bob Marley's (1980) lamentations in the name of Jamaica's emotionally erased – social outcasts, all – rang clear in my mind: *My* guilt from past and current silence and inaction reared up and would not let go of me. *I am the nation that called him, "Son!"*

On foreignness, hybridity, and the immigrant

Who is the foreigner? Or, perhaps more accurately, as Kristeva (1991) wonders, "Can one possibly be a foreigner?" (p. 41). In navigating this question, Kristeva (1991) offers the following thought, clearly steeped in relational sensibilities: "The foreigner is within us. And when we flee from or struggle against the foreigner, we are fighting our unconscious – that 'improper' facet of our impossible 'own and proper'" (p. 191). It follows, then, that a mind embedded in the apparent stability and security of cultural or national hybridity is an imprisoned mind. Such a mind is incapable of contemplating its own limits and limitations and cannot, therefore, imagine, or perceive, beyond rigid boundaries constructed between the self and the foreigner Other. *Who is the foreigner?* If the foreigner is theorized as a mark of difference from an established point of reference (non-foreigner, native), then she functions to shore up the self-proclaimed native's precarious sense of belonging – an anxiety of place within which foreignness is engineered. Why? *This anxiety, this defensive position, illuminates the existence of the unmentalized, repudiated foreigner residing implicitly within us all.* It is in manic defense (Altman, 2010) against conscious experience of this disavowed self-state that the "foreigner Other" must be constructed as felt Truth. Foreignness permeated Trevor's identity, as it did my own.

It is at the juncture of race and class that in Jamaica, the stranger-Other is wrestled into existence. Though not openly identified in polite company, "whiteness" – British whiteness, to be specific – was as integral to my identity as a Jamaican of lighter hue, as were the indulgences of class afforded me, not by any economic advantages I currently enjoyed, but simply by virtue of my ancestral "good" fortunes. For, despite our hybridity (as products of white and black races) – indeed, because of it – my ancestors were the recipients of economic and political privileges that were denied pure-blooded Jamaicans of African descent. This is a fact not lost on Jamaicans at home or in the diaspora. The author, Malcolm Gladwell (2008), discusses precisely this situation, for example, in relation to opportunities afforded his own light-skinned, Jamaican mother. Tracing his mother's ancestry to a white slave owner and an African slave, Gladwell comments upon:

> the extraordinary advantage that their little bit of whiteness gave the colored minority. Having an ancestor who worked in the house and not the fields, who got full civil rights in 1826. . . made all the difference in occupational success two and three generations later.
>
> (2008, p. 280)

Trevor understood well and associated this reality with what he perceived to be my ready fit into whiteness in America. But what we could not readily name was my unwitting participation in social structures that perpetuated his unfortunate plight.

We avoided talk of racial difference – a strange experience to hold in a country where, for the most part, I am regarded as a homogeneous "African-American," with all the vicissitudes of constructed Otherness. Instead, we focused on our common roots and delighted in the accomplishments of

Jamaicans across the globe. In particular, as our focus was on mutual discovery through music, we swelled with pride at Jamaica's intrepid influence on world music, including that of reggae artists and of our own DJ Kool Herc, "the sonic originator of hip-hop" (Bradley & DuBois, 2010, p. 2).

We dwelled in the safety of hybrid identities our motto constructed for us and connected as proud Jamaicans, pushed up against a less than welcoming American culture. Still, provocative anxieties nestled between the lines of our personal and analytic talk, signifying problems inherent in unreflected capitulation to hybridity as the natural order of things, under the flag of presumed sameness and unity. For my patient and me, one critical, yet unspoken, question seemed to be: In contexts of politically constructed hybrid structures, how do we secure subjectivity?

Trevor and I knew well the blurring of boundaries between self and country when hegemony cloaks hybridity, but we dreaded the destructive power that symbolizing this truth might potentiate. Too much was at risk here in America (where still he struggled to realize his dreams), to begin examination of his sense of foreignness in his nation home. He respected me too much, furthermore (enacting internalized power structures), to see me rendered vulnerable by any unwinding of our tightly coiled "secrets." And I did not want to face my vulnerability. I, also, felt too much on shaky ground in this place of "safety" he presumed me to occupy. How could Trevor have known the shock of racism and blatant *immigrantism* that I had encountered in my adopted home? How were my patient and I to negotiate the complexities of hybridity and foreignness within the context of our shared positions as "immigrants" in America?

We could not, of course, unlink our defining cultural histories from our current lives as "immigrants" in our encounter with strangeness. You see, like ghosts that emerge with the dimming of the light, their cultural language (by which I mean the tastes, the aromas, the dialects and accents, the sounds of hurt and the sounds of joy, the language that is the marker of their day and the poetry of their evening) lurks impatiently in every foreigner – in the shadow of her now – awaiting its moment. I am Jamaican. Yet, as I consider my identities I am, culturally, as American as I am Jamaican, and more – a full product of every culture, and of every culture within culture that I have inhabited, and which functions implicitly in me as lived experience. I defy hyphenation. And I embrace *this* hybrid, cultural complexity – not the historically pejorative, miscegenist construct of colonialism employed as descriptor of the mixed, mulatto class, who held the peculiar position of being "*neithered.*" Rather, I don the mantle of "hybridity" as a *Third*, subversive, anti-colonial garment (Bhabha, 1994) that promotes reconceptualization of "the foreigner/immigrant" and the "stranger/other." I embrace this *Third* as an inaugural space that activates movement toward resignifying identities (Butler, 1997).

In time, the process of negotiating our experiences as foreigners brought Trevor and me into creative joining that almost certainly would not have been possible were we in Jamaica, he being from downtown, and I from up; he from lack of opportunity and I from the safety of my position as "the inheritor of a legacy of privilege" (Gladwell, p. 280). But the "inside" and the "outside" and the "me" and "not-me" sensibilities swirling within and between us would garner meaning in the musical spaces that Trevor and I inhabited.

In the immigrant potential space dwells the subversive foreigner

In this discussion, I mean to travel well beyond contemporary theorizing of *the immigrant* as a chronic, inflexible state of being. I want, rather, to capture more complex, psychic dimensions, parallel to other such aspects physicists theorize to exist in the physical world, though they are imperceptible to the human brain. According to Greene (1999, pp. 47–50), time itself in relation to space is configured as *timespace*, and is, thus, a *fourth* dimension. For this discussion, these dimensions for which I search are living, active, psychic amplifications that, within the limits of our perceptual capacities, we can "envision" only as "transitional space." They afford a sort of twilight state intersubjectivity akin to being "lost" in music, a requirement of which is, at least temporarily, suspension of consciousness in time and space. Such a space transcends geographical limits and psychological boundaries, as when analyst and patient suspend awareness and all that matters in that moment is what matters in that moment: *The moment is the space, is the moment, is transformational.* What do I mean?

I invite you to consider this: Being in intersubjective spaces (with composer, author, artist, patient) or being embedded in the thing itself that is the product of their creative outpouring, demands momentary suspension of a conscious "I," who stands at the ready to impose unilateral structure, meaning, form. The *thingness[es]* of psychoanalytic moments are the seeds of possibility that grow in the fertile soil of relational spaces. But let's expand this further. Kristeva (1991) proposes that "uncanny strangeness . . . sets the difference *within* us in its most bewildering shape and presents it as the ultimate condition of our being with others" (p. 192, italics added). How is it possible that subjectivity is suspended from awareness in the service of intersubjectivity? Under one critical condition, I argue: *Interpersonal moments and spaces are transformational only in the certainty that "I" is alive in the mind of the other and is readily accessed within the context of an intersubjectively related "Us."* It is this experience that energizes subjective capacity for surrender into relational spaces where, *being simultaneously "there" and "not there," emerges as transformational possibility.* There is particular relevance in this that can be brought to bear on the question of the immigrant.

Recent papers addressing immigrant experience (e.g., Akhtar, 1995; Boulanger, 2004; Eng & Han, 2000; Grinberg & Grinberg, 1989) reflect the modern turn in psychoanalysis, which questions meanings when we speak of "knowledge" or "perceptions" that interrogates social constructs (such as language, race, class, gender, and, more recently, *the immigrant*); that embeds the individual broadly within the layers and circles of social, cultural, and political, contexts. These authors focus our analytic sensibilities upon that aspect of our work that encompasses the complexity of the immigrant experience, whether the immigrant is identified as the patient, the analyst, or both.

I offer the position that, even as the immigrant strives toward negotiating experiences of foreignness in a foreign culture, this very act insinuates him into interpellated (Althusser, 2000) positions that herald: "Look at you, you are interpellated, 'Immigrant!'" He is discoursed into the status, "Other." My patient, Trevor, one might say, is "verbed" – that is, projected into performance of that position as in: "I speak, I think, I dream, *I am* immigrant." His position in culture is imposed as his defining identity. So, no matter how sturdy the immigrant's attempts to "integrate" into the new culture, he is met with repeated acts of rejection as his difference marks him the imperfect Other. The power of social discourse to limit the boundaries of being are clearly delineated by Dimen (2011) as follows:

> Discursive formations . . . are power structures. They are networks of socially located ideas, beliefs, attitudes, behaviors, and action patterns that systematically fashion and inform subjectivity and its practices.
>
> (p. 5)

Is it ever possible to articulate a different understanding of the construct "immigrant" – one that encompasses a conceptual framework less limited than that enveloped in imposed Otherness? Might we not regard this conceptual framework as, itself, embedded in hope and relational possibilities? This reach toward the other is the message of roots reggae, what powers its life-giving impact on downtrodden people across the globe.

I am advocating a relational, intersubjective, approach to theorizing "the immigrant." By this I mean a different conceptualization of the term "immigrant" than one housed in legal briefs, or in socially constructed language. What if we thought of the construct "immigrant" not as a defined, observable phenomenon, but instead as a *thing in itself* – as a transitional space, invested with creative possibility? Might it be regarded as a potential space in which dwells the foreigner in transition between and within psychological and geographical boundaries? In this immigrant potential space multiplicity exists, and Otherness might be interrogated and challenged. In it, disavowed and dissociated self-states that carry culture are, in Boulanger's (2004) language, "made conscious, examined, mourned over" (p. 353) and are then re-linked and transformed into cultural identities molded in personal ambiguities and personal choice. I know it to be so, for without knowing it until we knew it, this is the dynamic space which launched the journey upon which Trevor and I embarked.

Over time, my patient and I questioned assumptions about each other along lines of our Jamaicanness – our complex identities, as determined by race and class. I did not wish to change my classical music, and I didn't. But I also knew that, foreclosing engagement with reggae music altogether would mean not only failure on my part to recognize and to bear witness to Trevor's existence as a repudiated Other, but would, also, perpetuate in me longings for unrealized aspects of *my* identity. Roots reggae was not his alone. It was also mine.

I invited Trevor to bring music into our sessions. We listened and permitted the sounds and playful accents to transport us back to Jamaica. And it did not take long before the political messages of the music, in alliance with rhythms that called out to the body, transported us from dissociated "memories" to recognition of realities that directly impacted our lives: Uptown, for example, I performed at "The Little Theatre," while downtown, he performed race and class as a "rude boy" with drugs and guns that secured the validation he craved. We listened to one powerful and raspy voice, unmistakably Marley (1977b), penetrating my uptown armor in my uptown office in New York City, shining a bright light upon the folly of mankind, living under false pretense, and purposefully eschewing consciousness of guilt. Shame clothed me, and I was frank. I openly acknowledged the security I gained from wearing dissociation and silence as protective shields against knowing. I offered apology:

> The truth is that the strangeness in you that frightened me is very much a part of me that I felt I couldn't allow myself to engage in Jamaica. I could have done more had I not been so afraid of being shamed. For that I truly apologize.
>
> Trevor was incredulous: "Nobody nevah tell me sorry, you know. Nobody, man. . . . Nobody. . . . And you?! You say that?"

In turn, *he* offered forgiveness. He would forgive me for the shield I placed around my privileged Jamaican heart so that I could, defensively, inhabit other self-states defined by denial and non-recognition. And Trevor could let go of his own guilt for secretly hating me and himself for the things he did and for losing sight of his dreams.

Trevor and I re-imagined our *kismet.*[1] We were not doomed to honor the disposition of providence. We expanded our perception of the identified, or constructed "foreigner": He is, in reality, multidimensional. His razor-sharp gaze penetrates multi-layered veils of indifference, disturbing the "non-foreigner's" essentialist sense of stability and belonging. The foreigner is not to be valorized as victim of his new cultural position, for in the immigrant potential space the foreigner challenges constructed truths about self and other. He asserts his revolutionary capacities as acts of subversion against colonial essentialism (Bhabha, 1994) in whichever culture, and in whatever form, it finds practice. Trevor is now an outspoken activist on behalf of undocumented "immigrants."

Exodus! Album of the century: Reggae, the stranger/ foreigner/other, and the world

In 1999, Bob Marley and the Wailers' triumphant album of spiritual reflection, redemption, and forgiveness (*Exodus*, 1977b) was voted *Time Magazine's* Album of the Century. That same year, the BBC named a song from

1 Kismet. (1953). *Stranger in paradise*. Musical: Kismet. Play: Edward Knoblock (1911). Book: Charles Lederer and Luther Davis. Lyrics: Robert Wright and George Forrest. Music: Alexander Borodin: *Gliding dance of the maidens* (Polovtsian Dances, 1890).

that album, "*One Love*" (1977a) the "Song of the Millennium." How is this possible? In so many ways when I listen to, and watch him perform, I experience Bob Marley (1977c) as a man standing in the wilderness of time, palms turned upward to the heavens – *Moses-like* – in spiritual conviction that, as surely as the sun rises in the morning, so, too, can humanity loosen its defensive grip upon the pedestrian, recognize its limits, resignify its motives, and forge new meanings and possibilities in the intoxicating experience of (reframing Sullivan, 1953), "*being as sublimely human as we are sublimely otherwise*."

Jamaica is a small country in the vastness of this universe. Yet, we have produced a musical genre that transcends geography, politics, culture, race, difference, and the psychology of hate. Representing this genre and message, Bob Marley's songs of hope and possibility have reached across geographical boundaries and awakened into action the weary spirits of displaced peoples in Zimbabwe, South Africa, South Korea, Eastern Europe, and Japan, to name a few. This influence grows stronger, as even unexpected causes embrace the power of *Roots Reggae* music. The aboriginal peoples of Australia and Native Americans find place in reggae's wisdom; and one Jewish reggae artist/activist, from Brooklyn, a former Chassid named Matisyahu (2004), found meaning for *his* searching soul in reggae's harmony.

Music is a powerful instrument for effecting change, and the music that is psychoanalysis is possessed of the inherent capacity to illuminate human anxiety and to articulate messages of hope, as we stumble into the experience of knowing and being known. This is one unwritten, yet critical, imperative that falls at the feet of psychoanalysis as theory and practice. We recognize that journeying from subjective experience into interpersonal relating is, at best, complex. But psychological transformation – the capacity to see ourselves in the other and to see the other in us – is, in the poetry of Philip Bromberg (2011), that "most valuable gift that any human being will ever receive – the gift of intersubjectivity" (p. 14). Can this *gift* of psychoanalysis, like the musical gift of reggae music, be transported across geographical boundaries as a safe enough instrument within which difference might be negotiated?

Intersubjectivity: unplugged

Moses (Deuteronomy 6:4) said unto his people: "Shima Yisrael, Adonai eloheinu, Adonai echad": "Hear, O Israel: The Lord our God, the Lord is

One." Bob Marley (1977a) recognized that perpetuating national, political, and psychological ideologies centered upon the construction of Otherness condemns the world to the prophesies of Revelations 16:16: *Armageddon*. In his song of hope in the human potential for unity and possibility, Marley (1977a) submits to us an alternative path to the dooming powers of Armageddon: UNITY. Bob Marley (1977a) – prophet – speaks unto *Us*, who locate our relevance in the work of reaching across aisles and miles of difference, with peace and reconciliation in mind; unto *Us*, who internalize our Earth's vulnerabilities and heed its urgent call to action; unto *Us* Bob Marley sings: "One Love." Indeed, for a rich and deeply moving experience of reggae's reach across real and constructed differences, I recommend to you the masterful rendition of the "Song of the Millennium" by an international group of performers who call themselves Playing for Change (2009).

Finally, from a little island in the Caribbean Sea – Jamaica – with the creative potential and the will to exert influence upon the world's conscience, including our own. . . . *Yeah, Man*!

References

Akhtar, S. (1995). A third individuation: Immigration, identity, and the psychoanalytic process. *Journal of the American Psychoanalytic Association, 43*, 1051–1084.

Althusser, L. (2000). Ideology and state apparatus. In S. Zizek (Ed.), *Mapping ideology* (pp. 100–141). New York, NY: Verso. (Original work published 1969).

Altman, N. (2010). *The analyst in the inner city: Race, class, and culture through a psychoanalytic lens*. New York, NY: Routledge.

Aron, L. (1996). *A meeting of minds: Mutuality in psychoanalysis*. Hillsdale, NJ: The Analytic Press.

Bhabha, H. (1994). *The location of culture*. New York, NY: Routledge.

Bob Marley and the Wailers. (1974a). Dem belly full (But we hungry). In *Natty Dread*. Label: Island, Tuff Gong. Producer: Chris Blackwell.

Bob Marley and the Wailers. (1974b). No woman no cry. In *Natty Dread*. Label: Island/Tuff Gong. Producer: Chris Blackwell and Bob Marley and the Wailers.

Bob Marley and the Wailers. (1975). Trenchtown rock. In *Live*. Label: Island. Producers Bob Marley and the Wailers, Steve Smith and Chris Blackwell.

Bob Marley and the Wailers. (1976). War. In *Rastaman vibration*. Label: Island; Tough Gong. Producers: Bob Marley and the Wailers.

Bob Marley and the Wailers. (1977a). One love/People get ready. In *Exodus*. Label: Tuff Gong: Studio: Harry J. Studio (Jamaica), Island (London). Producer: Bob Marley and the Wailers.

Bob Marley and the Wailers. (1977b). Guiltiness. In *Exodus*. Label: Island, Tuff Gong. Studio. Producer: Bob Marley and the Wailers.

Bob Marley and the Wailers. (1977c). Three little birds. In *Exodus*. Label: Island, Tuff Gong. Producer: Bob Marley and the Wailers.

Bob Marley and the Wailers. (1980). Redemption song. In *Uprising*. Label: Island, Tuff Gong. Producer: Bob Marley and the Wailers.

Boulanger, G. (2004). Lot's wife, Cary Grant, and the American dream. *Contemporary Psychoanalysis*, *40*, 353–372.

Bradley, A., & DuBois, A. (2010). *The anthology of rap* (p. 2). New Haven, CT: Yale University Press.

Bromberg, P. M. (2011). *The shadow of the tsunami and the growth of the relational mind* (p. 55). New York, NY: Routledge.

Bromberg, P. M. (2012). Credo. *Psychoanalytic Dialogues*, *22*, 273–278.

Butler, J. (1997). *The psychic life of power: Theories in subjection*. Stanford, CA: Stanford University Press.

Chang, K. O., & Chen, W. (1998). *Reggae routes: The story of Jamaican music*. Philadelphia, PA: Temple University Press.

Cliff, J. (1972). Many rivers to cross. Album: *The Harder They Come*. Label: Island Writer: Jimmy Cliff. Vocals: Jimmy Cliff.

Cohen, L. (2001). That don't make it junk. Album: *Ten New Songs*. Label: Columbia. Studio: Producer: Sharon Robinson. Writer: Leonard Cohen, Sharon Robinson. Vocals: Leonard Cohen.

Desmond Dekker & The Aces. (1967). *007 (Shanty Town)*. Label: Pyramid. Producer: Leslie Kong.

Desmond Dekker & The Aces. (1968). *Israelite*. Label: Pyramid. Producer: Leslie Kong.

Deuteronomy 6:4. The Holy Bible, King James Version. (2000). Oxford University Press.

Dimen, M. (2011). Introduction. In M. Dimen (Ed.), *With culture in mind: Psychoanalytic stories* (p. 5). New York, NY: Routledge.

Eng, D., & Han, S. (2000). A dialogue on racial melancholia. *Psychoanalytic Dialogues*, *10*, 667–700.

Fab Five. (2007). Retrieved from www.Fab5inc.com; www.youtube.com/watch?v=4do90wML2os

Fanon, F. (1963). *The wretched of the earth* (p. 308). New York, NY: Grove.

Garvey, M. (1937). The work that has been done. *Black Man*, *3*, 10.

Gladwell, M. (2008). *Outliers*. New York, NY: Little, Brown & Co.

Goldman, V. (2006). *Exodus: The making and meaning of Bob Marley and the Wailers' album of the century*. New York, NY: Three Rivers Press.

Greene, B. (1999). *The elegant universe* (pp. 47–50). New York, NY: W. W. Norton & Co.

Grinberg, L., & Grinberg, R. (1989). *Psychoanalytic perspectives on migration and exile*. New Haven, CT: Yale University Press.

Guralnik, O. (2011). Interpellating grace. In M. Dimen (Ed.), *With culture in mind* (p. 125). New York, NY: Routledge.
The Harder They Come. (1972). Producer: Perry Henzell. Director: Perry Henzel; Writer: Perry Henzel, Trevor Rhone. Starring: Jimmy Cliff. Studio: International Films, Inc. Distributor: New World Pictures. Country: Jamaica, WI.
The Holy Bible. (2000). King James Version. Oxford University Press.
Kismet. (1953). *Stranger in paradise*. Musical: Kismet. Play: Edward Knoblock (1911). Book: Charles Lederer and Luther Davis. Lyrics: Robert Wright and George Forrest. Music: Alexander Borodin: *Gliding dance of the maidens* (Polovtsian Dances, 1890).
Kristeva, J. (1991). *Strangers to ourselves*. New York, NY: Columbia University Press.
Kapuscinski, R. (2006). *The other* (p. 45). New York, NY: Verso, 2008.
Layton, L. (2006). Attacks on linking: The unconscious pull to dissociate individuals from their social context. In L. Layton, N. Caro Hollander, & S. Gutwill (Eds.), *Psychoanalysis, class and politics: Encounters in the clinical setting* (pp. 107–117). New York, NY: Routledge.
Matisyahu. (2004). No water. In *Shake off the dust . . . arise*. Label: Jdub Records. Producers: Daniel Seliger, Alon Cohen.
McGilchrist, I. (2009). *The master and his emissary: The divided brain and the making of the western world* (p. 73). New Haven, CT: Yale University Press.
The Melodians. (1970). *By the rivers of Babylon*. Label: Pyramid. Producer: Leslie Kong.
Nettleford, R. (2006). *Rex N.: Selected speeches* (K. O. Hall, ed.). Kingston: Ian Randle Pub.
Playing for Change. (2009). *Song: One love*. Producer: Mark Johnson. Studio: Hear Music. Writer: Bob Marley. Performers: Playing for Change playingforchange.org. Retrieved from www.youtube.com/watch?v=4xjPODksI08&list)
Schore, A. (2011). Foreword. In P. M. Bromberg (Ed.), *The shadow of the tsunami and the growth of the relational mind* (pp. vii–xxxvii). New York, NY: Routledge.
Sherlock, P. M., & Bennett, H. (1998). *The story of the Jamaican people*. Princeton, NJ: Marcus Weiner Publishers, Inc.
The Skattalites. (1967). Ball of fire. In *Ska authentic, vol. I* (Album). Label: Studio One. Producer: Lee "Scratch" Perry.
Stern, D. B. (1990). Courting surprise: Unbidden perceptions in clinical practice. *Contemporary Psychoanalysis*, *26*, 452–478.
Stern, D. B. (1997). *Unformulated experience: From dissociation to imagination in psychoanalysis*. New York, NY: The Analytic Press.
Sullivan, H. S. (1953). *The interpersonal theory of psychiatry*. New York, NY: W. W. Norton & Co.
Wailers, The (1970). 400 years: In: *Soul Rebel*. Label:Upsetter/Trojan. Producer: Lee "Scratch" Perry.

The Wailers. (1973). Get up/Stand up. In *Burnin'*. Label: Tuff Gong; Island. Producer: Chris Blackwell and The Wailers.

White, C. (2004). Culture, influence, and the "I-ness" of me: Commentary on papers by Susan Bodnar, Gary B. Walls, and Steven Botticelli. *Psychoanalytic Dialogues, 14*, 653–691.

White, C. (2012, April). *I sing, therefore I am*. Paper presented at Division 39 annual conference. San Diego, CA.

Winnicott, D. W. (1971). Creativity and its origins (p. 92). In D. W. Winnicott (Ed.), *Playing and reality* (pp. 87–114). New York, NY: Routledge, 2005.

Part IV

Clinical theory

Chapter 7

Intersectionality, normative unconscious processes, and racialized enactments of distinction

Lynne Layton

In this essay, I explore the complexities involved when two people, patient and therapist, each raised in conditions marked by a range of social inequalities (e.g., class, race), meet in clinical work. In doing so, I connect my concept of normative unconscious processes (Layton, 2006a, 2014, in press) to an intersectional understanding of the formation and enactment of the identity categories that inform subjectivity. The version of intersectionality theory that I draw on here has been elaborated over many years, largely by gay and straight feminist women of color. Because the premises of this theory are thoroughly relational, intersectionality theory fits well with many of the basic premises of the psychosocial version of relational analytic thinking that informs my work. Intersectionality theory, for example, posits that identities are built in relation to whatever other identity constructs are circulating in a particular historical moment and in the context of particular power relations (Brah & Phoenix, 2004). Black working-class cultural representations of what is "feminine," for example, are understood to be constructed in relations of dominance and subordination to black working-class representations of what is "masculine," as well as to white working and middle-class representations of what is "feminine," etc. (Layton, 2015). The relational matrices within which subject formation takes shape consciously and unconsciously convey the many and fluid ways of living these intersecting cultural categories, including ways that defy the constraints imposed by systemic and symbolic inequality and violence (Layton, 1998/2004; Hamer, 2002). Yet, we cannot escape the fact that the way identity categories are lived is marked both by the systemic and symbolic violence embodied in power relations in the present – the various ways hierarchies of class, race, sex, and gender are constructed and embodied in laws and institutions – and by the past, history that remains alive in intergenerational transmissions of the psychic effects of previous social constructions and inequalities.

The historical circumstances and power relations into which we are born, and in which we live the intersecting identity categories, affect how we experience emotional states like shame and anger, dependence, assertion, and all the many constructs that are basic to our understanding of subjective psychological experience. Thus, in my view, identity categories, the power-inflected relations of sameness and difference they both describe and prescribe, and social histories of oppression, are not add-ons to the psyche, not defenses against something deeper, but rather something found at the very deepest layers of psychic life (Layton, 2006b, 2015; Layton, 2018, in press; see also, Fors, 2018). Indeed, I have become convinced over time that what primarily keeps alive the claim in our field that psychic reality can be understood without reference to social location is precisely the race and class privilege enjoyed by the dominant social groups to which our theory makers generally belong.

My understanding of the intersectional formation of subjectivity in relation is indebted to more than forty years of academic and activist work. The manifesto of the Combahee River Collective (1977), a black feminist movement of the 1970s, called on activists to think intersectionally about identity formation and political practice. These antiracist feminists understood their political praxis to have been shaped by their own lived experience as black gay and straight women; that experience had clearly revealed to them that "major systems of oppression are interlocking," in particular, sexism, heterosexism, racism, and classism. In elaborating an intersectional approach, they were not merely setting out to understand intersectional dynamics but were committing to use that understanding to transform practices, disciplines, and institutions.

In her work on antidiscrimination law, Kimberlé Crenshaw, an African-American law professor and critical race studies theorist, further elaborated what came to be known as intersectionality theory. In an essay on the Anita Hill-Clarence Thomas hearings, Crenshaw (1992), who had assisted Hill's legal team, argued that Hill's story had fallen on deaf ears because dominant feminist and antiracist discourses had left her no way to lay claim to being both female and black. Thus, the Hill-Thomas hearings crucially exemplified the ways in which identity categories are constructed in relation to other identity categories – and to the weight of history on identities. Hill's complaint against Thomas was appropriated by a white feminist narrative of sexual harassment that rested on assumptions of white female sexual purity, assumptions that did not work for a black woman in a dominant white culture. Further, Thomas's use of the lynching trope made black men and their sexuality the true victims of white racism. A black woman's story was not a hearable story and was thus rendered not believable.

At around the same time Crenshaw was articulating her thoughts on intersectionality, African-American historian Evelyn Brooks Higginbotham (1992) wrote about Celia, an enslaved black woman in the 1850s who killed the white master who had raped her repeatedly. In the courts of the time, a woman who killed a man in self-defense after sexual attack would have had a case to bring against her attacker. But the enslaved Celia was not deemed to be a woman. She was deemed property, and, as such, she had no recourse to justice. Like Crenshaw, Higginbotham showed how racial, sexual, class, and gender identities are inextricably interwoven with the political and economic conditions, and the sets of power relations, that exist in the era in which they are constructed. Gender and sexual identities are constructed intersectionally, always already raced and classed.

As Cho, Crenshaw, and McCall (2013) have argued, any elaboration of an intersectional approach must attend "to the institutional and field-specific ways that intersectionality is articulated" (p. 792). An intersectionally informed psychoanalysis, then, needs to look both at the way that interlocking systems of oppression are playing out in the clinic as well as to how they play out in our field at large. Since our field is distinguished from most other fields by its attention to unconscious process, one important application of intersectionality theory to psychoanalysis should be a focus on the ways that people, including therapists and patients, unconsciously reproduce, and consciously and unconsciously resist reproducing the inequalities of race, class, gender, and sexuality. Another should focus on the ways our institutions, our training models, our theories (e.g., of development), our conferences unconsciously reproduce and resist a racist, sexist, classist, and heterosexist status quo. The concept of normative unconscious processes that I have elaborated over many years links the psychic and the social in a way that illuminates how intersecting binary and hierarchically defined identity categories are unconsciously reproduced in the clinic.

Intersectionality, normative unconscious processes, and subject formation

As post-structuralist theorists who focus on identity and power have argued, white/black, straight/gay, male/female are categories that are socially constructed in binary and dichotomous relation – what is white is in good measure defined by what is not black, what is male as not female, what is straight as not gay. Further, power inequalities work in such a way that the first of each pair is figured as the ideal. Thus, identity categories are constructed not only as different, but as superior versus inferior. In the best of circumstances, these distinctions do not fully determine the psyche, but they mark the psyche in very particular and very deep ways.

Academic identity theories are rarely thought about psychoanalytically and thus are rarely described in terms of the lived conflictual experience of individuals. To think about the way identities in relation are formed and lived, we need to add to these theories what we know about the force of unconscious process and dynamic conflict. A vignette drawn from everyday contemporary life offers one illustration of how hierarchically and intersectionally constructed categories develop and are lived psychologically (reported in Layton, in press):

Emily, the 8-year-old daughter of good friends, had been making movies with her 9-year-old male friend, Joe. While visiting one evening, we quickly discerned that the proud parents wanted us to watch the movies, so watch them we did. Although I was prepared to be bored, I found "Lovestruck I, II, and III" to be an astounding trilogy, in which Emily and Joe had enacted a rather sophisticated presentation of class, race, sex, and gender conflicts. The theme of these three movies was the social barriers to the love between an upper-class white girl and a lower-class white boy. At first, the young lady, draped in an adult's fur boa, told her single dad, played by her father, that she was repelled by this "boy," whom they both call an "amateur" (which seemed to be their word for lower class). The boy earns her love by being good to his mom and the best student in the class; as they work on their projects together and she comes to see how very considerate and ambitious he is, the cold and distant emotional shield she has erected against whatever it is she considers to be associated with the poor begins to erode.

In all three films, money worries feature prominently. "Lovestruck III" concerns the financial difficulties they face in their married life. Attention is diverted from this problem when Emily is kidnapped by what the film represents as a black lower-class thief who shows all of the attributes of poverty against which Emily had erected her upper-class defenses in the first place – he's unkempt, loud, and boorish; takes rather than earns money; and is a sexual predator. A happy ending resolves the tensions, but it masks the fact that the film's social conflicts are unresolvable – and that they are psychic conflicts as well.

Emily is struggling her way into a raced, classed, sexed, and gendered position. Her fantasy suggests that this position is created and maintained by splitting off and projecting certain ways of expressing feeling, certain kinds of desire, disallowing certain kinds of activity. Her conflictual raced, gendered, and classed desire for upward mobility, which may involve such psychic phenomena as guilt over privilege or a longing to be able to enact some of the forbidden behaviors associated with the lower class and with blacks, or anger and confusion at her family's concern with money, or Oedipal conflict, is expressed in her desire for the poor boy. Her conflictual classed desire for upward mobility is managed in fantasy by the way she gives him the attributes that make him safe for marriage (i.e., the attributes that make him a good bourgeois).

The notion of what was desirable did not come solely from within – although Emily had made her own brew of what she had experienced, the shape of her desire was intergenerationally transmitted and mediated by parents, peers, teachers, and the all-white structure of the gentrifying geographic spaces in which she was living her life. Those white spaces segregated her from intimate contact with people of color and their living conditions. And so, although she surely would come to know of these conditions, she would be taught how NOT to take notice of them. Not to know the history hidden in plain sight.

The failure of Emily's attempts at management of her conflicts surfaces in the appearance of the black kidnapper, who grabs sex and money without guilt. The black kidnapper represents simultaneously something desired, something feared, and something that has to be repudiated. But the word "represents" may be misleading: I would argue that Emily only *becomes* a white, middle-class girl by racializing parts of herself as black and classing parts as lower class. And she becomes ambivalently attached to these extruded parts of self. When those repudiated parts are too anxiety provoking to be owned and integrated, they are projected, thus appearing not as intrapsychic conflict but rather as interpersonal conflict that is played out in relationships – over and over and over.

Thus, besides being an example of both conscious and unconscious aspects of identity's intersectionality and the effects of power, the vignette reveals the way that, in the process of identity formation, the emotions and psychological structures that we work with every day in therapy – dependency, assertion, vulnerability, desire, emotion – are gendered, raced, classed, and sexed at the deepest levels. The Emily example suggests that an intersectional analysis at the very least complicates, if not runs counter to, our prevalent theories of development.

Finally, the vignette reveals the force of history and the intergenerational transmission of social inequalities. French analysts Davoine and Gaudillière (2004) have well described the powerful effects of social history on the psyche. They have argued that the task of treatment is to unearth the intergenerational truth that has not yet been able to be spoken and that has thus issued in symptoms. In their view, the unspoken can always be traced back to some breach of trust that has ruptured the subject's capacity to rely on the moral lawfulness of the social world (see also, Benjamin, 2004, 2017). The rupture in the social link abandons the subject to a dyadic realm of victimizer/victim, kill or be killed. The restoration of trust, however, requires that the therapist recognize his or her part in the BIG history.

Intersectionality, normative unconscious processes, and clinical enactments of distinction

As mentioned earlier, relational analytic theory and practice have fit very well for me with both feminist and post-structuralist theories of the intersectional construction of identity within relational matrices marked by power differentials. I have taken relational understandings of the co-construction of analyses (e.g., Mitchell, 1988), of the patient's interpretation of the analyst's subjectivity (e.g., Aron, 1996; Hoffman, 1983), of the questioning of analytic authority (e.g., Hoffman, 1998), of the assumption that the therapist's unconscious bears significantly on the treatment, and of the belief in the inevitability of enactments and impasse (e.g., Levenson, 1972), and I have added to these tenets the suggestion that the unconscious and conscious micro-processes that mark all analytic sessions are inflected by culture and by the cultural inequalities within which subjectivity develops.

Along with other psychoanalytic feminists in the '90s (Benjamin, 1988; Dimen, 1991; Goldner, 1991; Harris, 1991), I began to think about how culturally constructed gender binaries enforce processes of splitting and projection. Although I believe that subjectivity is formed in negotiations of two kinds of relational experience, one in which our various ways of expressing ourselves are accepted and one in which parts of us are not accepted (Layton, 1998/2004), I chose to explore the latter in more depth, focusing on the psychological effects of splitting, of assigning some human capacities to one side of the split and others to the other side. I also began to describe and theorize the kind of enactments in which identities are performed in such a way that social inequalities are not only expressed but reproduced (Layton, 2002, 2004, 2006a, 2018, in press). While identities are never performed in perfect conformity with social norms, I wanted to understand what happens to the psyche when love and social approval are given only for certain ways of being human and not others, when norms permit certain identifications and encourage disidentifications with what is socially considered undesirable. I wanted to understand what it is like to LIVE the splits mandated by various binaries – to look at what becomes experienced as me and what not-me and how the not-me gets projected onto others. Noting an increasing number of clinical papers on unconscious enactments of unequal power relations, and beginning to understand more about the intersectional nature of subject formation, I suggested an umbrella term, "normative unconscious processes," to describe both intrapsychic and relational dynamics that enforce the splitting demanded by binary social constructions of gender, race, class, and sexuality, splitting in which one of the binary pair is deemed superior and one inferior.

Normative unconscious processes, as described in the work of many clinicians, including Neil Altman (2000), Kimberlyn Leary (2000), Susan Bodnar (2004), Melanie Suchet (2004), Stephen Hartman (2005), Gillian Straker (2006), Gary Walls (2006), Sue Grand (2013), Sheehi and Sheehi (2016), Nancy Hollander (2017), and Yvette Esprey (2017), are effects of an intergenerational transmission of trauma, not the kind of trauma we generally think about when we think about intergenerational transmission – war, famine, political oppression – but trauma nonetheless. They result from the way that historically generated social inequalities – enacted, as we have seen, in laws and both formal and informal living arrangements and social interactions – are experienced on an individual level. Norms and practices that derive from social hierarchies of sex(ism), class(ism), race(ism), and heterosex(ism) mandate what counts as a "proper" versus "improper" identity – both within a subculture and within dominant upper-middle class white culture. Recognition (in the form of social approval, love, and conditions for social belonging) is granted, albeit often conflictually, to "proper" performances of identity. The risk of meeting with indifference, humiliation, shame, and loss of love discourages "improper" performances and encourages subjects to split off as "not-me" disapproved of ways of being and relating, ways that provoke anxiety or shame in significant others and thus remain unrecognized. Because, however, what gets split off in normative unconscious processes are human needs, capacities, and longings, these do not disappear; rather, they reappear in symptoms and in relational struggles.

In fact, the result of the splitting intended to make a part of the self "other" always keeps what has been split off near. Because we project what we repudiate onto others and keep what has been split off near, the ways *we* have been wounded will often stir up the wounds of those with whom we seek intimate contact (Layton, 2015). Distinction from others, the use of identity to establish superiority, is often sought when trying to defend against the possibility of being hurt and humiliated, when trying to defend against exposing shameful vulnerabilities that you fear will at some point be used against you. But because normative unconscious processes involve splitting off part of what it means to be human, we simultaneously engage in counter-normative processes that attempt to integrate the splits and lay claim to all parts of human experience. Psychic and relational life are replete with instances in which we try to negate inhuman binary structures and instances in which we reproduce them. Repetition compulsions, in and outside the clinic, are the very place where these struggles between coercive normative unconscious processes and counter-normative unconscious processes are enacted, particularly at moments of heightened vulnerability.

Longings for what has been disowned and devalued create the ambivalence of racial and other stereotypes. The conscious and unconscious conflicted motivation simultaneously to contest and to sustain norms also renders patient-therapist enactments full of seemingly impossible double-binds, the stuff of clinical impasse. I do not think of these kinds of enactments as clinical errors. Rather, they are relational repetition compulsions in which psyches shaped by social inequalities of all kinds unconsciously reproduce the very psychosocial structures that caused psychic pain in the first place. Given the binary and hierarchical nature of identity categories, we find that at the heart of many such repetitions is what I refer to here as "enactments of distinction."

Clinical vignettes

In the clinical material that follows, I look at examples of normative unconscious processes that involve relational repetition compulsions in which one or both parties take refuge in distinction. I also suggest possible counterhegemonic resistances to dominant norms in these clinical interactions, but my main focus is on the ways we unconsciously reproduce an unequal status quo in the clinic. Attention to the intersectional nature of categories, to interlocking systems of oppression, points us to the ways in which some aspects of identity can at times be used defensively to mask the salience of other aspects. In most of these examples, we can see how shameful vulnerabilities that emerge as the price of inhabiting certain identity positions are split off and return in enactments that sustain inequality and obfuscate awareness of the ways we can become implicated in each other's suffering. An intersectional approach opens up more ways to understand such enactments and work with their overdetermined complexities.

First vignette

In his ground-breaking essay titled "Black and White Thinking," Neil Altman (2000) described an enactment centered on unconscious processes resulting from a complicated history of racial positionings. Altman, a white Jewish analyst, described work with an African-American man, Mr. A, who, after an early history of acting out to such an extent that his parents had put him in foster care, ended up going to Ivy League schools and founding a law practice devoted to social justice issues. Mr. A's father had recently asked him to repay tens of thousands of dollars that he had loaned Mr. A. Mr. A had hoped the money was a gift; he did not, however, confront his father and he repaid the money. But the request had greatly upset him, and he felt that his father was deferring to his wife's wishes. In his mind, this repeated his childhood trauma, the placement in foster care, which Mr. A felt had been his mother's idea; his father, he felt, had not stood up to her.

From early on, the treatment was marked by cancellation and payment issues: Mr. A would often cancel sessions at the last minute, and, shortly into treatment, he began writing checks, for both missed and attended sessions, that bounced. At first, Mr. A blamed the bank, saying it was a tool of the capitalist system. Altman did not take up the comment, although he was aware that "the capitalist system" might have been a cipher for "white Jew." After three months of check bouncing, Altman finally confronted

Mr. A, and he agreed to pay cash. Altman had a hard time confronting the patient, and self-analysis suggested to him that his difficulty had to do with racial histories and stereotypes – although he greatly admired the patient, he became aware of shame and guilt about his own racist stereotyping. He felt that he was positioning himself as the responsible and good white citizen and positioning the patient as the irresponsible, black criminal – on some level, he realized he had expected to get stiffed[1] by a black man. He also began to feel ashamed about his anger over his wishes to get paid: feeling like a greedy Jew, he was aware of the tortured history of white Jewish landlords extorting high rents from blacks living in the rundown neighborhoods in which government policies forced them to live. At one point, Altman tried to get the patient to reflect on feelings he might have had about having to pay for so many missed sessions. The patient, who already had said that he thought it was totally fair that he was charged, because Altman had been waiting for him, now explicitly said he felt that Altman's needs have to be met. Altman was surprised and wondered about the patient's needs. The patient assured him that he felt happy with the treatment. Altman then suggested that perhaps the patient was letting Altman feel what the patient had felt in the face of his father's demand for money – like Mr. A, Altman felt he'd been promised money, thought he had it, and then found that the money was withdrawn.

Mr. A "looked stunned" (p. 595). And shortly after, he spoke about his pattern of letting relationships die, and how he did not want that to happen here and that's why he wanted to keep up with the payments. He specifically said he only keeps up with the people who keep calling him. Altman feels the double-bind of enactment: if I keep calling, he feels cared about. But if I'm calling constantly about money and missed sessions, he may feel my needs come first. It is not clear how soon after this Mr. A stopped coming, but he left without notice and owing Altman a fair amount of money. Altman wondered if his delay in confronting the bounced checks was experienced by Mr. A as racist, whether it had made Mr. A feel that Altman expected a black man to bounce checks. He analyzed his own fear of becoming the oppressive white male, but he also conjectured that his "level of anger may also have made the specter of racist violence too powerful a fantasy" (p. 598). Analyzing a vignette by African-American analyst Kim Leary, in which she had assertively and calmly confronted a white patient's aggressively racist comment, Altman wondered if Leary was more comfortable with confrontation because she is not impeded by white guilt.

Altman concluded that white therapists in racist societies need to be aware of countertransferential disavowals of white racism. He recognized that he and Mr. A were unable to transcend the interchangeable victim/victimizer binary. The truth was not spoken; the rupture in the social link was not acknowledged and not repaired. In her commentary on the case, African-American analyst Janice Gump (2000) offered another way of looking at the impasse, suggesting that the problem in this case is that Altman overlooked the patient's shame – shame stemming both from his personal history and from the intergenerationally transmitted wounds of slavery, in which blacks were and continue to be constructed as the inferior bad other. Gump argued that Mr. A must have felt internally split between being the responsible Ivy League graduate and the boy so bad he was kicked out of his parents' house. Mr. A, Gump thinks, was looking for acceptance of his "unconscionable performance" (p. 622), the acceptance he did not get from his parents. Altman should have kept calling. Gump believes that Altman's inability to recognize Mr. A's shame stemmed from a failure to feel empathy for him. Gump argues that the rupture slavery produced in the social link appears still in whites' inability to see blacks as same and not other, and in many black parents' difficulty allowing their children to express anger and sadness.

My sense is that the impasse in the treatment did indeed have to do with the disavowal of racialization and racism. I agree with Gump that one needs to explore not just stereotypes but the ways that feelings like shame become raced, gendered, and classed. But I also think that the question of who has needs was central to the impasse, a question that also is gendered, raced, classed, and sexualized and lived relationally in a particular historical moment. As Altman suggests, both patient and therapist seem to be enacting a split between the responsible white citizen and the black criminal. By 2000, when Altman published this paper, a primary cultural image and subject position for African-American males was "the entrepreneurial criminal," the degraded black complement to the neoliberal idealized white entrepreneurial self. The black male criminal was also the split-off other side of the black female welfare dependent, she who held *all* of the country's disavowed need. Reagan's race politics, including the mass incarceration of black men that vastly accelerated in the '80s, and countless media images, had produced this new version of an old racialized binary. Neoliberal politics and economics have produced new forms of an old classed, raced, and gendered split between autonomy and dependency – entrepreneurial selves and black welfare queens are two raced, classed, and gendered instances of neoliberalism's repudiation of dependency and idealization of self-reliance. Need is lower class and female; need is black. In this case, I hear an unconscious repudiation by both patient and therapist of need, which becomes a hot potato between them of back and forth splitting and projection. Such a repudiation might signal an autonomy/dependency split once played out between middle-class white men and white women; in neoliberal times, it is played out between entrepreneurial selves and those lowest on the social scale. But because the dominant cultural position of masculinity has long been constructed on a repudiation of need, men still perhaps struggle more than women with showing need, especially to other men (recall that for Freud, 1937, a man's repudiation of a passive relation to another man, inducing male homoerotic and heterosexist panic/castration anxiety, was bedrock). In this case, neither man wants to be the needy one: Altman is ashamed of being the needy, greedy Jew, but he's angry because, as he states, he *needs* the money. We never find out why. Need is projected onto the patient, and he's having none of it. Indeed, though Mr. A surely must have felt shame, I imagine that he unconsciously also must have gotten enjoyment from the thought of Altman waiting for him and needing the money – needing it more than he needed treatment. Might his exit from treatment and refusal to pay be read as a counterhegemonic defiance of capitalist relations that historically built U.S. wealth on the backs of enslaved Africans? A defiant unmasking of denied and projected white need/dependency/vulnerability? I think that bringing up race in this case would optimally include, among other things, talking about how the racializing, classing, sexing, and gendering of need/dependency/vulnerability might have been playing out between them.

Second vignette

Susan Bodnar (2004), a white woman of working-class origin, has also written compellingly about a case marked by the therapist's fear of bringing up the way that racial differences and racism were inflecting the treatment. Bodnar was working with an African-American woman, Lisa, who entered therapy because of inexplicable fits of anger that were damaging her relationships. Bodnar writes in an interpersonal frame. She posits that most of us with multiple and conflicting identity commitments end up dissociating those self-states that have not been met with acceptance and have become associated with pain and/or the fear of raising the anxiety of someone whose love and acceptance is important to them. Lisa, her very beautiful patient, was often late because of various interfering beauty treatments, like getting her nails done. This increasingly annoyed Susan,[2] but only after a while did she realize that the reason she didn't bring it up was because she was envious of the patient's beauty. Once she realized this, she brought it up. Unexpectedly, this self-disclosure brought race into the room for the first time. Lisa was astounded that a white person could be envious of a black person. Why? Because Lisa had been raised by parents (and a culture) who associated the good with white, the bad with black, and the less bad with less black.

Lisa then realized she'd been trying for some time to make Susan envious and that she had interpreted Susan's seeming indifference to these attempts as evidence of Susan's racism. In other words, Lisa was trying to prove that Susan believed, as she did, that envy only travels from black to white. This unconscious mutual collusion was, in my view, a resistance to treatment, a perverse pact (Gerson, 1996; Stein, 2005), and a traumatic re-enactment of an as yet unable to be spoken rupture in the social link, that is, the history of racist race relations (Layton, 2019). The enactments also suggest, however, that on some unconscious level Lisa must have hoped that Susan would somehow prove her wrong. And she did. Susan writes that her honesty broke this enactment and then allowed Lisa to talk more about family secrets, the rupture in the intergenerational social link that had led to symptoms. It turns out that her paternal grandfather had been a Southern bootlegger and alcoholic. Terrified as a young man by the frequent lynchings in the Jim Crow South, he had tried to keep himself and his family safe by going into a business that would provide whites with something they wanted: alcohol. He also beat his children. As Isabel Wilkerson (2011) writes in *The Warmth of Other Suns*, parental practices of Southern blacks were often authoritarian and strict, sometimes to the point of severely hampering their children's autonomy and exuberance. These practices were constructed in no small measure from the parents' terror of Southern racism and the violent reprisals whites enacted when blacks were perceived as transgressing Jim Crow laws – as noted earlier, black men were lynched for merely looking at white women. As Gail Lewis (2009) suggests, such historically produced everyday parenting practices are instances of how whites and blacks are co-implicated in the construction of blackness; the practices at once contest, conform to, mimic, and survive white racism. The very way love is given and felt, as anyone who has ever read Toni Morrison's novels (e.g., *Beloved*, 1987) can attest, is conditioned by the social circumstances in which love is allowed to be practiced.

In reaction to his own father's beatings, Lisa's father had sustained his sanity by demanding that the family live in the rigid world of white good/black bad. Bodnar writes that Lisa was left "with a peculiar set of dissociative symptoms that document traumatic events in our social history" (p. 596; on dissociative symptoms and cultural oppression, see Guralnik & Simeon, 2010). Most importantly, Bodnar recognizes that while, on the surface, Lisa's angry outbursts did not seem connected to race but rather to her father's rigidity, the deeper they went in treatment, the more apparent was the force of racialization and racism. The question to be answered was "whose rage is Lisa expressing, and what is that rage about?" The rage passed down in intergenerationally transmitted patterns of intimacy had everything to do with race.

These cases well exemplify my point that, in conditions of social injustice, parts of self are coded good or bad, and ways of living dependence, assertion, guilt, and love are socially inflected. Difference is not lived merely as difference, A versus B, but as distinction, A versus minus A, the latter the deficient version of the former. What emotions are allowed? Who is allowed to experience envy? Who allowed to be enraged? Who to be needy or assertive, accomplished, lazy? What have been one's models of loving? What Homi Bhabha (1994) has described as the ambivalence of the stereotype is the outcome of the narcissistic wounding that mandates splitting off human capacities and attributes, an impossible demand. Both sides of the split lack some important aspect of being human, so what the other has is both repudiated and desired; both sides of the split become deformed, and, as we see in the following case, damagingly stereotypical.

Third vignette: the couple and the conference – institutional-level enactments

For a while, I saw an upper-middle class African-American couple in weekly therapy. As in all couples therapies, one task of the therapist is to empathize with each member of the couple, but in this case feeling empathy was complicated by my own social positioning and by their very different ways of experiencing the wounds of racism, sexism, and class distinction. He was in a profession that was largely white, male, highly paid, and highly demanding. Although both were well-educated professionals, over time they had fallen into inhabiting traditional white, middle-class, split-gender roles in which he was the breadwinner and she the keeper of the home. He needed her to bolster his self-esteem, which repeatedly was battered by what they both felt was racism at work. She supported him, but at the same time she expressed the pain she felt at having so little time with him *not* by asking for time, which she thought would have gone nowhere since he felt he *had* to work as much as he did, but by giving moralizing lectures about how various aspects of his character were deficient. The ostensible purpose of these lectures was to help him be more successful at work. In therapy he would often rage at her for not having stopped him, many years ago, from working all the time. But it was clear to me and to her that his racial, class, and gender history had made him constantly feel he had to prove himself to his white and mostly male superiors. Indeed, she had supported his occasional job searches at black institutions, but it would soon become clear that, for him, a black institution did not hold the same allure as a prestigious white one. One thing that struck me was how their gendered relational pattern revealed the very different ways they experienced the wounds of racism – he felt that those moments in which he wasn't included or promoted at work had to do with racism and that there was nothing a black man could do to be rewarded in the way he felt he deserved to have been. She agreed that there was racism at work, but she felt that his frequent lateness for meetings and disorganization gave fuel to the racism and that, if he corrected his behavior, he'd be more respected – she believed that a black man *could* succeed – if he was extra good. In the end, he felt unappreciated and misunderstood not only at work but also at home. He spent less and less time at home, and thus more and more home work fell to her, reinforcing her sense of gender oppression. Both felt lonely; neither felt loved or seen.

What was hard for me was that, at times, to empathize with her was to empathize with a version of internalized racism in which she validated the norms of white success and seemed to suggest that color blindness is possible – what we might call a respectability politics. To empathize with him was to empathize with a version of cultural and personal sexism that had really harmed both of them, the splitting of roles into breadwinner and relationship-tender. To point to what that had done to her felt unempathic to him, as though I too didn't really get how much time and effort a black man has to spend in the workplace in order to find acceptance. When she described his lax behavior and harshness toward her, she appealed to me as a woman fed up with selfish male behavior.

To complicate the situation further, in several early sessions he brought his resumes and monographs to show me. He brought them to me as the white professional woman who has the power to confer worth. His problem feeling worthy had everything to do with race. But gender, sexuality, and the history of race relations in white supremacist culture complicated how the conflict played out in the clinic. His appeal to me to confer worth embroiled us in an old historical pattern in black/white relations, the one in which the black male repudiates the black female by seeking white female recognition, and in which the white female herself may well have unconscious desires propelling her toward protecting or desiring the black male. Historically, this pattern has set white women up against black women and has frequently interfered with the development of black/white female political solidarity (see, e.g., Breines, 2006). I think my female patient often felt I was too indulgent toward her husband, and I believe I was. Indeed, when I presented the case at a psychoanalytic conference in which there were a lot of women of color present, it was clear that they, too, felt angry that I had not challenged what he was doing in turning to me for validation. I did not acknowledge my role in the BIG history. But the anger of the women at that conference was not only about what I was doing with this couple. In fact, that conference was a good example of how enactments pile upon enactments when the intersectional wounds of racism and sexism are unspoken or just beginning to be spoken.

The conference was on diversity and treatment. Uncommon for that time was the number of women of color in the audience. On stage were three of the four invited speakers: two white Jews, one male and one female, and a British man of Southeast Asian origin. Absent was the invited African-American woman, who had to miss the conference because of family issues. The organizers had asked her to send her paper, but she declined. Nonetheless, the absence of the black woman was very much a psychic presence. This was manifest in several ways, first, in a difficulty dialoguing about whatever it was that had caused audience anger at both my paper and Altman's. But it was perhaps most manifest when a black female conference respondent, who had been asked to speak from the floor for five minutes, took the stage and delivered a forty-minute paper. I think there was an unspoken and perhaps unconscious group need to replace the missing black woman, but no dialogue about that was possible. Neither her paper nor subsequent conversations shed light, for me or for the other panelists and organizers, on what intergenerationally transmitted traumas between whites and blacks, men and women, were being enacted that day. I recall having wished that space had been made to process what had happened at the conference. From my current vantage point, I would say that at conferences bold enough to take up the wounds of history (Salberg & Grand, 2017), it is absolutely necessary to make space for processing the inevitable enactments that occur.

Such enactments exemplify the ways that intersectional normative unconscious processes play out at the institutional level (see also Lewis, 2013). Another such example occurred in a conference in which I was asked to discuss a case presentation by a young clinician on a panel set up explicitly to focus on intersectionality. The panel was titled, "The Trifecta: Gender, Race, and Sexuality." Here, a fourth category was unconsciously denied its place as an intersectional category: class. As it happens, the case was shot through and through with class, and, in fact, the major unconscious enactment in the case was around class distinction. Interestingly, when the presenter sent me the case, she told me that she had to delete some material because of time constraints, but she had left in what she had crossed out so I could see it. Each instance of crossed-out material was about class. This enactment of intersectional normative unconscious processes, like many, was overdetermined – the panel's title enabled the presenter to know and not know, to hide in plain sight what she later revealed to be a vulnerable part of herself, particularly in this context of being a clinician in training presenting to more senior colleagues.

To conclude, I want to summarize my main points: (1) In thinking about how identities are enacted, we need to recognize the effects of social inequalities, both as intergenerationally transmitted and as currently lived. (2) To do so, we have to look not just at racial inequalities, but at the multiple ways that systemic racism interlocks with systemic classism, sexism, and heterosexism. (3) And what I mean by looking at these intersections is that we think about how states, feelings, and capacities are culturally shaped as well as coded good or bad. Then we have to look at how the particular person with whom we are working has, from experiences of both acceptance and rejection, coded his or her various parts of self. (4) Finally, we have to be aware, as therapists, of the BIG history and our part in it, of what we have made "Other", what we ourselves have split off to become proper and loved raced, classed, sexed, and gendered subjects; what we split off to become less vulnerable to hurt and humiliation; what we split off to maintain privilege. Only then can we be aware of how our own enactments of distinction obscure our awareness of the ways in which we are different, similar, and mutually interdependent with our patients. Only then can we work toward addressing those ruptures in the social link that leave us all vulnerable to the double-binds of unconscious enactment, that can leave us foundering in the paranoid-schizoid realm of kill or be killed. In the spirit of the Combahee River Collective and other feminist and antiracist theorists of intersectionality, I hope that the intersectional understanding of conscious and unconscious process that I have elaborated here will be taken up in ways that transform our practices and our institutions.

Notes

1 In speaking a version of this essay, I stumbled over the word "stiffed," and I was tempted to change it in this written version. But I think that, unconsciously, I had used the word because I was "feeling" the sexual, homoerotic elements of the case that I had omitted from my analysis before fully recognizing them; the slip of the tongue and the stumble became clues that something was missing from my intersectional analysis, something known and not known.

2 In the same spirit, I found myself changing "Susan" to "Bodnar" once I had noticed that in the previous case, I was using "Altman" throughout to refer to the therapist. Upon further reflection, I thought that I should leave it as it was because I think that, among other possible meanings, the slip says something about my unconscious relation to female versus male therapists.

References

Altman, N. (2000). Black and White thinking: A psychoanalyst reconsiders race. *Psychoanalytic Dialogues*, *10*(4), 589–605.

Aron, L. (1996). *A meeting of minds: Mutuality in psychoanalysis*. Hillsdale, NJ: The Analytic Press.

Benjamin, J. (1988). *The bonds of love*. New York, NY: Pantheon.

Benjamin, J. (2004). Beyond doer and done-to: An intersubjective view of thirdness. *Psycho-Analytic Quarterly*, *73*, 5–46.

Benjamin, J. (2017). *Beyond doer and done-to: Recognition theory, intersubjectivity, and the third*. New York, NY: Routledge.

Bhabha, H. K. (1994). *The location of culture*. New York, NY: Routledge.

Bodnar, S. (2004). Remember where you come from: Dissociative process in multicultural individuals. *Psychoanalytic Dialogues*, *14*(5), 581–603.

Brah, A., & Phoenix, A. (2004). Ain't I a woman? Revisiting intersectionality. *Journal of International Women's Studies*, *5*(3), 75–86.
Breines, W. (2006). *The trouble between us: An uneasy history of Black and White women in* the *feminist movement*. Oxford: Oxford University Press.
Cho, S., Crenshaw, K. W., & McCall, L. (2013). Toward a field of intersectionality studies: Theory, applications, and praxis. *Signs*, *38*(4), 785–810.
Combahee River Collective. (1977). *The Combahee River Collective statement*. Retrieved September 1, 2018, from http://circuitous.org/scraps/combahee.html
Crenshaw, K. (1992). Whose story is it, anyway? Feminist and antiracist appropriations of Anita Hill. In T. Morrison (Ed.), *Race-ing justice, en-gendering power* (pp. 402–440). New York, NY: Pantheon.
Davoine, F., & Gaudillière, J. M. (2004). *History beyond trauma* (S. Fairfield, trans.). New York, NY: Other Press.
Dimen, M. (1991). Deconstructing difference: Gender, splitting, and transitional space. *Psychoanalytic Dialogues*, *1*(3), 335–352.
Esprey, Y. (2017). The problem of thinking in Black and White: Race in the South African clinical dyad. *Psychoanalytic Dialogues*, *27*(1), 20–35.
Fors, M. (2018). *A grammar of power in psychotherapy*. Washington, DC: American Psychological Association.
Freud, S. (1937). Analysis terminable and interminable. *The Standard Edition of the Complete Psychological Works of Sigmund Freud*, *23*, 209–254.
Gerson, S. (1996). Neutrality, resistance, and self-disclosure in an intersubjective psychoanalysis. *Psychoanalytic Dialogues*, *6*(5), 623–645.
Goldner, V. (1991). Toward a critical relational theory of gender. *Psychoanalytic Dialogues*, *1*(3), 249–272.
Grand, S. (2013). God at an impasse: Devotion, social justice, and the psychoanalytic subject. *Psychoanalytic Dialogues*, *23*, 449–463.
Gump, J. (2000). A White therapist, an African American patient – shame in the therapeutic dyad: Commentary on paper by Neil Altman. *Psychoanalytic Dialogues*, *10*(4), 619–632.
Guralnik, O., & Simeon, D. (2010). Depersonalization: Standing in the spaces between recognition and interpellation. *Psychoanalytic Dialogues*, *20*, 400–416.
Hamer, F. M. (2002). Guards at the gate: Race, resistance, and psychic reality. *Journal of the American Psychoanalytic Association*, *50*(4), 1219–1237.
Harris, A. (1991). Gender as contradiction. *Psychoanalytic Dialogues*, *1*(3), 197–224.
Hartman, S. (2005). Class unconscious: From dialectical materialism to relational material. *Psychoanalysis, Culture & Society*, *10*(2), 121–137.
Higginbotham, E. B. (1992). African American women's history and the metalanguage of race. *Signs*, *17*(2), 251–274.
Hoffman, I. Z. (1983). The patient as interpreter of the analyst's experience. *Contemporary Psychoanalysis*, *19*, 389–422.
Hoffman, I. Z. (1998). *Ritual and spontaneity in the psychoanalytic process*. Hillsdale, NJ: The Analytic Press.

Hollander, N. (2017). Who is the sufferer and what is being suffered? Subjectivity in times of social malaise. *Psychoanalytic Dialogues*, *27*(6), 635–650.
Layton, L. (1998). *Who's that girl? Who's that boy? Clinical practice meets post-modern gender theory*. Hillsdale, NJ: The Analytic Press, 2004.
Layton, L. (2002). Cultural hierarchies, splitting, and the heterosexist unconscious. In S. Fairfield, L. Layton, & C. Stack (Eds.), *Bringing the plague: Toward a postmodern psychoanalysis* (pp. 195–223). New York, NY: Other Press.
Layton, L. (2004). That place gives me the heebie jeebies. *International Journal of Critical Psychology: Psycho-Social Research, 10*, 36–50. Reprinted in L. Layton, N. C. Hollander, & S. Gutwill. (2006). *Psychoanalysis, class and politics: Encounters in the clinical setting* (pp. 51–64). New York, NY: Routledge.
Layton, L. (2006a). Racial identities, racial enactments, and normative unconscious processes. *Psychoanalytic Quarterly*, *LXXV*(1), 237–269.
Layton, L. (2006b). Attacks on linking: The unconscious pull to dissociate individuals from their social context. In L. Layton, N. C. Hollander, & S. Gutwill (Eds.), *Psychoanalysis, class and politics: Encounters in the clinical setting* (pp. 107–117). New York, NY: Routledge.
Layton, L. (2014). Normative unconscious processes. In T. Teo (Ed.), *Encyclopedia of critical psychology*. Retrieved from www.springerreference.com/docs/html/chapterdbid/307088.html
Layton, L. (2015). Beyond sameness and difference: Normative unconscious process and our mutual implication in each other's suffering. In D. Goodman & M. Freeman (Eds.), *Psychology and the other* (pp. 168–188). Oxford: Oxford University Press.
Layton, L. (2019). Transgenerational hauntings: Towards a social psychoanalysis and an ethic of dis-illusionment. *Psychoanalytic Dialogues*, 29(2), 105–121.
Layton, L. (in press). *Toward a social psychoanalysis: Culture, character, and normative unconscious processes*. New York, NY: Routledge.
Leary, K. (2000). Racial enactments in dynamic treatment. *Psychoanalytic Dialogues*, *10*, 639–653.
Levenson, E. A. (1972/2005). *The fallacy of understanding*. Reprinted with *the ambiguity of change*. Hillsdale, NJ: The Analytic Press.
Lewis, G. (2009). Birthing racial difference: Conversations with my mother and others. *Studies in the Maternal*, *1*(1), 1–21.
Lewis, G. (2013). Unsafe travel: Experiencing intersectionality and feminist displacements. *Signs*, *38*(4), 869–892.
Mitchell, S. A. (1988). *Relational concepts in psychoanalysis*. Cambridge, MA: Harvard University Press.
Morrison, T. (1987). *Beloved*. New York, NY: Vintage Books.
Salberg, J., & Grand, S. (Eds.). (2017). *Wounds of history: Repair and resilience in the trans-generational transmission of trauma*. New York, NY: Routledge.
Sheehi, L., & Sheehi, S. (2016). Enactments of otherness and searching for a third space in the Palestine-Israel matrix. *Psychoanalysis, Culture & Society*, *21*(1), 81–99.

Stein, R. (2005). Why perversion? "False love" and the perverse pact. *International Journal of Psychoanalysis*, *86*, 775–799.

Straker, G. (2006). The anti-analytic third. *Psychoanalytic Review*, *93*(5), 729–753.

Suchet, M. (2004). A relational encounter with race. *Psychoanalytic Dialogues*, *14*(4), 423–438.

Walls, G. (2006). The normative unconscious and the political contexts of change in psychotherapy. In L. Layton, N. C. Hollander, & S. Gutwill (Eds.), *Psychoanalysis, class, and politics: Encounters in the clinical setting* (pp. 118–128). New York, NY: Routledge.

Wilkerson, I. (2011). *The warmth of other suns: The epic story of America's great migration*. New York, NY: Vintage Books.

Chapter 8

Intersectionality encountering Laplanche

Models of otherness and the incomprehensibility of perpetration

Julie Leavitt and Adrienne Harris

Introduction

In this essay, we take up the concept of intersectionality along interwoven threads of inquiry. In one thread we extend Crenshaw's term "mutual elision" (Crenshaw, 1991, p. 1252), which she uses to describe the driving force behind intersectionality that operates in social systems of domination. Here, people who are caught[1] among multiple, marginalized identifications are consequently multiply vulnerable to subordination, through the denial of certain dimensions of their identity enabled by these mutually eliding convergences within such systems of power. Considered psychoanalytically, we elaborate "mutual elision" as a psychical force operating at the interface between individual- and social-unconscious. As such it obscures the awareness of the one perpetrating the intersectional subordination, because of the blinding effect of one's *incomprehensibility*[2] to see oneself as capable of enacting such insidious, socialized violence toward another.

Extending this thesis along a second thread, we cross Laplanche's "enigmatic transmission" with Crenshaw's idea of intersectionality. We illustrate how his model, in which subjectivity 'arrives' from the other, is imbricated in "mutually eliding" aspects of multiple subjectivities: gender, sexual desire, racial identity, class and cultural formation. Through the negation that mutual elision incites culturally, these enigmatically transmitted identifications may become, across generations, harboring sites for historical trauma. In the United States, this is perhaps most acutely true in regard to race.

To illustrate these ideas, we give complex clinical examples involving white, female patients, whose whiteness – intersecting with their (specifically female) sexuality – elides race in ways that were incomprehensible to them, their white analysts and psychoanalytic theorizing itself.

Part I: Intersectionality, mutual elision and the incomprehensibility of perpetration

As a backdrop, we begin by briefly explaining the idea of "mutual elision" which, as the driving force behind intersectionality, becomes a nidus of socialized patterning that propagates an 'incomprehensibility of perpetration' from the individual to the collective.

Kimberle Crenshaw (1989) explains "intersectionality" as a phenomenon with detrimental social and political consequences, in which two or more potentially powerful axes of socialized identity are "inertly juxtaposed": for example, in her thesis on antiracism and feminism, "to the extent that they can forward the interest of 'people of color' and 'women,' respectively, one analysis[3] often implicitly denies the validity of the other." "These *mutual elisions,*" Crenshaw concludes, "present a particularly difficult political dilemma for women of color. *Adopting either analysis constitutes a denial of a fundamental dimension of [her] subordination*" (Crenshaw, 1991, p. 1252, italics added).

With mutual elision, in other words, people who straddle two or more subordinated categories in the social field fall through a socially established (if also collectively unconscious) hole in the floor of political allegiance, where the "denial of a fundamental dimension of [their] subordination" is enacted. It is around this double-denial of a person's subjectivity – first through their subordination at one identity dimension, then through the concealment of that subordination by another, "inertly juxtaposed" identity dimension – that we ask: who is doing the denying, what is being denied, and why? In other words, from a socio-psychical perspective, where are the actual sites of intra- and interpsychic denial of subordination: by what forces do they emerge? In whom? And how might one then confront and disarticulate them? We can use the lens of psychoanalysis while also critiquing that lens, to explore how intersectionality not only reveals the denial of certain people's subordination but also uncovers an active, if unconscious, 'perpetration' of socialized othering accompanying that denial. Further, the 'incomprehensibility' in those who perpetrate blinds them to their perpetrating acts. The blinding force of incomprehensibility circularly reinforces systems of power precisely because its presence functions to elide: it seeds and disseminates from the psyches of individuals to societal groups and systems that hold power along axes of identification, including race, gender, class, etc. Historically, psychoanalysis has been one such group: in its belief in its own relative neutrality, it has been vulnerable to blindness of its incomprehensibility to perpetrate intersectional subordination through unconscious cultural identifications and biases in its theories and praxis: namely as white, phallocentric/patriarchal, heteronormative and class-elitist.

We have chosen the word 'perpetration' carefully, recognizing the charge that this word carries in its potential association to externalizing blame, which risks inflaming feelings of guilt that prohibit rather than motivate deep self-inquiry toward change. However, perpetration names the socialized, violating act that results in the subordination of people caught at the intersection of marginalized groups that Crenshaw describes, making it accessible for interrogation and dismantling. Perpetration also problematizes our thesis: because of its cultural link with acts of 'sexual' aggression, it implicates not just sexuality as an identity but also the sexual act itself as among the power axes that drive intersectionality socially. Here, Laplanche's idea of "enigmatic transmission" (Laplanche, 1997, 1999), in which the enigma of "the sexual" is unconsciously passed from mother to child, can be extended as a useful model for understanding these socially unconscious, mutually eliding forces at work in intersectionality.

Laplanche's unconscious: asymmetrical transmission from parent to child

Laplanche continuously and insistently uses the term "maternal seduction" to convey the experience in which messages, remaining initially unconscious to sender and receiver, are an inevitable experience of early parent-child engagement (1997). He is most insistent on the matter of asymmetry. It is this insistence that led him to organize this aspect of his theory under the rubric "The General Anthropological Situation." The persons involved in the transmission from the adult side will vary: parents, caretakers, siblings and others the child encounters. But while the person varies, asymmetry in the relation of adult to child is a constant. Stein (2005), Saketopoulou (2014a, 2014b, in press) and others draw on these ideas in order to think of the message as inherently containing excess.

Messages, which are passed from the unconscious of the adult to the child, transmit in an enigmatic, unpredictable process. To a large degree the messages are uncoded by sender or receiver, at least at the point of transmission. Laplanche's central and brilliant insight/discovery is that it is these enigmatic messages that come to constitute the unconscious in the child. Infantile sexuality in the child is the outcome of enigmatic intrusions from the other: one outside the child but deeply entrenched. The child is not empty, but initially helpless. This particular intrusion happens over time and over a child's development.

Whatever sensory and receptive/enactive processes are in the child, sexuality, in the form of the infantile sexuality of the adult, arrives from an alien source. It is this part of the theory that adds so powerfully to the concept of intersectionality: namely the sensitivity and susceptibility of the child to sexualization from 'others.' This work is a definitive move from the notion of innate drive and endogenous forms of sexuality. Laplanche argues that we are sexed, male and female; we are gendered: that arrives as an ascription; and we are sexualized via messages from the sexual unconscious of others.

What makes Laplanche such an important theoretical partner for Crenshaw is his commitment to the power of the other, parental sibling, someone other than the child as a transmitter of messages (conscious and unconscious) to the child which slowly and inexorably constitute the child's sexuality and infantile unconscious sexuality as these messages are translated. This is a theory of sexuality, one of the crucial elements in Crenshaw's model that is socially and interpersonally constituted. Laplanche offers a model of development in which the forces of history, social experience and desire arrive inevitably in, to and for the child. It is a model of interpersonally derived forms of identity that constitute the relational mechanism through which Crenshaw's conflicting identity experiences are instantiated in the individual child, in a way and at a stage of early helplessness and vulnerability.

Case material – preamble

We present two clinical examples: one historic, from Joan Riviere's famous and frequently cited "Womanliness as a Masquerade" (Riviere, 1929), the other a contemporary, actual analytic case.

We offer this as a preamble to the case material:

It is critical to recognize that white analysts are ill equipped to write about non-white patients around racial projects in the consulting room, until we exhaustively explore race from within, in the context of working with patients who are white. If that confuses the reader, then behold!

You are right now caught in a moment of mutual elision. In fact, the refusal to explore race, whether implicitly or explicitly, between white analyst and white patient, reveals an intersectional, mutual elision of race in psychoanalysis itself. Here, race is white-washed so to speak, within the presumed-white matrix that comprises and reinforces the normative unconscious (Layton, 2002) of the profession. However, analysts might struggle to understand how it could be possible, never mind useful and even imperative, to think about race in a white-on-white analytic encounter. Indeed in the realm of "sameness," the notion that "difference" could be taken up as part of the transference is apt to evoke concerns of straying from one's role as psychoanalyst qua analyst, for the analyst bringing in her 'social' subjectivity. Contrarily, it is *de rigueur* in contemporary psychoanalytic circles to include race dynamics between analyst and patient when there is a perceived *difference* there, lest the analyst be caught in a countertransference reaction of avoiding the analysand's presumed transference at that interface of difference. This is also true in the assumptions we inevitably make in any analysis with regard to how gender and sexuality differences are perceived and performed in the analytic encounter. These assumptions, based on our own identities and those we spontaneously construct about patients (and which are generally plotted within binary system), live implicitly in the conceptual identity matrices we weave, which fundamentally set the stage of our analytic formulations around these two bedrock identity vectors. These implicit constructs of identity difference become central to our transference/countertransference formulations (think maternal/paternal transference, erotic transference, etc.)[4] (see work of Dimen, 2003). So mapped onto race, might we also conjecture that race gets performed – experienced, enacted – in all manner of ways between white people as it does between different races?

Breaking out of this mutual elision in the field necessitates including the ways race lives in white-on-white analytic treatments as part of the transference-countertransference matrix. Equally important, by taking up 'white' from within, one avoids the risk of making patients of color a projective screen for the in-process work of disassembling racialized beliefs and exposing white-ness blind spots in psychoanalysis. This forces them to do that work for white people, which is not only reprehensible[5] but also does nothing to break through the incomprehensibility barrier in the field, so fraught with the corrupting vicissitudes of guilt and projection.

Case material proper: Laplanche, intersectionality and Joan Riviere's masqueraded woman

In the first 'case,' intersectionality is engaged with Laplanchian models of enigmatic transmission, through a key clinical elaboration of material discussed by Joan Riviere in 1929. Intersectionality is examined for its interpenetration and interpellation of racial violence into a Southern girl's fantasy. The meaning of these excitements and fantasies has been, over nearly 100 years, elaborated in terms of femininity and homosexuality, and almost never of race. We use this material to reflect on how intersectionality may be drawn into discussions of the elaboration and developmental trajectories of female sexuality.

Laplanche built his unique theory of sexuality in the individual in a dialogue with Freudian one-person psychology and metapsychology. He made a radical step to place the origins of any person's sexual identity as emergent from enigmatic transmissions from 'the other.' He made some attempts to expand this model to include gender. For psychoanalysis, at this point in its evolution in which we are bound to consider social unconsciousness as well as the intersubjective and the intrapsychic, we have the possibility of a very rich account of how historical and socially derived categories of experience interact in unique, unpredictable and emergent forms. Laplanche's models of enigmatic transmission, otherness, and après-coup synthesize a very new and unique developmental model, with many similarities and common elements to nonlinear dynamic systems theories (Harris, 2009) and other field theories (Lewin, 1951; Baranger & Baranger, 2008; Stern, 2013a, 2013b).[6]

Womanliness as a masquerade[7]

Joan Riviere, very much immersed in Kleinian accounts of identification and unconscious fantasy, drew an intriguing picture of female anxiety in relation to agency, power and sexuality. She was outlining with clinical material many women's anxious turn away from an experience of subjective empowerment or ambition, an undoing designed to reassure others – mostly men – that there was no threat. It is in the mutual elision which we can see operating here in Riviere's theorizing, that misogyny does its destructive work. But buried in this text is another perpetration scene, a mutual elision where race, gender and sexuality are simultaneously criminalized and eroticized.

So as to think about intersectionality and mutual elision, we focus on one example, taken from a woman in treatment, presumably in the 1920s. As background, the following is the text from Riviere that is importantly put in question. Riviere is detailing a childhood masturbatory fantasy of the patient, whom she identifies as an American from the south:

> This phantasy, it then appeared, had been very common in her childhood and youth, which had been spent in the Southern States of America; if a negro came to attack her, she planned to defend herself by making him kiss her and make love to her (ultimately so that she could then deliver him over to justice). But there was a further determinant of the obsessive behavior. In a dream which had a rather similar content to this childhood phantasy, she was in terror alone in the house; then a negro came in and found her washing clothes, with her sleeves rolled up and arms exposed. She resisted him, with the secret intention of attracting him sexually, and he began to admire her arms and to caress them and her breasts.
>
> (1929, p. 309)

Riviere herself analyzes this material as an instance of Oedipal dynamics. The dream and the fantasies are stripped of context and history, viewed as the endogenous product of drive, anxiety and conflict. Butler (1990, p. 53) reads the entire essay as an obfuscation and erasure of female homosexuality. This is surely an appropriate reading of the essay but incomplete as we can now see. Harris (1997) writing about this essay was initially focused on the material as it related to gender and femininity. Only at a conference on race and racism could she actually look at the material and see what had been utterly obvious.

In looking at this material now, with intersectionality and mutual elision in mind, it seems important to distinguish the agenda of the writer, Riviere, a woman in the early part of the twentieth century in England not attuned to American racism in its ugliest formation. Our concern here is the amnesia in North American readers over nearly a century. Much later this paper, with its ideas of masquerade, was of interest to Lacan (1960). He too, but not surprisingly, missed the important implications about race and gender. For our purposes here, the interest is in examining the underlying message, with its complex agendas of perpetration, murderous attacks on black male sexuality and black men: all of it hidden in the interiority of a child's sexual fantasy. It seems to us important to register that the racial implications of this material was not publicly commented on by psychoanalysts. Butler (1990) was concerned with Riviere's failure to theorize or privilege a discussion of homosexuality. Race went unnoticed, or at least uncommented on.

One of us (Harris, 1997) wrote about this, with an initial attention to race. But in an era without the cultural scaffolding within psychoanalysis to explore race in this way, the insight is too easily occluded. Now we are all struggling to notice our own race blindness, for example to critique – with fresh eyes – this interpretation written in 1997:

> Now an American woman in the 1920s dreaming of sending a black man to the authorities for the crime of sexual advances is a woman with lynching on her mind. In the dream the fate of a dangerous desire is to be degraded. It must be policed and destroyed. Heterosexual and homosexual longing is masked; masculinized, blackened, apprehended and headed for execution.
>
> (Harris, 1997, p. 305)

There is an appreciation of the racial implications, but these ideas are still recruited to an understanding of the repression of femininity and female desire. Again, race is present but occluded.

The sole writer who has taken up the race aspect of this clinical material is Pellegrini (1997). Operating out of a more racially sensitive world of cultural studies, she unpacks in detail both the theoretical edifice and the clinical vignette that constitute Riviere's argument regarding the psychic function of "masquerade." Pellegrini notes that Riviere's paper has been an anchoring conceptual base for feminist theories of performance and studies of female spectatorship, and in more explicitly psychoanalytic quarters for looking at women's relation to agency, and to competition and rivalry in dyads and triangles.

The argument, which Riviere develops, is that women – despite skills, capacities and motivations to thrive and compete – often blanket and disguise their competitive and aggressive motives and actions by a strange performative display of a flirty 'femme': often slightly comic, it is an enactment of vulnerability in the stereotypic sexy, unthreatening girl. It's a masquerade in which the deep plan to win – to outdo others, particularly men – is covered by 'play.'

It is a psychic, social and even 'political' move that is still remarkably robust. A young patient, who finds herself in situations in which in her training she is publicly called on to answer questions, teach junior people and display her knowledge, is horrified and furious with herself as she has to notice that she does perform well. She is considered exceedingly capable and reliably smart in her cohort of trainees but always speaks in an odd, high, girly voice, sometimes twirling her hair with a finger. She is deep in disguise.

It is possible to see this as a strategy for more than gender, though Riviere in her essay focuses on the women who must hide her (for Riviere) masculinity/homosexuality under a cover of femme style. This may be kin to Bhabha's concept of minstrelsy (1994), in which he sees the enactment of racial stereotypes as a ploy to defuse racial attacks and anger or shaming.[8] There is perhaps a similarity also to 'flaming': a practice in gay male culture, perhaps sometimes entangled with drag and/or camp, in which the (already misogynist) stereotypes that are used to shame and degrade the gay man are taken up/taken over in a performance designed to maintain a working social plane.

All these moves that Riviere makes are fascinating addenda to feminist theory and to thinking of the complexity of negotiating social and cultural space where there is ambition, envy and competition, the holdover of Oedipal dynamics and social pressure that makes for glass ceilings, uneven playing fields and significant anxiety. We certainly might see the playing out of some of these issues in the #MeToo harassment situations involving women approaching power or visibility in interaction with men who hold power.

In psychoanalysis, as we see, one kind of identity (white femininity, as well as its equally enigmatic twin: white female sexuality) may be founded on the destruction of another (black masculinity). Fanon (1961, 1967) would argue this is true of white identity across genders. This veiled destruction of one socially marginalized identity in the service of constituting another is mutual elision at work, at the intersection of these identities.

What Pellegrini does in 1997 – and in psychoanalysis we are only now beginning to see – is how in this material the brilliant analysis of gender is built on the repression (there can be no other term) of the entwined complex of experiences of race, gender and sexuality as they operate at all levels in individual psychic life and social culture. To make her case for feminine conflicts around Oedipal strivings as well as envy and competition, Riviere remains blind to the racist practices, the terror and draw of cross-racial desires in white men and women and the scenarios of destruction and murder in which excitement and punishment is played out.

Let us now link Laplanche and Crenshaw to consider that in this fantasy, what has been conveyed from some alien other (parental, cultural, intimate or large scale, explicit and unconscious) is installed as alien, that is, unconscious and untranslated, in the child. These messages are what constitute both sexuality and unconsciousness. Here we can see in the untranslated messages, that is, which would remain unknown to sender or receiver (in some degree), the installation into female sexuality (in this southern subgroup) a destructive aggressive attack on a black man. This is, after all, what Riviere describes as a core sexual fantasy of her patient. Feminine excitement emerges from a scene of racial destruction, probably a prequel to murder and lynching. Is this not one way of reading Crenshaw's idea of mutual elision?

Laplanche talks of the work of "après-coup" (House, 2017), when the traumatic installations at time zero become available for re-narratization and recovery at a later time. Here, as we see in 1929, no one patient or analyst could activate the tools which would unpack the traumas. It has evaded any such après-coup for nearly a century. So now, in our collective après-coup, we (contemporary North Americans for sure, but indeed all others sitting with white privilege/fragility [DiAngelo, 2011]) understand racism and colonial domination to be worldwide.

What could we imagine as the message(s) through which this organization of excitement and satisfaction might travel? Laplanche centered his idea of the message as transmitted from a mature person with an infantile sexual unconscious, an adult psychosexual structure with conscious and unconscious formations. We would also need to consider that children in situations in which mass violence is a too-regular event are infused both by the social unconscious (Rozmarin, 2009; Guralnik, 2016) and the tightly intense parent-child bonds in which the child is immersed and dependent. In both registers, the irreducible mixture of sexual excitement and racial hatred/domination is present and transferable in messages both explicit and implicit.

What Riviere has produced is a clinical story about femininity and the crippling of agency that is also a template through which we can understand the intergenerational transformations of racism. This core fantasy of a young girl carries at its heart a pervasive scene (actually reproduced many times over decades) in which a black man is destroyed because of beliefs held by whites about his sexuality and aggression. This form of transformation and messaging seems particularly insidious. We can imagine that this unconscious formation may have actually augmented and underwritten the tenacity of this most dangerous practice of racism. What is revealed to us in this sexual fantasy is the transfer and implantation of messages that sexualize a child in a particular direction. Riviere remarks in the paper that this fantasy appeared frequently in the clinical material. Apparently, this is a core fantasy based on and anchoring a conviction that the black man is exciting, dangerous and forbidden, and must be punished. Here we can see the pernicious hold that racism may have on the unconscious as well as conscious sensibility of generations of white persons, veiled in an already culturally obscured "white feminine sexuality."

What is crucial to consider in this regard is what this kind of unconscious fantasy, with its eliding of racism, female sexuality and the endangering of black masculinity, tell us about white fragility. Here we see that "mutual elision," to return to Crenshaw's concept, is an insidious process in which one form of identity is built on the erasure and in this case the potential destruction of the other. But most importantly, what does it mean for a serious dismantling of racism that much of the core of such ideology lives in deeply unconscious forms of desire and excitement?

Intersectionality: from twentieth to twenty-first century and from theory to practice

Crenshaw's thesis on intersectionality has historical roots in the black women's feminist activist community: in 1974, a group of black feminists formed the Combahee River Collective,[9] and in 1978 they wrote a statement that included the following:

> [W]e are actively committed to struggling against racial, sexual, heterosexual, and class oppression, and see as our particular task the development of integrated analysis and practice *based upon the fact that the major systems of oppression are interlocking. The synthesis of these oppressions creates the conditions of our lives.*
>
> There have always been Black women activists . . . who have had a shared awareness of how *their sexual identity combine* [sic] *with their racial identity to make their whole life situation and the focus of their political struggles unique.*

> We also often find it *difficult to separate race from class from sex oppression* because in our lives they are most often experienced simultaneously.
>
> Our situation as Black people necessitates that we have solidarity around the fact of race, which white women of course do not need to have with white men, unless it is their negative solidarity as racial oppressors. *We struggle together with Black men against racism, while we also struggle with Black men about sexism.*
>
> (Eisenstein, 1978, italics added)

In the development of her seminal thesis on intersectionality, Crenshaw elaborates this phenomenon through an exhaustive review of legal cases, deeply unpacking these "interlocking systems of oppression" and their "synthesis" in the real-time, actual experiences of women of color. From them, she reveals how laws themselves may fall through mutually elisive cracks, failing to protect women of color – or *poor* women of color; or poor *immigrant* women of color; or poor, immigrant, *non-English-speaking* women of color – and so on. At the intersection, features of these women's identities – already vulnerable to systemic discrimination – are erased so that they remain unacknowledged in the legal system. One cultural casualty is that black women's sexuality remains entirely unnamed and unaddressed. This is a form of insidiously perpetrated violence that goes unrecognized because of the powerful, blinding effects of mutual elision socially.

How does this eliding system become culturally embedded? Sue Grand's conceptualization of the effects of "banal evil" (Grand, 2000) helps underscore the sites from which the ill effects of "mutual elision" arises:

> Generation after generation, evil has assumed subtle, pedestrian forms. Sometimes sadistic but more often banal, these interpersonal acts may be perpetrated with *or* without the conscious intent to destroy . . . even as [evil] is everywhere, it is everywhere denied: perpetrator and bystander collude in its obfuscation.
>
> (Grand, 2000, p. 10)

Applied to the nefarious effects of intersectionality, we argue that, unconsciously, the perpetration-*as*-bystanding threatens to become unconsciously sequestered in those who occupy positions of relative power deeply embedded in systems of social privilege – including in our legal systems purporting to 'protect.' Of course, these positions can be occupied consciously as well, but the dangers of completely disavowing these aspects – through an unconscious [dis]identification with the "banal-evil" aggressor – are uniquely toxic. Here, the denial is redoubled intrapsychically in the individual by the forces of incomprehensibility. In fact, informed by historical and contemporary critical race theories aimed directly at whiteness and white fragility (Fanon, 1967; DiAngelo, 2011; Rankine, 2014; Coates, 2015; Morrison, 2017), we argue that the bystander of intersectional violence perpetrates precisely because she appears to innocently happen upon the violence as if *not* implicated in the structures that create and perpetuate it socially. She cannot see herself as perpetrating even the kinds of subtle "pedestrian, banal evil" of everyday social injustice, precisely because she experiences herself as benignly outside of the oppressive systems and projects of her time and operating within the law, and thus has no overt role in the perpetration of such forms of harm toward the other. Further, the groups in which she dwells, likewise blinded by her incomprehensibility of perpetrating such harm, serve to reinforce systems of socialized, targeting hatred, reifying those who inhabit and inform her individual psyche and her near-relational field. Finally, the guilt undergirding white fragility seals the deal to completely foreclose the (incomprehensible) self-recognition as implicated in the perpetration against the other.

Referring to what is specifically denied here as "cultural traumas," Dorothy Evans Holmes describes the internal site of this denial: "the layer within the psyche that contains and secretes crimes of humanity and their history" (Holmes, 2016, p. 642). This is not just white fragility[10] but white terrorism: the "negative solidarity" (of racial oppression) described by the Combahee River collective, mentioned earlier. It is a selective identification in certain groups who share sites of social[ized] privilege. It is negative, errant and mischievous – and overrides the unconscious bias or overlays it.

Indeed, as analysts with a likelihood of enjoying at least some unconsciously held privilege across various social vectors (race, class, gender, sexuality, creed, education, etc.), we are uniquely implicated here because of the ways we may become inured in our complicity, refusing to acknowledge these forms and vehicles of prejudice that afflict our patients on both the delivering and the receiving ends of that prejudice. Holmes theorizes about why "[p]sychoanalysis in general has largely excluded cultural history and its traumas":

> (a) Psychoanalysis still maintains individual and institutional identifications with the silence established and promulgated by the founders of psychoanalysis; (b) psychoanalytic institutions maintain defenses against embracing these factors – the defenses include dissociation and projective identification, and (c) it is difficult to work clinically with cultural trauma because of the first two factors just summarized and because most cultures continue to perpetrate and condone crimes against humanity.
>
> (Holmes, 2016, p. 653)

In particular, working for days, months, then years with patients who necessarily live in a world in which they are targets of such systemic oppression that "make[s] their whole life situation and the focus of their political struggles unique," (Eisenstein, 1978) but not addressing it within and beyond the transference matrix, the analyst can herself become the perpetrating bystander; even more so, perhaps, when the patient himself dwells in life-assuming privileges (e.g., white patients working with white analysts, or male patients working with male analysts, or wealthy-class patients working with wealthy-class analysts), albeit by and large unconsciously, along vectors of socialized power. Here "bystanding" is an act of non-recognition that can perpetrate erasure of parts of self and experience (White, 2007; Suchet, 2007, 2011). Thus, this "bystanding," experienced as "innocent" because it is incomprehensible as an identification, is the hidden accomplice that weaponizes whiteness, patriarchy, class elitism, etc., including within the clinical and theorizing practices of the psychoanalytic field.

The case of Sorrow

We explore the unconscious hold of racism – as it arises out of intersectionality, the genetic and social enigmatic transmission of sexuality and race, and the incomprehensibility of perpetration – in a more nuanced scenario, through analytic work with a patient called Sorrow. As with Riviere's case, both analyst and patient are white and female. However, here the scene is situated in the early twenty-first century American West.

The complicated layering of identifications in Sorrow's family involve class, sexuality, dis/abled bodies and race. These mutually eliding identifications, deeply embedded in Sorrow's psyche and body, surfaced in the shared social identifications between herself and her analyst.

Raised by a single mother from a white, openly (if insidiously) bigoted family, Sorrow transcended profound childhood neglect and poverty by sheer will and determination. The small family lived in extreme, peripatetic circumstances, moving from place to place because of unstable finances. This was detrimentally exacerbated by the unending need for care of Sorrow's severely disabled sibling, whom we'll call Drama. Mother's love, on the one hand, seemingly as abundant as her overwhelm, was nevertheless mainly reserved for Drama's care. Sorrow was left feeling both deprived of being recognized in her mother's eyes, and indeed undeserving of attention in the face of so much existential non-existence that was Drama's tragic life.

Danger followed Sorrow's family, embedded in the chaos of their daily existence. First, the eruptive physical manifestations of Drama's disability frequently shattered their days into fragments. Second, there was a constant stream of strange men that somehow found their way, with hungry lust, to Sorrow's mother – according to Sorrow a "classic blond beauty." It was hard for Sorrow to know which was more disturbing: Drama's unpredictable, violent episodes or mother's body in sexual rapture with a strange man's. Sorrow frequently witnessed both. The grotesqueness of bodies out of control colonized her psyche and sexuality, but not with the typical, complex-PTSD kind of traumatic mark. In the context of Drama's unrelenting precarity and suffering, Sorrow possessed no internal justification for being recognized as a traumatized person, so these memories pervade her mind and body more like abject, unthinkable dread.

Sorrow's internalized early environment is feral: an encapsulation of simultaneous deprivation and depravity. From that constellation of factors, excess and deficit haunt her being in equal measure, with no room for being-enough and having-enough. Consequently, her self-actualization became weighted with a complex of resentment, envy and guilt that can afflict victim-survivors.

Oh yes, and Sorrow's father. According to a history shrouded in vague mythology, he abandoned the family early on, seemingly when the picture of a life dragged under by Drama's permanent illness and constant, expensive medical need became clear. The mythic father was despicable: "selfish" and "ugly," a monster for having abandoned the struggling family. The monstrousness was not just incessantly pointed out in his behavior, but his physical appearance as well. Mother often reminded Sorrow that both she and her sibling looked "just like" father – with their shadowy-dark complexion and black-brown eyes – and that Sorrow had a personality to match: opaque, untamable and relationally eschewing.

For Sorrow then, the weight of class, sex and [dis]ability prevailed as the intersectional axes that shaped and constricted her identity development. Race was strangely buried in an unspoken, insidious layer that linked "dark" features with an exoticized remoteness: as Sorrow began to embody her own sexuality, it seemed for her mother that Sorrow's elusiveness became a refusal of Mother herself, and Sorrow became seductively untamable, impelling in Mother a sexualized, cloying intrusiveness with regard to her daughter's body and emotional states.

In all, these degrading cultural stereotypes around race, gender and sexuality were, for Sorrow, woven with the too-muchness of bodies and sexuality and not-enough-ness of somato-psychic containment. The collision of these corroded identity vectors mutually elide various aspects of Sorrow's internal and external experience, including her erotic self – entangled as they are at the intersections of privilege and shame, self-possession and objectification – but also by the disturbing allure of race intertwined with feminine sexuality that becomes dehumanizing in the realm of socialized systems of racial – overlapping with feminine sexual – objectification. This was the enigmatic transmission of sexuality between Sorrow and the hungry, excessive, erupting bodies around her, and its complex entanglement with the racialized body.

Being normatively, sexually appealing and able-bodied has, of course, afforded Sorrow real advantages. She already feels deeply undeserving for possessing these advantages, especially vis-à-vis the tragic lack of them in her marginalized sibling. As well, these social advantages obscure her deep class and female body shame, which render her self-hating while also resentful of those around her who, to her mind, don't have to struggle with such knotted feelings about themselves. These links have been extensively pulled apart and analyzed in her treatment. They involve excess and deficit that have defined and pervaded Sorrow's sexual and gender experiences throughout her life.

For years race had been elided, sequestered in the negative of Sorrow's life and of the analytic work for its being correlated with what is dehumanized and hated. Within and between two self- and socially conscious white women race, as a speech-act and an embodied trait, has nonetheless been concealed in incomprehensibility. This is the enigmatic transmission of race socially, the twenty-first century version of the "interpenetration and interpellation of racial violence in a Southern girl's fantasy" hidden in and colonizing the psyche of Riviere's masqueraded woman described earlier.

Only recently has race emerged as another powerful vector of identificatory experience for Sorrow. Highlighted earlier, phenotypic "dark"ness hovered in Sorrow's early self-identification, associated with her father: despicable, unattractive, remote, eschewing need for others. She ended up marrying a black man, whom I call Salman, whose family is in so many ways more stable and tight-knit than Sorrow's. Salman's family immigrated to the U.S. from North Africa when Salman was a child. He is warm, attentive, desiring and devoted toward Sorrow, who herself struggles to take in his warmth and sensuousness for fear of being taken over. At the same time, the relational matrix between them is awkward and alienating for Sorrow because of fundamental cultural differences. This exacerbates the agonizing alienation Sorrow already suffers, in which she is alone in a world with no potential for recognition. While they try to discuss their strained sexual divide, race itself hides behind the cultural/ethnic assumptions in their near-world about her husband being "foreign," "Arab," or simply, "black." In the past it routinely arose around his frequent international travel, because of the ways, since 9/11, he was ethnically/racially profiled: invariably pulled aside, questioned and searched by "security." That dehumanizing assault is not new, and in fact came to be expected. What is new is how Sorrow is beginning to understand the hidden, shameful incomprehensibility concerning her own racialized ideas and feelings – both in identificatory and dis-identificatory ways – and how those ideas and feelings squelch her sexual desire, and desirability, toward Salman.

These racialized beliefs and her incomprehensibility about harboring them not only directly affects Sorrow in relation to her partner, but also to their brown-skinned, biracial child as well. Pierce, now 13, is the love of Sorrow's life. Their relationship is quirky and fun. Clearly, Pierce brings out an otherwise hidden, easy, embodied lightness in Sorrow, who has worked very hard to have even boundaries with Pierce that allow for closeness *and* independence and privacy. Pierce is growing up in a city that, priding itself as an enclave of cultural openness, is itself historically racially segregated and now caught in the national political cataclysm around race, class and extreme marginalization of the other. In the Bay Area of California, this is amplified by gentrification and the massively widening income disparity in the city,[11] within a state – California – that is trying to combat the racialized, immigrant-phobia[12] that's becoming ever-more deeply entrenched at its border with Mexico.

However while Sorrow, within herself and with her analyst, has understood race in her world only through the lens of her husband's and now child's experience, it has recently come into the conscious analytic field to consider her own racial experience as a white person, which includes 'white' as another complex identificatory marker that intersects with Sorrow's emotional-relational entanglement around pride and guilt, shame and privilege: as a daughter, sister, mother, partner and analysand. In her family of origin, there was already an explicit familial bias toward lighter complexion even within their white family, with roots in the anti-black racist bigotry that haunts U.S. society. Here, Sorrow was identified as (dark) like her father and disabled sibling, with its violent, degrading stereotypy, and in the case of her exquisitely vulnerable sibling horribly entangled in shame of the judgment of someone already so tragically outcast. The race vector was the one that, between analyst and patient as two white women, had been mutually elided from sexuality, gender, class and the traumatically afflicted body. Race now hovers in the treatment field, as each member of the dyad works to make *comprehensible* their histories and experiences at the intersection of race, gender and sexuality. White race has become explicit in the treatment as a mutually eliding vector with sexuality, class and able-bodiedness, as Sorrow increasingly brings in the insidiousness of structures of racism that terrorize her own family and complicate her closest relationships.

For example, race as a socio-developmental recognition has begun to emerge with her child, who, in beginning to embody an emergent sexuality, is now starting to dis-identify with (and no doubt developmentally separate from) Sorrow. Pierce specifically expresses this dis-identification around racial-ethnic differences. Pierce had already in the past several years overtly established a strong identificatory bond with Salman's racial/ethnic heritage. It wasn't until after the 2016 U.S. presidential election that

Pierce began explicitly naming the racial differences within their immediate family. Consequently, Sorrow is starting to speak explicitly in my presence of her (white) race, including the ways that she feels aligned with her analyst as two white women, as opposed to the complicated mis-alignment with her child. One day when Sorrow and Pierce stood together before a mirror, Pierce asked sympathetically, "Mom, are you sad to be white?" In that moment Sorrow not only felt "ugly" but simultaneously ashamed of her "whiteness," and the pain and humility born of being the outsider to the father-child bond between Pierce and Salman. Salman and Pierce openly align with each other's experiences of difference and alienation from the world around them even as Sorrow, herself always having felt alienated and now alienat*ing* in relation with Salman, likewise watches them struggle – and live in real fear – in ways that she herself doesn't. This confluence around identity-difference with Salman and Pierce highlights in Sorrow the cold, distant aspects of herself-in-relation: as not just rejecting, but defending against the exclusion/rejection she feels. She watches with envy and disturbance as her brown-skinned child receives a complicated attention in the world for possessing an exoticized, envied, sexualized body and presence, while "going-on-being" in amidst the relative benefits of a more emotionally attentive, socioeconomically stable, able-bodied family. This is the complex arena of Sorrow's relational world, where intersections of race, gender, sexuality and dis/ability are at once criminalized, objectified eroticized and differentially valued along historical-cultural lines, in the exquisitely vulnerable, lived experience of herself and her family.

From intrapsychic to social: making the incomprehensibility of perpetration comprehensible

By what intra- and interpsychic processes do we inadvertently collude in the perpetration – as analysts and as human collectives? Perhaps it is possible to liken such unconscious acts of intersectional perpetration to Judith Butler's explication of the socially constructed and unconscious aspect of the violent and violating racial slur:

> The racial slur is always cited from elsewhere, and in the speaking of it, one chimes in with a chorus of racists, producing at that moment the linguistic occasion for an imagined relation to an historically

> transmitted community of racists. In this sense, racist speech does not originate with the subject, even if it requires the subject for its efficacy, as it surely does. Indeed, racist speech could not act as racist speech if it were not *a citation of itself*; only because we already know its force from its prior instances do we know it to be so offensive now, and we brace ourselves against its future invocations. The iterability of hate speech is effectively dissimulated by the 'subject' who speaks the speech of hate.
>
> (Butler, 1997, p. 80)

Butler insists here that we recognize the slipping of linguistic signifiers that perpetrate hate in that liminal (and also veiled) space between the "subject" and the group: the site, we argue, from which "incomprehensibility" emerges. She recognizes and targets not just the speech that harms in real time, but also the identificatory systems of sociopolitical hegemony that continually enact harm to individuals (including, as Ta Nehisi Coates[13] so vividly and wrenchingly illustrates, to certain bodies [Coates, 2015, p. 10]). These identificatory systems keep harming into the future by their power to move along trajectories of prejudicial domination and hatred, woven through the social order by way of the "dissimulating" – concealing – subject.

This subject who is "required" for the insidious efficacy of racism is a critical focus for psychoanalysis. Yes, we can expose the slippage in racial slurs as a construct of *racism* itself: race as, per Coates, "the child of racism, not the father" (Coates, 2015, p. 7). But then there is the moment when I speak a racial slur (or more insidiously, unconsciously collude in a racial project such as maintaining the elitist/subordinating status quo in my profession by avoiding the racial slurriness within), when it bubbles up iteratively from my unconscious, embedded in my "whiteness"-as-reiterative-power – which already refuses to comprehend my collusion – and I perpetrate an other, and others by association, in that moment and for many subsequent moments going forward. This is not dissociation. Rather, it is an incomprehensibility that, refusing to take account of itself-within-me, nonetheless perpetrates harm toward others.

We might add here the work of Moss (2003) who has written very original theory about the complex structure of hatreds, carried socially, individually and unconsciously. He argues that the generic quality of hate speech is its odd but inevitable occurrence in the first-person plural. The ones that hate are 'we.' It is general, social, universal perhaps. We hate X, and race, class, gender, sexuality, culture, belief, each may come to be hate's objects. Moss goes on to deconstruct this plural, this universal 'we hate' and to notice that it masks and disguises a first-person singular state which will contain some form of 'I desire' – a series of statements that might come to include envy, appropriation, excitement, greed, and even love. The intolerable mix of the libidinal longing and the need to degrade and destroy the hated/hateful other does its damage in all directions. Shame and guilt undermine but do not deter the violence of these hatreds, in whatever direction they are flowing.

In psychoanalysis historically, there has already been, through patriarchy-as-reiterative power, grave mis-interpretations and presumptions about the origins, variabilities and vicissitudes of female sexuality, and indeed of gendered sexuality. There have been voluminous and sophisticated feminist and queer critiques of those patriarchal theories, beginning at the dawn of psychoanalysis with articles such as Joan Riviere's "Womanliness as a Masquerade." But lying concealed beyond those critiques, and indeed buried within their folds is a racial violence that draws female sexual fantasy into layers of white, proprietary fantasies of the black, sexual body. These layers are complex, embedded in a strangulating matrix of differential power, dehumanization and socialized terrorism – sometimes blatant, other times subtle, but always perpetuating cultural, racialized violence. As with Laplanche's enigmatic transmission of the "excessive" sexual occurring intersubjectively between mother and child, there is an enigmatic transmission of such mutually eliding, racially dominating systems at the intersection of race, sexuality, gender and, indeed, bodies. This violence approximates the death drive and must be endlessly reckoned with: intrapsychically, relationally and collectively.

Conclusion: toward comprehensibility

Unbeknownst to Sorrow, simultaneous to her own race-awakening her analyst is likewise engaged in such an awakening: personally, professionally and socio-politically. As two white women who are each in our own lives already somewhat sensitized to the effects of "othering," we manifest a tandem struggle to bring intersectional elisions around race into the conscious field of our analytic engagement. For each, this is a step toward making the embeddedness in whiteness-perpetration comprehensible, toward exploration and interrogation, grief and reckoning, atonement and reparation.[14] Of course, this is a delicate walk for the analyst to not explicitly disclose her own process; but in fact the two engage in the work in the intersectional field of the analytic relationship, where the social contextualizes and permeates the analytic field. It matters that at the level of transference-countertransference both can simultaneously, in each other's presence and through the matrix of their analytic relationship, look and tease apart the complex of identities that constellate each of them, toward recognition of socialized truths and true-self experiences that gradually [in]form them.

There is an incomprehensibility of perpetration that lives between Sorrow and her analyst, in their trying to discover how race, complexly interwoven with extant and emergent sexuality, plays out in Sorrow's relationships with her husband and child, *and* in the socially bound analytic relationship itself. It slips beyond the explicit encounter into the unconscious ether, as the struggle to understand how the presence of whiteness/race constructs are always imbricated with gender and sexuality – sites of misunderstanding and misrecognition – in the struggles of incomprehensibility with immigrant marginalization, in a nationalist cultural environment like the U.S. For this analytic pair, it can be spoken to and spoken about, but can never be spoken from within. This impossibility is threaded through the very exercise of psychoanalysis, which purports to make space for understanding and meaning but can never quite do so until, in our communities, we call ourselves and one another to task to interrogate our selective incomprehensibility with race, sexuality and gender, that pervades our theories and seduces us to remain unquestioning in our collusion with mutually eliding projects, including in our institutions.

Notes

1 "Caught" is perhaps a provocative word. Here, we deploy it to underscore the power of competing identifications to impose complex demands and conflicts upon individuals. We are increasingly attentive to the complexity of multiple identifications: race, class, gender, sexuality, cultural and religious identifications, etc.: a lengthening list of identity demands *and* conflicts that burden,

especially those bearing the vulnerability of marginalization at multiple axes of identity.

2 We use the term "incomprehensible" to highlight that for many, identifying prejudicial acts of perpetration in oneself is abject, and thus disavowed: not simply "that is not me" but "there is no part of me that could *ever* be that."

3 By "analysis," Crenshaw means understanding through interrogation, which she is positing is undermined by mutual elision: "The failure of feminism to interrogate race means that the resistance strategies of feminism will often replicate and reinforce the subordination of people of color, and the failure of antiracism to interrogate patriarchy means that antiracism will frequently reproduce the subordination of women (Crenshaw, 1991, p. 1252)."

4 And to push that a bit further, what about gender "difference" between analyst and patient purportedly of the same gender? Can we *presume* gender-sameness? Given the myriad ways that gender is performed and lived in societies across the globe, it seems it would be another case of avoidance not to entertain the possibility of gender variability in any gender-identified analytic dyad.

5 Jeff Chang illustrates this in his critique on institutions 'including' black faces in their promotional materials perhaps more to attract whites rather than being truly inclusive toward people of color. He asks: "[Is] diversity for everybody, for people of color, or just for white people?" (Chang, 2016, p. 17).

6 Field theory, originally developed by Kurt Lewin in Europe in the 1920s, was a model of structural evolution as an outcome of experience in context. This model influenced the evolution of cognitive theories like Piaget, speech act theory, gestalt psychology and later, the psychoanalytic models developed by Bion, and extended by developments in Latin America and North America. These points of origination and the subsequent developments are extensively discussed by Stern (2013a, 2013b).

7 Material here is drawn from an essay in press, "The Perverse Pact" (Harris, in preparation).

8 Eng & Han, 2000, take up some of these questions in their analysis of "racial melancholia."

9 The Combahee River Collective members and contributors included Cessie Alfonso, Cheryl Clarke, Demita Frazier, Gloria Akasha Hull, Eleanor Johnson, Audre Lorde, Chirlane McCray, Margo Okazawa Rey, Sharon Page Ritchie, Barbara Smith and Beverly Smith. More on their origins and history may be found in *How We Get Free*, Keeanga-Yamahtta Taylor (2017).

10 It is important to situate this concept in relation to Robin DiAngelo's thesis on "White Fragility," which she defines as "a state in which even a minimum amount of racial stress becomes intolerable, triggering a range of defensive moves." DiAngelo focuses on "the outward display of emotions such as anger, fear, and guilt, and behaviors such as argumentation, silence, and leaving the stress-inducing situation" which "function to reinstate white racial

equilibrium." While incomprehensibility might be seen as another "defensive move" resulting from white fragility, the focus here is to isolate and characterize the doubly *unconscious* aspect of incomprehensibility. It is perhaps no more or less damaging than other defenses undergirding white fragility, but because of its embeddedness in the mutually eliding power of intersectionality it is uniquely difficult to identify and interrogate within oneself.

11 San Francisco, California, census data. Retrieved April 3, 2019, 08:43, from http://worldpopulationreview.com/us-cities/san-francisco-population/ www.bayareacensus.ca.gov/historical/corace.htm; http://censusviewer.com/city/CA/San%20Francisco

12 Retrieved April 3, 2019, 08:50, from www.sfchronicle.com/bayarea/article/Bay-Area-Muslims-facing-backlash-try-reaching-6716320.php. Retrieved April 3, 2019, 08:52, from https://hoodline.com/2017/01/sfs-muslim-community-faces-reality-of-trumps-america.

13 "But all of our phrasing – race relations, racial chasm, racial justice, racial profiling, white privilege, even white supremacy – serves to obscure that racism is a visceral experience, that it dislodges brains, blocks airways, rips muscle, extracts organs, cracks bones, breaks teeth. You must never look away from this. You must always remember that the sociology, the history, the economics, the graphs, the charts, the regressions all land, with great violence, upon the body." Coates, T-N. (2015). *Between the world and me* (p. 10). New York, NY: Spiegel & Grau.

14 In the final pages of *The Autobiography of Malcolm X* (and less than a year before he was assassinated), Malcolm X shares what he had said to Harlem street audiences after his spiritual awakening in Mecca in 1964. "I said that on the American Racial level, we had to approach the black man's struggle against the white man's racism as a human problem. . . . I said that both races, as human beings, had the obligation, the responsibility, of helping to correct American's human problem. The well-meaning white people, I said, had to combat, actively and directly, the racism in other white people. . . . Where the really sincere white people have got to do their "proving" of themselves is not among the black *victims*, but out on the battle lines of where America's racism really *is* – and that's in their own home communities; America's racism is among their fellow whites" (Haley & Malcolm, 1964, pp. 431–432).

References

Baranger, M., & Baranger, W. (2008). The analytic situation as a dynamic field. *International Journal of Psychoanalysis*, *89*(4), 795–826.

Bhabha, H. (1994). *The location of culture*. New York, NY: Routledge.

Butler, J. (1990). *Gender trouble: Feminism and the subversion of identity*. New York, NY and London: Routledge.

Butler, J. (1997). *Excitable speech: A politics of the performative*. New York, NY and London: Routledge.

Chang, J. (2016). Is diversity for white people? In *We gon' be alright* (p. 17). New York, NY and London: Picador.

Coates, T-N. (2015). *Between the world and me*. New York, NY: Spiegel & Grau.

Crenshaw, K. (1989). Demarginalizing the intersection of race and sex: A Black feminist critique of anti-discrimination doctrine, feminist theory and antiracist politics. *University of Chicago Legal Forum*, 139–167.

Crenshaw, K. (1991). Mapping the origins: Intersectionality, identity politics, and violence against women of color. *Stanford Law Review*, *43*, 1241–1299.

DiAngelo, R. (2011). White fragility. *International Journal of Critical Pedagogy*, *3*(3), 54–70.

Dimen, M. (2003). *Sexuality, intimacy, power*. Hillsdale, NJ: The Analytic Press.

Eisenstein, Z. (1978). *The Combahee River Collective statement*. Cited from *Home girls, a Black feminist anthology* (Barbara Smith, ed.), ©1983. New York, NY: Kitchen Table: Women of Color Press, Inc. Retrieved January 15, 2019, 10:45, from https://combaheerivercollective.weebly.com/the-combahee-river-collective-statement.html

Eng, D., & Han, S. (2000). A dialogue on racial melancholia. *Psychoanalytic Dialogues*, *10*(4), 667–700.

Fanon, F. (1961). *The wretched of the earth*. New York, NY: Weidenfeld.

Fanon, F. (1967). *Black skin, White masks*. New York, NY: Grove Press.

Grand, S. (2000). *The reproduction of evil: A clinical and cultural perspective*. Hillsdale, NJ: The Analytic Press.

Guralnik, O. (2016). Sleeping dogs: Psychoanalysis and the socio-political. *Psychoanalytic Dialogues*, *26*(6), 655–663.

Haley, A., & Malcolm X (1964). *The autobiography of Malcolm X*. New York, NY and Toronto: Random House Publishing Group.

Harris, A. (1997). Aggression, envy and ambition: The circulating tensions in women's psychic life. *Gender and Psychoanalysis*, *2*(3), 291–325.

Harris, A. (2009). *Gender as soft assembly*. Hillsdale, NJ: The Analytic Press.

Harris, A. (in preparation). *The perverse pact*. Paper at Program on Race (April 16, 2018, BIPSE).

Holmes, D. E. (2016). Culturally imposed trauma: The sleeping dog has awakened. Will psychoanalysis take heed? *Psychoanalytic Dialogues*, *26*, 641–654.

House, J. (2017). The ongoing rediscovery of après-coup as a central Freudian concept. *Journal of the American Psychoanalytic Association*, *65*(5), 773–798.

Lacan, J. (1960, September 5). *Guiding remarks for a congress on feminine sexuality: 1958*. Presented in Amsterdam.

Laplanche, J. (1989). *New foundations for psychoanalysis*. London: Blackwell.

Laplanche, J. (1997). The theory of seduction and the problem of the other. *International Journal of Psychoanalysis*, *78*, 653–666.

Laplanche, J. (1999). *Essays on otherness*. London: Routledge.

Layton, L. (2002). Cultural hierarchies, splitting, and the heterosexist unconscious. In S. Fairfield, L. Layton, & C. Stack (Eds.), *Bringing the plague: Toward a postmodern psychoanalysis* (pp. 195–223). New York, NY: Other Press.

Lewin, K. (1951). *Field theory in social science: Selected theoretical papers* (D. Cartwright, ed.). Oxford: Harpers.

Morrison, T. (2017). *The origin of others*. Cambridge, MA: Harvard University Press.

Moss, D. (2003). *Hating in the first person plural: Psychoanalytic essays on racism, homophobia, misogyny, and terror*. New York, NY: Other Press.

Pellegrini, A. (1997). *Performance anxieties: Staging psychoanalysis, staging race*. New York, NY: Routledge.

Rankine, C. (2014). *Citizen: A lyric*. Minneapolis: Graywolf Press.

Riviere, J. (1929). Womanliness as a Masquerade. *International Journal of Psychoanalysis*, *10*, 303–313.

Rozmarin, E. (2009). I am yourself: Subjectivity and the collective. *Psychoanalytic Dialogues*, *19*, 604–616.

Saketopoulou, A. (2014a). Mourning the body as bedrock: Developmental considerations in treating transsexual patients analytically. *Journal of the American Psychoanalytic Association*, *62*(5), 773–806.

Saketopoulou, A. (2014b). To suffer pleasure: The shattering of the ego as the psychic lie of perverse sexuality. *Studies in Gender and Sexuality*, *14*(3), 245–252.

Saketopoulou, A. (in press). The draw to overwhelm: Consent, risk and the retranslation of enigma. *Journal of the American Psychoanalytic Association.*

Stein, R. (2005). Why perversion? "False love and the perverse pact". *International Journal of Psychoanalysis*, *86*(3), 775–799.

Stern, D. B. (2013a). Field theory in psychoanalysis, part I: Harry Stack Sullivan and Madeleine and Willy Baranger. *Psychoanalytic Dialogues*, *23*(5), 487–501.

Stern, D. B. (2013b). Field theory in psychoanalysis, part 2: Bionian field theory and contemporary interpersonal/relational psychoanalysis. *Psychoanalytic Dialogues*, *23*(6), 630–655.

Suchet, M. (2007). Unravelling whiteness. *Psychoanalytic Dialogues*, *17*(6), 867–886.

Suchet, M. (2011). Crossing over. *Psychoanalytic Dialogues*, *21*(2), 172–191.

Taylor, K-Y. (2017). *How we get free*. Chicago: Haymarket Books.

White, C. (2007). Fertile ground at the edge of difference: Self, other, and potential space: Commentary on paper by Gillian Straker. *Psychoanalytic Dialogues*, *17*(2), 171–187.

Chapter 9

Intersectionality

From politics to identity

Neil Altman

The notion of "intersectionality" evolved in a political context when it was noted that individuals who were assigned to two or more oppressed identity categories (e.g. black women) were doubly oppressed (McCall, 2005). The concept also called attention to the complexity of belonging to an oppressed and a dominant category, for example black men or white women. In a feminist context, intersectionality noted that black women and white women sometimes needed to take account of race and social class when seeking to ally as women (Davis, 1983; hooks, 1984). Sometimes alliances function well until a "hot spot" arises when the interests of one or more identity categories clash. Recently, people of Jewish identity may be inclined toward a political alliance with people of color, until Israel's oppression of Palestinians becomes a "hot button" issue.

In this chapter, I take up "intersectionality" at the level of the individual and the dyad. On the individual level, the context is not primarily political or strategic, but rather the process of the individual's personal identity formation and the social context in which it evolves. In the process of identity formation, individuals draw on categories extant in the culture, for example race, culture, social class, gender, and sexual orientation, among others. These categories, especially those related to race, gender, and sexual orientation, are often polarized, though the either/or structure of these identity categories is rapidly breaking down. In a dyadic interaction, such as the psychoanalytic one, personal identity categories meet and interact in complex ways, as is detailed later.

On this personal, individual level, the process of identity formation may appear deceptively straightforward, but in fact, the intersection of a few categories that can be seen, thought about, and experienced as polarized and/or continuous, over time, and in interaction with each other, quickly becomes extremely complex. The lived experience of being a woman or a man, a black woman or a white woman, a gay black man or a heterosexual white woman are all bound to vary in accord with the individual's position on these dimensions and refracted through each unique personality, itself evolving in time and in response to an ever-changing social context. The dimensions themselves are abstractions, polarized conceptually but, as noted, continua in experience. Race, gender, social class, and sexuality are stereotypes that have a poor fit with the way any given individual lives and experiences him or herself (from moment to moment) as a raced, gendered, classed, and sexually oriented individual. At the same time, one cannot deny that these categories are extremely salient organizers of experience.

Non-linear dynamic systems

This complex interaction of factors and forces constitutes a non-linear dynamic system of identity formation. "Non-linear" in this context means that there is no straightforward cause and effect relationship between one's position on any of the identity categories and one's experience or sense of self. The impact of one's position with respect to an identity category, for example man or woman, gay or straight, black or white, or anyplace in between, is modified by one's position on the other dimensions, and by other non-identity–related factors. One's identity-related experience, in turn, feeds back to one's other identity-related experiences. "Dynamic" in this context refers to the interaction of many parts that are continually changing, depending on context.

Self and identity as "Strange Attractors"

Non-linear dynamic systems are thus chaotic and organized, unstable and stable. Non-linear dynamic systems theory gives us a language for thinking and talking about the mind-boggling complexity that characterizes identity development and interactions among people. Although non-linear dynamic systems can be described as "chaotic" (Gleick, 1987), they do have their own emergent organization, called "attractors"; non-linear dynamic systems tend to be attracted toward specific forms of organization (Harris, 2004; Seligman, 2005). When these organizations have a fractal structure – that is, when each part has the same structure as the whole – they are called "strange" attractors. The "self" is an attractor that emerges from the complexity of an individual's life; the self is a strange attractor in that each of us is recognizable to him- or herself and to others from our behavior. Other examples of strange attractors include psychotherapy sessions, so characterized by one of my early supervisors when he said, somewhat recklessly to my mind, that if I told him about the first interaction of a session he would tell me about the whole session. The navigation of such complex and multi-layered psychic and interpersonal situations is the stock in trade of clinical psychoanalysts. This chapter draws on clinical vignettes to illustrate what can be learned about intersectionality from psychoanalytic work, as well as how an understanding of intersectionality can enrich clinical psychoanalytic therapy.

Race and sexual orientation intersect

I received a call from Mr. C in which he said he was looking for a therapist and would like a consultation with me. He had gotten my name and contact information from a friend who knew of me from my writing. I was flattered and anxious to live up to what I imagined was the expectation that I would be a person whose consciousness was at a high level about social issues in psychotherapy, all the more so when he arrived and I met an African-American man who described himself as a successful entrepreneur. He said he was depressed after a break-up with his male partner. He said he was interviewing two or three therapists and would soon make a choice. I suggested that we meet one more time, at least, as I believed it was helpful to be able to process the initial consultation together as part of getting to know how we might work together.

When Mr. C came for the second session, he said he had decided to work with me. I asked whether race had been a factor in his choice. He said he did not want an African-American therapist because he thought a black therapist might expect solidarity on racial issues and he did not want that. I thought I was showing my openness to exploration of racial issues with my question, but his response took me aback. His response seemed to expose self-hating prejudice. I turned away from this response, however, in favor of feeling pleased that he wanted to work with me, and we set up our next session.

When the time arrived for our follow-up session, Mr. C did not show up. In fact, I never saw him again despite my efforts to reach out to him.

At first, I thought perhaps he was showing me a prejudicial attitude that he thought I had, but I was at a loss as to how I had exhibited my prejudice. I was not aware of the narcissistic pleasure I felt at being chosen; I was too immersed in my narcissism to be reflective about it.

From an individual and dyadic point of view, and over years of trying to imagine and process what happened between us, I have come to think that perhaps he had indicated that my question about race as a factor in his choice to see me made him think that I was unduly preoccupied with race. Indeed, why had my question focused on race and not on sexual orientation or gender, for example? It seemed plausible to me that he would think that I had a blind spot, at least in that moment, around sexual orientation. I think I had a narcissistic investment in being a "good" white person, that is, a white man with a high level of consciousness about race, concerned about what it might be like for him to be in therapy with me, a white man. Did he register my blind spots around these issues? I will never have an opportunity to inquire.

Looking at this interaction through the lens of intersectionality, Mr. C seemed to identify as a gay black man of upper-middle class, while I identify as a heterosexual white man of similar social status. These categories, however, being polarized stereotypes, fail to do justice to the complexity of our racial, sexual, gender, and social class self-experiences. Rather than embarking on a shared exploration of this complexity, I defensively and narcissistically stereotyped myself as a self-aware white man, producing the question that exposed my inattention to sexual orientation, the play of sexuality between us, my narcissism, and so much else in our interaction. I suggest that out of the complexity, indeed the chaos, of the multi-faceted interplay among race, social class, gender, and sexual orientation in the culture in which Mr. C and I were situated, a strange attractor emerged into which I, at least, was swept up. This strange attractor could be characterized as white, male, heterosexual narcissism and defensiveness, a pattern that, evidently and ironically, can be detected even in those, or perhaps especially in those, who presume to have studied it. The irony here emerges from a central aspect of strange attractors: their fractal structure ensures that efforts to observe, reflect upon, and transcend their "gravitational" pull will reproduce the pattern. Here is an overlap with the contemporary psychoanalytic notion of enactments, in which it is repeatedly found that efforts to transcend enactments tend to reproduce them, sometimes usefully (Bromberg, 2002; Mitchell, 1997; Stern, 1997). As Freud

(1912) noted with respect to the reproduction of the past in transference, "it is impossible to kill anyone *in absentia* or *in effigie*" (p. 108).

Social class, gender, and culture

Ms. D called me to say she was looking for a therapist and wanted to know what my fee was. I told her that it was $150 per session. She said she would think about whether she could afford that fee and would call me back. I did not hear from her for one year. One year later, she called me to ask if I would adjust my fee. She was working as a mid-level administrator and would find it difficult to pay my fee every week. I told her that I would charge her $125 if she came at an off hour in my practice (i.e. mid-day). She said she would be able to come in the middle of the day, and we made an appointment for a consultation.

When we met, Ms. D told me she had decided to pay my full fee. She said she did not want to be a "second-class citizen" in my practice. We began meeting once weekly. As a mid-level administrator, Ms. D supervised clerical staff in her organization, reporting to upper-level staff. Ms. D felt protective of her subordinates, tending to believe that they were exploited by the upper-level staff whom she saw as lazy and uncaring. Several years into our work, Ms. D began to feel exploited by me in ways that I found surprising. For example, she felt it was unfair that she had to pay for missed appointments, whereas I was free to cancel appointments with her with no penalty. Ms. D enjoyed exposing the hypocrisy in my denial of my power to set the terms of our engagement. I began to make the link between Ms. D's identification with, and feeling of protectiveness toward, "her" staff, and her choice to pay more so as not to be a second-class citizen in my practice. I had not previously grasped the significance of the fee in relation to her sense of our relative status.

Ms. D had grown up in a working-class family in Brooklyn. Her father was an alcoholic, and her mother was periodically addicted to amphetamines. She remembered having to catch crabs for family dinners when money was scarce. Ms. D, herself, had become an alcoholic during her adolescent years, until she joined Alcoholics Anonymous in young adulthood. Ms. D had gone on to college, received a graduate degree, and lived a middle-class life as a member of the professional/managerial class

(Ehrenreich & Ehrenreich, 1979; Dimen, 1994). She remained strongly attached to her sense of identity as a working-class woman.

I had grown up upper-middle class. My father was an attorney, my mother a homemaker. There always seemed to be enough money, though in recent years, when money was short, I sometimes remembered my father's anxious calls to his office to see if any checks had arrived in the mail. As a child and adolescent, money seemed to me like water: you turned on the faucet when you needed it.

When I began seeing Ms. D I had two young children and had begun to know about money as a scarce and precious commodity. I wanted to make enough money so that my children would know that they could do work that they loved and found meaningful, free from anxiety about making ends meet. The social class difference between me and Ms. D was deep and wide. One reflection of the divide was that I was oblivious to the ways in which personal value could be measured by the amount of money one had at one's disposal (Cobb & Sennett, 1972).

Reading Cobb and Sennett's book *The Hidden Injuries of Class* I began to appreciate some of the influence of social class on self-esteem in a capitalist economy that had been a blind spot for me, certainly when I had negotiated a fee with Ms. D. Our social class differences came into focus on one occasion when Ms. D found a job that looked to me, and to her, at first, as a move up: more money, a higher-level supervisory position with more responsibility. On her first day on the new job, she was told that among the perks she was *not* being offered was access to the executive dining room. She was insulted and wanted to quit right then and there. No, she would *actually* quit over this issue. I was dumbfounded; why sacrifice so much over a superficial symbol of status? After all, she was planning to eat lunch at her desk anyway. Ms. D accused me of trying to make her middle class. To her, I was not only dumbfounded; she had found me to be dumb. Working-class people, she said, were very sensitive to such slights; there were so many of them in their lives. Working-class people sometimes reacted with action, not with detached reflection. To me, the whole premise of psychotherapy seemed at stake. At the same time, what was more psychotherapeutic than for me to try to understand where she was coming from? I stood my ground, with reservations, and Ms. D resigned on her second day on the job, or, rather, she quit. Soon thereafter she presented me with a book about working-class women. It is now years later, and

I must say, Ms. D has landed very well on her feet. It has become a kind of joke between us that from time to time, Ms. D believes I am secretly rolling my eyes when she mentions quitting a job, or pulling up stakes and moving out of state to a less trendy part of the country, or some such thing.

Ms. D rolls her eyes at my cluelessness about the values and traditions that inform her background. She has made her move into the middle class in many ways, but I think she maintains a connection and a kind of loyalty to her roots that makes her sensitive to the exploitation of the people she supervises and the hypocrisy of the people who exploit them. I am part of the middle class that she has chosen, but she wants her roots in the working class to be recognized and honored. Ms. D frequently feels misunderstood and insulted by me, but she pulls her punches with a half-joking, sardonic tone as she calls my attention to my unreflected-upon middle-class values and my efforts to impose them on her.

The system that formed the matrix for my work with Ms. D is capitalism such as it has evolved in the United States, along with a denial of class differences and associated cultural differences. These blind spots have roots in the early European immigration to North America to escape the oppressive and unchangeable bonds of class in Europe. The mythology of a classless society obscured the way in which people's lives were shaped and bounded by social class, for all the vaunted social mobility of the new world. In fact, the myth of social mobility made a failure to come up in the world a personal failure rather than a property of the system, as Cobb and Sennett (1972) had pointed out. What Ms. D might have called middle-class values have infiltrated the self-esteem systems of working-class as well as middle-class people.

These considerations form my view of the complex and dynamic system that formed the matrix of our therapeutic relationship. The strange attractor here was social class difference; the fractal structure was created and reinforced by the denial that social class and money were so fundamental to our lives and to our relationship. Wherever we looked, or failed to look, social class lurked.

The power structure of our relationship was also shaped by the differences in our gender and religious identification. While social class was in the foreground most of the time, gender remained in the background, its impact perhaps unformulated between us, the book on working-class women notwithstanding. Most of the upper-level administrators with whom Ms. D worked were men, lazy and exploitative of women, to her mind, while upper-level women were experienced as insidiously competitive and envious. Jewish men, like me, were the main supportive figures, mentors, in her life. Her exposures of my hypocrisy were good natured and condescending, rather than deadly serious. Social class differences were the focus of difference and conflict between us, for the most part, while gender and religion formed a supportive background, the basis for a working alliance.

Conclusion

My work with Mr. C and Ms. D took place in a complex, multi-dimensional matrix of interaction and intersection between social and personal factors. Complexity does not yield to chaos, however. No matter how complex the system, it seems, organization emerges, somewhere between the property of the human mind to search for and make links, and something in external reality that lends itself to being organized in the ways that we find satisfying and appropriate.

An intersection between psychoanalysis and non-linear dynamic systems theory is to be found in the way that strange attractors, organizers of complexity, take shape in what contemporary analysts call enactments (Bromberg, 2002; Mitchell, 1997; Stern, 1997). These are unconscious or unformulated interactions for which analysts have learned to grow antennae. These enactments have a fractal structure, as if playing hide and seek with us, daring and tempting us to look for what is hidden in plain sight, everywhere.

References

Bromberg, P. M. (2002). *Standing in the spaces: Essays on clinical process, trauma and dissociation*. Hillsdale, NJ: The Analytic Press.

Cobb, J., & Sennett, R. (1972). *The hidden injuries of class*. New York, NY: W. W. Norton & Co.

Davis, A. (1983). *Women, race, and class*. New York, NY: Vintage Books.

Dimen, M. (1994). Money, love and hate: Contradiction and paradox in psychoanalysis. *Psychoanalytic Dialogues*, *4*(1), 69–100.

Ehrenreich, B., & Ehrenreich, J. (1979). The professional-managerial class. In P. Walker (Ed.), *Between labor and capital* (pp. 5–48). Boston: South End Press.

Freud, S. (1912). The dynamics of transference. *The Standard Edition of the Complete Psychological Works of Sigmund Freud*, *12*, 99–108.

Gleick, J. (1987). *Chaos: Making a new science.* New York, NY: Viking Books.
Harris, A. (2004). *Gender as soft assembly.* Hillsdale, NJ: The Analytic Press.
hooks, b. (1984). *Feminist theory: From margin to center.* New York, NY: Routledge.
McCall, L. (2005). The complexity of intersectionality. *Signs: Journal of Women in Culture and Society, 30*(3), 1771–1800.
Mitchell, S. A. (1997). *Influence and autonomy in psychoanalysis.* New York, NY and London: Routledge.
Seligman, S. (2005). Dynamic systems theories as a metaframework or psychoanalysis. *Psychoanalytic Dialogues, 15*(2), 285–319.
Stern, D. (1997). *Unformulated experience: From dissociation to imagination in psychoanalysis.* New York, NY and London: Routledge.

Index